SNAPSHOTS:
An X-ray of Cameroon's Democracy, Governance and Unification

Sam-Nuvala Fonkem

Langaa Research & Publishing CIG
Mankon, Bamenda

Publisher
Langaa RPCIG
Langaa Research & Publishing Common Initiative Group
P.O. Box 902 Mankon
Bamenda
North West Region
Cameroon
Langaagrp@gmail.com
www.langaa-rpcig.net

Distributed in and outside N. America by African Books Collective
orders@africanbookscollective.com
www.africanbookcollective.com

ISBN: 9956-791-77-6

DISCLAIMER
All views expressed in this publication are those of the author and do not necessarily reflect the views of Langaa RPCIG.

Table of Contents

Preface

When I was asked to do the preface for this book, the first thing that came to my mind was a humiliation I once suffered as a second-year journalism student in Lagos Nigeria, many years back. A mutual friend had mailed me some Cameroonian newspapers, which I excitedly took to class and was showing them off.

If my class mates were wary about pointing out the very appalling stuff of the watered down, highly censored and insipid nature of Cameroonian journalism at the time, my Mass Communication teacher, the very renowned Professor Ralph Akinfeleye shot from the hip. To make matters short, he leafed through some of the pages and announced to the entire class that going by what he had in his hands, Cameroonians were practising "cocktail" journalism, adding that his students would be doing themselves a world of good by not as much as having anything to learn from a "tamed media" under President Ahmadou Ahidjo's dictatorship.

To make matters worse, these papers had come in just at the time the learned Professor was taking our class on the various theories of mass communication. Thus, my highly treasured newspapers became pedagogic material for what obtains in a totalitarian state, or better still, the authoritarian model as opposed to the libertarian or social responsibility theory of the press. Granted that I reluctantly submitted myself to Professor Akinfeleye's piercing lessons, yet, the humiliation of my country's media being consigned to the dustbin of mediocrity hurt very much.

From then on, when I listened to Radio Cameroon, I would even switch off my transistor as soon as a Nigerian or any other foreign colleague was approaching. Until one day at about 4.00pm local time, I heard Sam-Nuvala Fonkem's booming voice on Radio Yaounde airwaves. He was reading an up-dated version of what had been the national and world news an hour earlier. It became a delight to daily follow his newscasts, scripted in impeccable, well-articulated English and delivered in this rare baritone voice of his.

I was to regularly invite my classmates to, at least, listen to some Cameroonian Journalist, who was not, after all, "His Master's Voice", as our Lecturer had depicted every Cameroonian media practitioner.

On one of my vacations to Cameroon, I was informed that because of his sterling journalistic qualities, Sam had been appointed Chief of the International Channel of what was then Radio Cameroon.

It was, small wonder then, that several years later, when I was recruited by the Cameroonian Public Service and seconded to what later became CRTV, Sam instantly became one of my mentors. This relationship was to continue long after we had both "voted with our feet" from the national broadcaster in search of greater freedom in the independent media. May I quickly add here that following his chosen path as a free press crusader, Anglophone Cameroon and human rights activist, it was a matter of time before Sam Nuvala Fonkem parted ways with the establishment.

Appointed to the rather inferior and redundant post of Adamawa Provincial Chief of Service of Media Observatory in 1993, Sam turned down the appointment on the same day in a strongly worded letter to the then Information and Culture Minister, Augustin Kontchou Kuoumeni. The latter summoned him and clearly told him that he had denied his request to be transferred to Buea in Anglophone Cameroon, "where you would be carrying out your brand of politics". We are told that Sam's appointment to the Adamawa Province, which came in September, was coming barely some five months after the All Anglophone Conference (AAC-1) in Buea, where as leader of the "Free West Cameroon Movement" the hard-hitting Journalist had called for the secession of what was once the Federated State of West Cameroon.

Sam then dropped the microphone for the pen, and embarked on writing for several newspapers, including "Cameroon Post", which I edited at a point in time, and "The Post" Newspaper which I have served as its Editor-in-Chief, since we founded it seventeen years ago this year.

It must be noted here that he did so with the same verve, the same commitment and forthrightness for which he was noted in the heydays of the Sunday morning- must listen- highly critical and analytical programme, "Cameroon Report".

Cameroon's Anglophone independent media "lost" Sam and his targeted 'SNAPSHOTS' when the prolific writer joined the United Nations Operation in the Ivory Coast (UNOCI), in Abidjan in February 2010, as Public Information Officer. However, with the publishing of a collection of his 'SNAPSHOTS' in a single volume, what was lost to the UN by way of this journalistic talent, is about to be regained in this single collection.

Hopefully, also, the book is a recapitulation of sorts that would serve both the informative, nay, historical interests of those of the younger generation, who, as it were, were not opportune to live the era when the true journalism heroes of Cameroon were being made.

Charly Ndi Chia,
Editor-In-Chief,
The Post Newspaper,
National President, Cameroon Union of Journalists, CUJ

Introduction

I began writing for the private press in 1991 that is on the dawn of multipartism and the struggle for civil liberties. This was the only option open to me after having parted ways with Radio Cameroon. I had spent a period of incarceration in police cells and the maximum security prison of Nkondengui, Yaounde along with my colleagues Ebssiy Ngum and Johnnie McViban from June to October 1986 as a result of the controversial news talk I delivered titled "Enemies of Democracy" which can be found in a separate collection of writings titled: *Incisive Journalism: The Best of Cameroon Report (1978-1986)* by Langaa Publishers.

As a result of the democratic wind of change blowing from Eastern Europe, Parliament in late 1990 had passed a corpus of laws pompously referred to as "liberty laws" which had considerably eased conditions for setting up a newspaper enterprise and this saw the mushrooming of dozens of newspapers both in English and French.

Paddy Mbawa had just returned from journalism training in Nigeria and negotiated with publisher Mr. Ngalim to revive Cameroon Post that had gone comatose for something like two decades. So I began writing in Cameroon Post not as a staff member but an independent contributor. After all I was still a civil servant even if my professional career had been dashed against the rock.

The roaring 1990s was marked by a new spirit of self-expression. Anglophone Cameroon whose voice and those of its leaders had not been heard for decades began to find expression. The Anglophone teachers' union CATTU, the Civil Servants Union, the Parent/Teachers Association and other civil society groups began to emerge as they organized street marches to demand more freedoms and better working conditions. Bamenda was the main theatre of the groundswell of this activism. At the national level, there was mass agitation for a national conference bringing together all the active forces of the society to find solutions to the myriad of problems plaguing the country since independence.

The government's response was to sell the idea of a limited constitutional reform process which it could conveniently control. Anglophone political activists however saw the prospects of a constitutional conference as an opportunity to go back to the drawing board regarding the unification of Anglophone (Southern Cameroons) and Francophone Cameroon. They saw the possibility of a second "Foumban Conference" to work out more concrete constitutional guarantees for what was once the mandated territory (under the League of Nations) and later the Trust Territory of Southern Cameroons (under the United Nations) which had now been chopped up into the North-West and South-West provinces of La Republique du Cameroun and its citizens reduced to second class citizens.

On the outset, Cameroon Post (which later became The Post in 1998) and the Herald newspapers were the leading English-language tabloids. My preoccupation at the time obviously was the plight of the Southern Cameroons as evidenced by my write-ups of 30 May 1991 (Suggestions for an Ambazonia Caucus-Ambazonia being another name for Southern Cameroons) and 6 June 1991 (What Future for Cameroon Integration?).

Writing for Cameroon Post was an on-and-off romance giving the exploitative attitude of all Anglophone newspaper publishers. In-between, I wrote for Cameroon Life Magazine, the only English-language news magazine at the time and a one-off publication "The African Star" in 1996. In 1997, I resumed writing for Cameroon Post and introduced for the first time the SNAPSHOT column. By 1998, Francis Wache and Charlie Ndi Chia split from the dictatorial management of the paper over fundamental managerial issues and created The POST in 1998. I went along with them. These two men had been running the paper ever since Paddy Mbawa was forced to go on exile in the mid- 90s following his exposure of an insurance scam at the agro-industrial corporation CDC which earned him a long prison detention, harassment and threats to life.

I later (2001) withdrew my collaboration with The POST because of what I have described as the "exploitative attitude" of publishers.

In the meantime I wrote for other publications such as "Insight Magazine", The Witness tabloid and Manyu Millennium magazine, a regional publication created by the talented Augustine Ayuk Augustine aka AAA. "BOBA Today" was also one of those one-off publications created specifically to commemorate the golden jubilee of the Cameroon Protestant College, Bali- my alma mater. BOBA stood for Bali Old Boys Association. Selections from such non-professional publications have been included to bring variety and spice up this collection.

Press Freedom

It would be erroneous to assume that because there was a new political dispensation, press freedom had been handed down to media practitioners on a silver platter. Far from it. The newfound freedom of expression that accompanied President Paul Biya's accession to power in 1982 and the regime's remarkable exercise of tolerance toward the growing independent press whose discourse was mainly in defence of Biya's position against Ahidjo and the remnants of Ahidjoism was later in the 1990s to be replaced by a more intolerant Biya regime that was sceptical and hostile to the advent of multipartism and political competition. Mass public rallies and marches were organized throughout the nation by stalwarts of the regime, all of whom were raised in the one-party mould to say NO to multiparty politics. It was un-African, it was an imported western model, they cried.

Granted that the so-called "Liberty Laws" decree of December 1990 which provided for a set of civil liberties including the freedom of assembly and the press had abolished prior censorship (prior restraint which consisted in editors presenting the dummies of every edition of their paper to the Prefet – local administrator – for approval before going to the printers), newspapers published issues with whole pages furrowed by the censor's stamp. It took some time for the decree to be implemented and even then newspaper editions carrying what was considered offensive and subversive could still be seized from the kiosks and destroyed.

I had done very little writing between 1991 and 1997 so did not come under the censor's axe. The harsh censorship did not only make newspaper publishing a non-viable business proposition but also rendered newspapering a hazardous occupation. Even the 1996 constitutional reform still upheld censorship and although prior restraint had been lifted, newspaper editions could still be seized from the kiosks.

Issues forming the bulk of SNAPSHOTS were mainly political and economic. While democracy was of paramount concern, the plight of Anglophone Cameroon constituted my war horse. Some of the write-ups were actually exposes such as the one on the "CDC Privatisation Palaver" which I believe must have cautioned the government to tread carefully on the issue. A lot of research went into some of the articles because I could afford the time and resources, as an independent columnist, to take on whichever topic whenever I was inclined to do so. Economic derivation with regard to the Southern Cameroons, human rights issues, bilingualism, the Biya regime and the ineptitude of the opposition, political violence and street power were among the issues that captured my attention.

The imbroglio between Cameroon and Nigeria over the Bakassi Peninsula was one issue which undoubtedly captured the critical attention of every current affairs commentator. I have not in this collection included magazine cover stories I wrote as editor of Cameroon Life such as the ones on Bakassi and Barrister Ben Muna because of their length. However I would like to briefly relate in passing an incident concerning a Bakassi cover story I did in 1994 and whose publication incidentally coincided with the holding of the Second All Anglophone Conference- AAC-2 in Bamenda.

Two days before I was to leave Yaoundé for Bamenda, a truck load of 30 anti-riot police surrounded my residence at Etoug Ebe at about 5 am, knocked on my door and announced they had come to search my house. This was not the first such encounter I was having with these strange characters, but this was the first time they came knocking when my wife and children were at home. I did not quite know at first how many of them had come visiting but I recall that one uniformed gendarme and two plain clothes showed up at my door and vaguely introduced themselves. As usual I received them courteously, offered them seats and later woke up my wife to serve them tea, something I always did to disarm them morally. At that time also my uncle-in-law, a retired policeman who had come to Yaoundé to chase his pension files flew into a rage when he sensed what was going on. He insisted the men show a search warrant. It took me quite a while to calm him down and explain that Francophones were strangers to search warrants and that he had nothing to fear as I had nothing to hide anyway.

After ransacking the whole house-living room and bedrooms, I even suggested they climb up the ceiling or else tell me what they are looking for so I can give them and save everyone the embarrassment and waste of time. They kept at it, asking me if I had any communication or radio link with Nigeria. To cut a long story short, after an hour or so they did not seem to have found what they wanted but for two Nigerian weekly news magazines which were on the coffee table in the living room: Concord and Newswatch. It was just normal for me to update myself on what the Nigerian media were saying on the Bakassi issue as part of my research on the cover story. Their leader, the uniformed one, asked me if he could borrow one of the magazines to show his boss as proof that they had paid me a visit. I obliged, reminding him to tell his boss to make budgetary allowance for news magazines because I was not in the habit of borrowing magazines to security officers as they never returned them. He persuaded me to sign the copy of the magazine as further proof that they actually met me at home. I did. Needless to say I never got the magazine back.

As I opened the door to let them out, lined up on an open esplanade in front of my house were some 30 "ninjas" armed to the hilt with bowed heads and a downcast expression on their faces as they saw me shaking hands with their squad leader. At the shady hours of pre-dawn when I opened the door to receive their team leaders, members of the "anti-gang" squad had taken cover, I was later told by neighbours, in a corn bush behind my house, ready to foil any escape attempt. From that incident on, the people in my neighbourhood began greeting me with an unmistakable expression of awe on their face. They all knew I was a journalist but the squad that came calling that morning was reserved for the likes of Osama bin Laden who had not yet achieved global notoriety.

On arrival in Bamenda the day after, we learnt the whole consignment of Cameroon Life magazine had been held by security agents at the Nigerian border and several copies dispatched to the SDO in Mamfe for censor's clearance before entry into Cameroon. For cost effectiveness, Cameroon Life was printed in Calabar, Nigeria.

Plans to make huge sales of the magazine during the AAC conference were not only scuttled by the delay but also because an armada of troops from French Cameroon had been dispatched to Bamenda to disrupt the conference, harass, beat up and arrest participants. Bamenda was in turmoil close to the one that took place during the launching on 26 May 1990 of the opposition SDF party in Bamenda.

I wrote little about personalities except for a few eulogies and memorials for certain personalities and friends who exemplified certain shared values i.e. Rt. Hon. John Ngu Foncha, Dr. John Kale, Justice Dan Kisob, Miriam Makeba and others. There is also a poem for three Southern Cameroons activists who were slain in broad daylight in Kumbo by the goons of la Republique du Cameroun while they held a peaceful march on October 1, 2001 to commemorate the 'independence day' of the Southern Cameroons.

In all fairness, the Biya dispensation (and it had little choice in the matter owing to international pressure) was bound to allow the press considerable breathing space. Journalists and writers became more daring and outspoken. I for one began questioning the validity of the unitary state and the dubious foundations of national integration. We tried to expose the falsehood on which unification was founded and the historical revisionism of the Yaoundé regime which bordered on distortion, if not outright obfuscation of historical facts. All this could not have been possible under the Ahidjo regime. The difference however was that while the Ahidjo regime listened and took judicious note, the Biya regime developed a thick skin, deaf ears and continued its autocratic governance in a manner as if to say "Le chien aboie mais la caravan passé – the dog barks but the caravan passes on". It couldn't care less!

This brings us to the question of impact. What impact can the sum total of our crusading journalism be said to have had in changing Cameroon society? Some have argued that the question of impact should be a matter of academic curiosity and should not bother the journalist or social critic whose job is to chronicle and comment on current affairs; whose job is to create public awareness whether or not the public avails itself of this awareness to change its condition of living.

The media are a watchdog of society but how often has society paid a heavy price for failing to heed to this thankless role of the journalists? The journalist is neither a clairvoyant nor a doomsday prophet but as a watchdog it can send early warning which those of the "la caravan passe" mind-set have always ignored to the detriment of society. Consider the following:

My Snapshot of 6 June, 1991 titled "What Future for Cameroon Integration" had this to say inter alia concerning Cameroon's relations with Nigeria: On May 22 (1991) the Voice of Nigeria in its newsletter programme traced the uneasy border relations from the time of the killing in 1981 of five Nigerian soldiers by a Cameroon naval patrol and the continued harassment by Cameroon gendarmes of Nigerians moving in and out of Cameroon. I warned, "When Nigeria begins to open old wounds such as this, only a fool would take it lightly, especially at a time when Cameroon is experiencing violent socio-political upheavals." By December 1993, Nigerian troops had moved into the Bakassi Peninsula for what was the beginning of a border war of attrition which took 13 years to resolve with the signing in New York of the Greentree Accord of 6 June 2006.

The caravan may pass and ignore us, but we will keep writing because the pen is mightier than the sword and the force of argument shall prevail over the argument of force.

Suggestions for an Ambazonia Caucus
May 30 1991

Since it has become decisively clear that West Cameroon's continuation of its political arrangement with la Republic du Cameroun ought to be predicated on the restoration of the 1961 federation, I would like to join my voice with those foresighted and concerned citizens who have called on West Cameroonians to close their ranks and put a common front at the proposed national conference aimed at determining the future of the entire nation.

The need for a pre-conference consultation by Anglophone Cameroonians (irrespective of ethnic origin) is dictated by the disolidarity and disarray that characterized the Southern Cameroons (West Cameroon) delegation to the 1961 constitutional conference in Foumban. And we know the political blunder that was committed at that conference and the consequent marginalization and eclipse of Anglophone Cameroon.

That West Cameroon has a specific geographic, historic, linguistic, socio-cultural and political character that makes it different from la Republic du Cameroun can never and has never been a subject of debate. Rather, it constitutes a point of departure for any pre-conference concertation. History would judge the present crop of emerging Anglophone politicians even more severely than their predecessors if they fail to restore the dignity and autonomy of West Cameroon. Their predecessors' crime is mitigated by one fact: ignorance. They have confessed to have had little knowledge of that other side of the Mungo; hence they were ignorant of its cannibalistic political instincts. That excuse cannot hold today.

We must correct (not regret) the errors of the past. To this end, I suggest a pre-conference consultation grouping leaders of the ruling and opposition parties, elderly statesmen, paramount chiefs (including those who have sold out, since room must be allowed for repentance), eminent lecturers, professors and dynamic student leaders, prominent members of the Bar and the media as well as other professions, trade union and women's leaders, retired governors, police commissioners and army officers. It's my belief that the elderly statesmen, paramount chiefs, veteran trade union leaders and retired senior officers of the police and armed forces are privy to certain political and strategic intelligence that could be vital to such a concertation. This pre-conference concertation could be styled the Ambazonia Caucus, since Ambazonia is the original and authentic geographical expression for West Cameroon.

For fear of embarrassing certain personalities, I have refrained from unilaterally proposing a list of persons one would expect in such a caucus. However, the proposed caucus should not be chaired by an executive member of any existing political party so as to ensure that such a chairman is not hindered from playing the role of an objective moderator.

The task of the caucus should be to examine perceived and actual points of contention, politico-ethnocentric antagonisms, as well as the allocation and re-allocation of political power and economic control among the various components of the Ambazonia political chessboard. The spirit of such an examination should be to emphasize convergence and commonality as well as mutual interest and survival.

The caucus shall be expected to re-examine the 1961 federal constitution with a view to identifying loopholes that made it possible for East Cameroon to embark on the assimilation (disguised as integration) of West Cameroon as well as review the constitution of the federated state of West Cameroon for possible weakness. A re-examination of the 1961federal constitution should envisage in unequivocal terms the accession of a West Cameroonian to the presidency of the federation and, perhaps the possibility of an alternating presidency i.e. sharing of the presidential mandate by West Cameroon and la Republic du Cameroun.

The caucus should be prepared to put forth proposal for a more equitable system of development that would respect the principle of derivation (natural endowment). There is no reason why an area that provides all the potential for diamond and gold exploitation should remain the most backward in any given country. For example, an agreed quota of oil proceeds exploited in Ambas Bay should have been set aside for the development of the Victoria deep sea port in Limbe or the Korup forest conservation project or the fish canning and bitumen industries.

We recall that the successive ruling oligarchies in Yaounde, in order to split the Anglophones, have been in the habit of making fake and vague promise especially to citizens of Fako division, giving them the false impression that they were the favourite babies amidst the wretched lot of Anglophones. We know what became of these promises.

Granted, the government has just announced plans to transform the university centre in Buea in to a full-fledged university fashioned after the Anglo-Saxon tradition. Although from the surface the decision is commendable, it is at best a belated trade-off and at worst a cheap bribe.

The above suggestions for the agenda of the proposed Ambazonia Caucus are not exhaustive. However, given the limited time that such a caucus might have before an eventual national conference, it is important that proponents concentrate now on the broad outlines while details would be subsequently worked out after a consensus is reached on these outlines. Once again it is imperative that every step is taken to avoid a repetition of the Anglophone comedy staged in Foumban in 1961.

S-N F.

What future for Cameroon integration?

June 6, 1991

Authentic political scientists who have surveyed the pre and post-independence political landscape of Cameroon can today pat themselves on the shoulder for having apprehended, if not foreseen the outcome of Cameroon's experiment in political integration. The integration of Anglophone West Cameroon and Francophone East Cameroon is far from a success story as the lopsided process has tended towards assimilation of the Anglophone minority.

Abundant information and empirical data are available to support the fact that efforts towards integration have been misguided by the selfish interests of the ruling class, thus resulting in the alienation of Anglophone Cameroon (See S.T Muna's Memorandum on the Anglophone situation, 1985; J.N. Foncha's letter of resignation from the C.P.D.M; letter of Anglophone elites in Douala 1985; Free West Cameroon Movement pamphlet: The First October Eyewash 1985; Anglophone university students letter to parents 1984; Gorji Dinka's New Social Order: Diffuse The Time Bomb 1985; CRTV Anglophone journalists petition to Head of State 1990 etc., etc.).

The apprehension of political scientists can be summed up in the following pertinent observation about Cameroons experiment in political integration. Professor Kofele Kale had pointed out the unequal nature of the Cameroon union and its one-side process of integration stating that national integration did not necessarily mean an exercise in assimilation.

Referring to Cameroons one party system (1966) which ushered and sustained the unitary form of government since 1972, J. F. Bayart noted that the politics of unification , in denying diversity and particularism, impinged on a strong national consciousness resulting in a growing ethnic (or Anglophone)discontent. He made a general observation to the effect that some minority groups experience national unity (integration) as alienation.

In their attempt to achieve a synthetic integration, Cameroon's post-independence leadership waged a dogged crusade against diversity and particularism in the blind hope that the Anglophone personality would be neutralized and eventually absorbed. Their watchword was integration at all cost. Their method consisted of constitutional manipulation, marginalization of Anglophone human and natural resources as well as the English language, promotion of the notion that Anglophone Cameroon was an ethnic group and recently the use of military force to cower the Anglophone community.

What the leadership ignores is the historical fact that political integration is a voluntary process and has never been achieved by coercion. The regime deliberately or inadvertently ignores a number of indelible characteristics of the Anglophone minority and that Southern Cameroons (later, the federated state of West Cameroon) joined the Cameroon union as an autonomous entity with the clear understanding it would preserve its originality. It should be recalled that West Cameroon was endowed with a fairer notion of balanced development; that West Cameroon has always been wary of the possibility of being engulfed by the Francophone majority; that West Cameroon, unlike most national minorities, is fixed to a particular segment of the territory; and that West Cameroon shares borders with the giant Federal Republic of Nigeria with whom it also shares the same civilization, same language and same way of life. According to Maurice Duverger, the problems posed by this last factor are more complex and this brings us to the question of West Cameroon and the Nigerian connection.

The geopolitical position of West Cameroon is a decisive and crucial factor which daily haunts the Cameroon leadership but which it prefers to overlook. The great risk as Duverger states is that "the minority community (West Cameroon) will turn to its large neighbour to defend itself against the state it belongs to and sometimes even attempt to break it up.

6

Cameroon's nightmare over Nigeria has been translated into the deliberate neglect to forge a meaningful trade, cultural and scientific relationship with our giant neighbour. Relationships have been reduced to protocol and diplomatic niceties at the same time as little or no attempts have been made to improve communications links since independence.

On May 22, the *Voice of Nigeria* in its newsletter programme traced the rather uneasy border relations between the two countries from the time of the killing in 1981 of five Nigerian soldiers by a Cameroon naval patrol, the continued harassment of Nigerians moving in and out of Cameroon by Cameroon gendarmes, Cameroon's lukewarm diplomatic response to these harassments etc. The point I am trying to make here is that when Nigeria begins to open old wounds such as this, only a fool would take it lightly, especially at a time when Cameroon is experiencing violent socio-political upheavals.

The question we should be resolving now is how to save the remaining shreds of national unity that have survived three decades of despotism, political chicanery and constitutional manipulations. First of all to do this, we must admit that the manner in which the leadership has gone about the business of integration has been high handed and lopsided and that the experiment to a very large extent has failed. Secondly it is incumbent on the emerging Francophone political formations to dispel from the minds of their militants once and for all the notion that Anglophone Cameroon is a tribe or is synonymous to one. When these two conditions would have been fulfilled, then one can hope for a necessary change of mentality and the proper frame of mind that should facilitate the tackling of the question of national unity.

It is my view that the most realistic solution to the problem of Cameroon unity and integration in the federal system of government as I have suggested on several occasions and I see no reason why some people insist on regarding this solution as an advocacy for national disintegration. Far from it. In a multi community or, in Cameroon's case, a bi-cultural situation wherein each group refuses assimilation and preserves its originality, federalism, as Duverger explains, is the most common solution. He cites the case of Switzerland which has proven it can succeed very well. Numerous examples, says Duverger, show that preservation of originality does not prevent the formation of highly unified and closely integrated nations in which patriotic feelings are strong.

No one can honestly assert that Cameroon's unitary state and its highly centralized government have helped promote a strong sense of patriotism, public accountability and social justice. Far from it. On the contrary, as Kofele Kale had noted and experience has shown, centralization has resulted in the decline in the enjoyment of human rights and intolerance to opposition.

Frankly speaking, if the proposed national conference aimed at defining the political, cultural and socio-economic future of Cameroon fails to pay reasonable attention to the solution proposed in this article, then West Cameroon would have no choice but to rely on its originality and perhaps the Nigerian factor to find a solution that would restore its dignity. This is a warning not a threat.

S-N F.

Parliament's Queer Sense of Patriotism

August 05, 1991

Towards the close of this year's budgetary session of the National Assembly, the "progressive" faction of the ruling CPDM parliamentary group issued a statement to the effect that the new budget was inspired by the International Monetary Fund (IMF) and is therefore not Cameroonian.

The statement said the budget was bad and advanced several reasons why it would not serve the public interest. These reasons include the increase in taxes on imported industrial inputs which would affect small and medium-size industries and salary cuts in the public sector which will severely reduce the purchasing power of tax payers.

The "Progressive" deputies, who, one may assume, were also speaking on behalf of the majority of the people's representatives who are too lethargic and dumfounded to openly identify with any line of thought, did register certain reservations over the budget which they said would have disastrous consequences on the tax payer. Despite their reservations, the deputies said they voted for the budget "out of sheer patriotism." And what a queer sense of patriotism?

The fundamental contradiction inherent in this justification only helps to cast more doubts as to the validity of what is now referred to as the "progressive wing" of the ruling CPDM party in the present political context. Indeed, by voting an anti-people's budget, the deputies have lent credence to the observation that if at all there is any such thing as a progressive wing, its place is certainly not within the ranks of the CPDM because any truly progressive minded deputy ought to have voted against a budget that does not serve the public interest.

It can be accurately deduced that the invocation of patriotism as a justification for adopting the budget was a shameless act of political camouflage. While it is true that patriotism is the natural (not artificial) love for one's country and the readiness to defend it, political sociologists have identified a certain kind of "patriotism which serves to establish an artificial sense of solidarity between the oppressed and the oppressors within a given nation."

In their attempt to take cover behind the altruistic motives of patriotism, the CPDM "progressives" have only succeeded in exposing their ineffectual reformist posturing, political emasculation and lack of guts.

It is most exasperating and certainly not edifying to witness the people's representatives endorse the economic suicide (which they want to make us believe is the economic survival) of the nation which they claim to love so well and later mount the rostrum to bleat like castrated he-goats that they did it out of love of nation.

Love of nation is not enough. A patriot must also defend the nation, not become an accomplice to its destruction. But at last, comforted with an "IMF invasion, our "patriotic" deputies preferred to play Judas and proceeded to outdo Pontius Pilate; a desecrated form of patriotism that has been the hall mark of the Cameroon's political hypocrisy since its flag independence.

Indeed, the real sentiment behind all the crocodile tears shed by the deputies can be deduced from their very statement in which they complained that the new fiscal measures should have been carried out in 1987 (when the one-party system was still intact) and not at present when the country is in the process of setting up a multi-party democracy.

Their fear is that the suicidal (not survival) budget they adopted would aggravate the swelling disaffection amongst the electorate who "in the coming months, it would appear, shall arbitrate between us who are voting austerity today and candidates of the emergent opposition who will be presenting an untainted parliamentary and political past record." In short they fear the June session was

10

probably the last they shall ever attend. Therein lies the truth: concern for their personal interest.

The public derision provoked by the deputies' political capering has been further compounded by their pathetically desperate hope that posterity shall judge them leniently because of their contemptible reservations about the budget. In effect, they are hoping that history might acclaim them for their cowardly leadership. Maybe they shall be rewarded in their own coins but certainly not acclaimed.

They should not pretend to bother about posterity's judgment because they have already been tried and it only remains for the verdict to be passed - at elections. It is the height of cynicism when people presume to bother about the opinion of the unborn while completely ignoring the survival of the living.

It could be said that the widespread vexation caused by the recently adopted budget and finance law is not only due to the fiscal burden on the tax-payer but more so because of the democratic principle which holds that there can be no taxation without representation. And who were represented at the budgetary session? Of course, the "fire brigade" of the ruling CPDM clique-that is one political party out of about thirty. (Note: the deputies accused government of pyromania, charging that every time it sparks a fire, it calls on parliament to extinguish it). Thus, until a multiparty parliament is put in place, there is reason to doubt the moral authority and legitimacy of all decisions taken by our "patriotic" deputies who seek comfort in the proverb that when the ship of state sinks, "the crocodiles do not distinguish between the bodies of those who 'chopped' and those who did not 'chop'," as the Secretary of State for Finance Ephraim Inoni stated wisely in a recent radio interview.

There is yet another truth, though less poetic, which all maritime dwellers are well acquainted with and it is that before we allow a boat to sink, everything must be done to throw all burdensome cargo (the 'choppers' of state coffers) overboard. If the boat sinks thereafter, then posterity would attribute it to the wheel of destiny.

11

God forbid!

S-N F.

4

Western Conspiracy against Cameroon's Democratic Transition
12 October 1991

In a bid to counter charges that Cameroon had lost the confidence of Western donor countries, the national media mounted the usual hosanna choir, incanting a scanty catalogue of recent aid packages granted by certain European countries as well as Japan.

Highlighting these assistance and investment packages, which included Australian commitment to quarry some rare mineral in Akonolinga, Chinese aid for the Lagdo Dam, Japanese grant of F.M. radio studio and Switzerland's granting of debt-relief, the government media hoped to establish that Cameroon still enjoyed external credibility despite the opposition's contrary view.

While the claims of the government on the one hand and the opposition's on the other could be convincingly argued with a good dose of demagogic acumen, the fact that the West is still providing any amount of financial and investment assistance at all is a question which merits critical examination.

Continued Western assistance to the ruling CPDM government puts a big question mark on Western declarations since last year that further aid would depend on the extent to which recipient countries are willing to democratize their political systems (political conditionality).

At the Franco-African summit in Baule, France, in June 1990, French President Francois Mitterrand reiterated this condition. At the Bretton Woods Committee meeting in Washington in April 1990, the American Assistant Secretary of State for African Affairs, Herman Cohen announced that in addition to economic reforms and human rights, democratization would become a third condition for US assistance to Third World dictatorial regimes. The US congress equally declared that limited aid would be awarded to 'newly forming democracies' and not wasted on autocratic grimes.

In the light of the above and the fact that aid continues to flow gives any observer the impression that the West has failed to live by its own very principles and may not be willing to pay more than lip service to Cameroon's transition to democracy.

The realization that the West is in a conspiracy with its local compradors to thwart the democratic process has been widely expressed by the local press questioning the dubious role of Western countries in the process. *Le Messager* (August 31ˢᵗ) flashed the headline "A Quoi La France and *Cameroon Post* (Sept 6-13) ran the caption: "France will intervene on Biya's Behalf: America Wants Biya because of Our Oil and Gas. *Le Messager* also carried an eloquent cartoon in which the French President was seen to be pondering over a card table, playing what appeared to be a game of Solitaire in a bid to find the joker among the emergent political parties in Cameroon. In that same cartoon, President Biya is depicted as crossing his fingers in a desperate superstitious effort to jinx the French President so he doesn't find the joker.

It is very disappointing to realize that even Mr. Mitterrand believes he can facilitate a breakthrough in the present political stalemate by a game of hazards and therefore leaving the future of the country to chance.

In trying to find a political joker, one gets the impression that the West is trying to find a suitable alternative to Mr. Biya and at the same time realizing it may not find one who would be popularly accepted and still be conducive to its imperial interest. Cameroon Post suggested that the US is bent on ensuring "that Biya lasts long enough to conclude the unholy oil and gas deal with Uncle Sam."

The West is not only frustrating the democratic process by pumping aid but its financial institutions such as the International Monetary Fund (IMF) and the World Bank have kept the credit line open under the auspices of the Structural Adjustment Plan (SAP) whose disastrous effect on the masses such as mass unemployment, wage freeze and cuts, withdrawal of government subsidies, and inflation have become a stark economic reality. The effect of this has been to instigate bitter discontent, indignity and the worst kind of poverty which have in turn sparked widespread bloody demonstrations and the repression of the masses by armed government forces.

A part from generating political opposition and armed reprisals, SAP has caused incomes to fall to an intolerable level. As Claude Ake (Journal of Democracy Vol. 2 No 1 Winter 1991) has rightly observed, "to implement SAPs, governments have been forced to resort to a large dose of coercion. For this reason African regime have become more, not less, authoritarian…" Since this is the case, how can we reconcile such a consequence with Western commitment to democracy?

Pro-democracy forces in Cameroon have called on the West to withhold further aid but the call appears to have fallen on deaf ears. The basis on which the West rationalizes continued assistance is unfounded. Western governments project the disproved argument that withholding aid will hurt the economy and the people, but as Ake has questioned: "how can aid given to violently repressive leaders rather than through Non-Governmental Organisations possibly help the people as opposed to helping these leaders to remain in power?" The argument that aid must continue in order not to impede development, Ake observes, "overlooks the fact that most African leaders have been under developing the continent for years in spite of aid – indeed probably because of it."

The West is showing a lack of foresight by not heeding to calls for sanctions. By propping inept and authoritarian governments because of attractive short-term gains, the West is pushing the present democratic forces to adopt extremist ideologies that would make it difficult for Western governments to pursue meaningful relationships of mutual interest when the anti-dictatorial forces eventually control the political machinery.

S-N F.

5

The Falling Standard of English:
A Political Perspective

March 1992

I followed with unusual interest a late October 1991 edition of the TV programme 'English with a difference' in which the argument focused on the falling standard of the English language in Cameroon. The host of the programme, Peter Esoka, exerted so much effort to find out from his guest, Mr. Ambe Andoh, a Cameroonian research fellow in communication studying in Nigeria, whether he thought the standard of English in Cameroon had fallen and if so, what could be the cause.

In a rather tedious and circumlocutions performance, Mr. Andoh admitted there was a drop in standard, adding that this decline was temporary. Temporary? Now what's he up to, this fellow? I asked myself. Then came the next question. Cause of decline? The environment, said the expert. What do you mean by the environment? A hungry man cannot express himself as well as a well fed man. But what has hunger got to do with language? While the host was progressively losing his patience, mine had already been replaced by a growing sense of irritation and distress. By the end of what I considered the most tortuous and torturing argument on CRTV, Mr. Andoh revealed that by environment, he meant the political setup in Cameroon. (Now you're talking). The question of standard is not merely linguistic but runs across the whole gamut of the Anglo-Saxon tradition. (Come on boy!). The question of language has to do with identity. (Bravo my man!).

Just when we expected the real argument to begin, seeing that the premise had clearly been stated at last, the programme came to an end to the greatest disappointment of most Anglophone viewers, I imagine. Had the host been less mischievous, he should have pursued his interview, cut out a good portion of the first part and presented viewers with a more exhilarating and enlightening programme, but that's beside the point. The point is why did Mr. Andoh (a communication research fellow of all persons) take such a tremendous effort to arrive at this point?

I submit that Mr. Andoh's performance in itself was a scientific validation of his thesis about environment affecting the quality of language. He was demonstrably ill at ease and not quite sure of what position to take until he was virtually bullied into it. Anyone who is familiar with Cameroon's highly censored media environment would readily sympathise with him. Mr. Andoh inadvertently found himself exercising self-censorship which resulted in the devious trajectory his argument took before landing. One could easily sense what was going on in his mind: "This is CRTV, his master's voice of the CPDM oligarchy, one wrong move and the Gestapo may come calling; I could land in Nkondengui or some concentration camp, watch your words; any slips and I'm doomed, no more research, no future, safest thing to do ...be vague, beat about the bush...". This might have been an exaggerated impression, but it does not hinder me from congratulating Mr. Andoh for having touched on the crux, namely that the root of the falling standard of English is hanging on the lopsided political landscape of the Anglophone/francophone divide; a tenuous political marriage that resulted in the annexation of the Anglophone federation state of west Cameroon in 1972 and the subsequent persistence by the francophone polity to assimilate the Anglophones.

Sadly enough, most writers on the issue of falling (fallen?) standards have shamelessly circumvented the crux, preferring to heap the blame on English language teachers or the pupils or on the both. Some have gone as far as advancing unfounded theories that hold Pidgin English as the scapegoat for falling standards. I entirely agree with Mr. Andoh when he stated that the matter of falling standard is closely related to the question of identity. And if we agree that since the reunification of west and east Cameroon in 1961, the francophone-dominated government in Yaoundé has done everything to undermine and destroy the Anglophone identity and to relegate the Anglophone to the status of second class citizen and that the Yaoundé regime has been denying this assertion for the past 30 years- which only goes to validate the truth of the statement-then, in that case, what standard of linguistic performance would you expect from someone who is made to feel he is second class, someone whose political status has been usurped, whose culture and language are regarded as inconsequential, if not a nuisance? What performance do you expect of a teacher or pupil who feels that the mere utterance of his language of communication identifies him with political and cultural rootlessness and exposes him to public scorn? What performance do you expect when there is lack of confidence and loss of cultural pride and identity resulting from political machination?

A recent government-sponsored public health campaign adopted the bright idea of erecting giant slogan-bearing posters at strategic locations in the capital city which read : "SWEEP, CLEAN AWAY, TO GATHER DIRTINESS IS GOOD, NOT TO MAKE DIRTY IS BETTER". That's Cameroon bilingualism for you; a calculated attempt to make a mockery of the English language. One may ask, was that translation from French to English (since French is constitutionally the authentic official language of Cameroon and translations can only be done from French to English) an evidence of falling standard or political machination? Can anyone assert that any Anglophone above class seven levels was involved in the conception of such an important campaign? The argument over falling standards reminds me of a similar debate, a decade ago, concerning the paucity of literary works produced by Anglophone Cameroonians. This debate ,which was quite spirited and took up the centre spread of several issues of the then weekly English version of Cameroon Tribune, featured two protagonists, 'honest Man' Sankie Maimo (writer) and the late professor Emeritus, Dr Bernard Fonlon (R,I.P). The one held that the paucity of Cameroon literature of Anglophone expression was due to the dictatorial political atmosphere marked by censorship and oppression while the other attributed paucity to the British colonial emphasis on vocational education. Until the learned

19

professor (who lost his spear at first cast in the polemics) passed away, he could never explain how Nigeria, a former British colony, managed to produce literally giants like Wole Soyinka (Nobel laureate) and Chinua Achebe as well as Ayi Kwei Armah of Ghana and Ngugi wa Thiongo of Kenya.

I have often asserted that any attempt to shift the focus of the Anglophone problem to linguistic mechanics is sheer papering over the cracks. It is broad daylight chicanery. This issue is political not pedagogic and can only be resolved as such. That is probably why Mr. Andoh considered the question of falling standard of English as temporary and suggested that standards would be regained when the situation changes. That is probably why Nigerian leader Ibrahim Babangida in a summit meeting with Cameroon's Paul Biya in 1991 spoke of Cameroons (with an s) because there are indeed two Cameroons, different in geography, history and socio-political culture.

S-N F.

6

End of the oil monopolies?
April / May, 1994

On February 17, 1994, The Prime Minister of Cameroon and Head of Government, Hon. Simon Achidi Achu signed a letter of intent to the International Monetary Fund, IMF soliciting confirmation of 68 billion CFA loan over a period of 18 months. The amount represents 60% of the country's quota of a 1.400 billion CFA standby loan 90% of which has been allocated for the settling and servicing of external debts.

Hon. Achidi Achu's letter was accompanied by a medium term economic and financial policy statement, including a time table for economic measures that spells the end of the monopoly enjoyed by SNH and SONARA in the petroleum sector.

The era when oil-related matters were regarded in Cameroon as the strongest taboo subject may soon be over. Every informed citizen is aware of the occulted secrecy that has shrouded the oil business in Cameroon ever since it became known that the country started its first shipment of black gold' in 1978.

In most of the Middle East countries, especially the Persian Gulf States, the discovery of oil was like manna from heaven that was used to develop public facilities and infrastructures such as roads, schools, hospitals etc. but not so for francophone African States, especially Cameroon.

From former President Ahidjo's time to the present Biya regime, Cameroon has maintained an irresponsible silence over matters related to oil exploitation and revenue and up till date oil operations and financial accounts are not open to the scrutiny of the highest legislative body of the country, the National Assembly. Most observers would recall the disdainful and arrogant manner in which the late General Manager of the National Hydrocarbons Corporation

(SNH – French acronym) Mr. Jean Assoumou came on television two years ago to insult the intelligence of the population by declaring that the oil business was too complicated a matter for the simple minds of the citizens to comprehend. He most tactlessly revealed that the oil business remained a secret between him and the Head of State Paul Biya.

The taboo imposed over Cameroon's petroleum sector has been such that no journalist in a press conference dares to ask the Head of State any question related to oil. Sometime in the early 1980s', the Chief of Station of Radio Buea, Mr. Asonglefac Nkemleke, after a visit to the national oil refinery, SONARA in Victoria, in the company of a top government official questioned why Cameron's oil production was being measured in tons instead of barrels per day as is the universal tradition. He was promptly relieved of his duties.

Cameroonians would recall how sometimes in the early 1980's, the nation woke up one morning to the stunning news of the gruesome murder of Mr. Mpondo, a top level Cameroonian executive of Gulf Oil Company in Douala. He had been strangled with his wife and buried hurriedly behind his Bonaberi residence by armed thugs who locked up their few months old baby in the wardrobe. The nation lost one of the few early oil executives whose experience would have been an asset today – all because he was suspected by Ahidjo's regime to be in possession of very sensitive information on oil production.

The government's intention to play down the importance of oil revenue and its reluctance to inject same into the economic mainstream was informed by the disastrous inflationary effects the oil boom had created in certain African countries. It took the wise decision to put oil revenue into a special account (compte hors budget), which in reality was Ahidjo's personal account in Switzerland and other secret bank accounts abroad. His successor Paul Biya has not changed that policy. Any amount trickling into the national budget from oil revenue was a matter left to the discretion of the Head of State.

Point 17 of Cameroon's policy statement to the IMF acknowledges that the increasing financial instability of the country as of 1992/93 was caused by the sudden fall in SNH's payment of rents, levies and taxes to the national treasury. It would be recalled that for the past two years or so, rents and company taxes destined for the local treasury of Victoria (Limbe) were carted with impunity to an undisclosed destination by special tax collectors from the nation's capital, armed with authority from above. Hence local contractors and civil servants have been constrained to pay a 30% kick-back in order to cash payment vouchers whenever they have been lucky to do so at the local treasury.

Cameroon's letter of intent to the IMF pledges to install a quarterly procedure of accountability with regard to oil revenue and that henceforth, treasury payments would be determined by the value of crude oil exports and domestic sales to the national oil refinery.

Cameroon's programme of economic reforms and time-table envisages that before the year 1994 runs out, SNH's monopoly over oil supplies to SONARA would have been eliminated. To be very honest, SONARA, for pragmatic reasons of survival had recently sought alternative sources of crude and has for some time been refining the Brass River brand from Nigeria.

S-N F.

Epitaph for Papa John
March 25, 1997

I am deeply aggrieved by Cameroon Post's immature, disjointed and rather superficial handling of the political career of Dr. John Kale Kale who was laid to rest in his native village of Mokunda, Buea on March 15.

Papa John or Pop as he was fondly called by his close friends lived the life of a country squire who was attached to the gentleman's code of fair play, public service, human dignity and integrity. For Cameroon Post obituarist of last week to suggest that "nobody knows in which political party cloak he was clad before his death" is to betray a woeful lack of understanding of and empathy with the personality he was dealing with. To suggest that Dr. Kale, whom the obituary acknowledges was endowed with political vision, after seven years of public office as first deputy Mayor of Buea had "recoiled to the rather familiar terrain and took to a low profile political life. Political somnambulism"…

Take note of the underlined. The first suggests that he, who, after a daunting public stewardship under the one-party polity, had availed himself of the promises of multi-partism and democratic culture and "embraced, and for quite some time savoured power to the people political slogan" – an unmistakable reference to the opposition S.D.F party – ended up committing political apostasy by hob-knobbing with the CPDM regime. The second phrase, 'political somnambulism', implies that John Kale, Esq. later drifted into some kind of limbo, without a sense of direction, yet he is in the same obituary credited with ambition and vision. He was not only a visionary but he is correctly portrayed as an advocate of "tolerance, respect for opposing views, respect for public property/office, love of country and respect for fellowmen…" as well as probity.

I wonder how such a personality as the above could be said to have vacillated. Should caution in political pronouncement be interpreted as vacillation? Does the fact that he refused to declare the platform on which he planned to stage a political comeback necessarily mean that he had re-joined the ruling CPDM regime? Feeble faculties! So the logical sequel of abandoning the SDF platform (if he ever thought of doing so) is joining the CPDM?

Such muddle-headed logic calls for a brief lecture on political priorities and strategies. To make a tactical retreat, as in any battle, is not to be interpreted as abandoning the cause for political change which he whole heartedly embraced. Political liberation is not synonymous to political somnambulism. No one can contest the fact that Dr. John Kale, more than any of his kith and kin, was most instrumental in establishing the SDF in the entire Buea district-stretching down to the West Coast. To suggest that he was going to jump boat is simply outrageous.

Apart from upcoming legislative and presidential elections, there are also senatorial and regional elections in the pipe line. The Cameroon Post obituarist should have done well to find out from the squire which rung of the ladder he was aiming at.

As someone who was privy to his intimate political thought, vision and plans, I should abbreviate my observation by stating that Dr. John Kale's political integrity was never in doubt. The fact that he fraternized with people of all walks of life, shades of opinion and political platforms only emphasizes commitment to democratic culture.

He may have felt betrayed, but was never bitter. He was obviously mistreated by the administration and denied his due privileges, but he bore no grudges. The fact that he did not formally resign from the CPDM party while serving his community – the Buea Municipal Council – on the CPDM ticket was simply predicated on the pragmatic realization that service to his people was a duty that stood far above partisan political interests.

As deputy Mayor on CPDM ticket, John kale Esq. was a radical among conservatives and reactionaries. He might have failed to

26

change the system from within, but he must be credited for not giving up trying until he was finally destituted by decree. He had slowed down his political activism and vanguardism to concentrate on an equally noble and desirable occupation i.e. teaching, but he had never abandoned the cause.

May God grant it that John Kale Esq. did not die in vain and his legacy shall remain a shining example.

Item: Scrapping G.C.E Board is playing with Fire

If reports of a secret presidential decree annulling the autonomy of the GCE Board are true, then decidedly the Biya regime or at least some of its hatchet men have gone berserk. We are told the Board would, under the yet-to-be published decree, be put under the direct control of the national education ministry and that its linkage with the University of London to give the certificate international credibility has been severed.

While these measures are the hand work of the devilish francophone network in Yaounde whose adamant and senseless ambition has been to destroy the Anglo-Saxon educational tradition in English speaking Cameroon (Southern Cameroons), there is a fifth column of Anglophone quisling proxies that has been hired to execute a hidden agenda including the exclusion of pro-Anglo-Saxon exponents of the GCE Board, elimination of its militant leadership as well as set up a financial probe of the outgoing executive. While probity is one of our most cherished values, we hope such an audit does not turn out to be an exercise in witch-hunting on the executive which should be commended for its successful management despite financial constraints.

The francophone conclave in Yaounde ought to be reminded that in 1993, Southern Cameroonians stood up like one man to rescue the GCE from the brinks of disaster and repatriated it to where it rightfully belongs. The Anglophobic clique has been sufficiently warned that any attempt to reverse what Southern Cameroonians regard as a cultural victory that restored a vital part of

27

their sovereign identity shall see Ambazonians rise again like one man, fearless and steadfast to defend the last frontier of their God-given territorial, political, and socio-cultural space on this planet. This is a warning, not a threat!

Indeed, since the satanic forces of francophonie are bent on destroying the vestiges of our down trodden identity, we are kindly requesting them to politely withdraw thousands of their siblings who have overcrowded our private elementary schools such as the PNEUs as well as our lay private and missionary colleges. Our own children can hardly get admission into our own schools because of the congestion created by the francophone influx. God forbid!

And to think of the whole hypocrisy and ambiguity of it all. How can francophones flood our schools with their wards and at the same time seek to destroy the foundation of the very same educational system? The answer is a reverse assimilation whereby the greater the number of francophones who can speak English (without necessarily adopting Anglo-Saxon values) the easier it would be to neutralize and minimize Southern Cameroons' claims to its share of power, public office, and the commonwealth. A pathetically erroneous theory based on the assumption that every francophone (born and bred in the francophone mind-set) who can speak English is a numerical replacement for every Southern Cameroonian who aspires to high office on the basis of his identity. The more francophones can speak English, the more justification for appointing them to all positions of public authority on the grounds that they too are bilingual and all you "Anglo fools can go to hell!"

To hell we shall proudly march, but please kindly withdraw your offspring from our schools. They are choking and, probably, contaminating our children. Por favour, for God's sake.

S-N F.

28

8

The Falsehood of the Northwest-Southwest Divide: Mola Musonge disappoints admirers
April 1, 1997

The trend of ethnic hate literature seems to be on the rise as a call by Prime Minister Peter Mafany Musonge on settlers in Fako division "to vote for the ruling CPDM party in appreciation of hospitality" is being translated into hostility with subtle messages of ethnic exclusivity being bandied around by agents and errand boys of the francophone regime in Yaounde.

No reasonable person can deny the fact that so-called 'settlers' or 'strangers' should "think and reason with the natives" i.e. show active concern for the development of where one resides. But I take exception to the notion that such freeborn Cameroonians, now labelled as 'strangers' should show appreciation of the hospitality of natives by voting for a ruthless regime that is notorious for destroying the welfare of the people.

In fact there is some meaning beyond the mere demand for 'strangers' to show gratitude. The feeling one has is that the so-called stranger who should go on his knees and against his conscience to show gratitude is, in effect, being made to feel like an intruder, a "perche" or squatter, who ought to be apologetic about his/her settlement.

Come to think of it, it would appear that the so-called stranger is expected to behave as if he were living on some kind of charity of the natives. Charity indeed! The notion that 'strangers' are living off the charity of natives has resulted in their being made to feel as if they were beggars. The hostility against Graffis is so misplaced, hypocritical, vicious and mischievous when we know as a fact that the arch-apostle of 'South-west' puritanism, his Excellency Peter (again another Peter) Oben Ashu's trusted domestic staff and

29

retainers are nearly all honourable Graffimen. The Graffi-coastal hate-love relationship is regrettably tilting to the negative side when political mercenaries like Dr. Chief Atem-Ebako in resolutions adopted by the South-west Chiefs General Assembly held in Kumba on March 8, 1997, endorsed the fickle notion that "Today South-Westerners are like strangers in their homes and it is only a matter of time and they shall cease to exist as a people…"

Well enough. The paradox is equal to the confused and confusing mind-set of the paranoid i.e. the indigene now identities himself as a stranger. And instead of calling on the World Wide Fund for Nature W.W.F. to rescue them from imagined extinction, they are rather calling on people to vote for the CDPM regime as a means of salvation. Who is fooling who?

Traditional healers and modern doctors: mutually exclusive or complimentary?

The first national forum on health that brought together medical practitioners in both the public and private sectors including traditional healers in Yaounde two works ago, seemed to have brought one major controversy to the limelight i.e. how much importance should be given to traditional medicine (or is it traditional doctors) in our public health delivery system?

While traditional healers have been pressing for statutory measures and legislation recognizing and regulating their profession, modern doctors regard the moves as an attempt by what are now known as tradi-practitioners to equate their profession with theirs. They view demands by traditional healers for the establishment of a department of traditional medicine in the Ministry of Public Health as a claim to unmerited status.

Some liberal intellectuals say they would not mind if traditional healers set up their own training school, but on no account would they entertain the notion of carrying out joint diagnosis and treatment of patients under the same roof because their respective methods are at variance (or is it different?).

While the majority of traditional healers have had very little or no formal modern education, it is erroneous to consider African traditional medicine as unscientific, as Peter Essoka suggested on Hotline last week, because it lacks a data base (or that it has no written literature or documentation). Balderdash. What is based on observation, formulation of theory (be it on paper or brain, it after all begins from the brain), experimentation and repeated evaluation of the process in order to establish a logical and incontrovertible truth and basis for diagnosis can be considered as scientific. Is Peter suggesting that the practice of traditional medicine does not fulfil the above criteria? Of course, it does. Whatever differences there are between the two methods, what counts is the result.

Besides the controversy over the place of traditional medicine in society, it was not clear what criteria (scientific?) were used by the organizing ministry in the choice of delegates representing traditional healers to the national forum. It is surprising that the legitimate and recognized authority on traditional medicine in Cameroon, the National Association of Cameroon Traditional Doctors led by the country's pioneer organizer of the profession, Dr. Fai Edward Ngu Fominyen was not even consulted as to the participation of his sector in such an important forum, let alone invited. For nearly three decades, Fai Fominyen has tirelessly fought to give traditional medicine its deserved status in Cameroon and his ardent efforts were crowned in Kampala, Uganda last May when he was elected Coordinator of the committee for the organization of Traditional practitioners in Africa, an organ of the Scientific and Technical Research Council of the Organization of Africa Unity.

Unfortunately, our penchant for 'man- know- man' business deprived the forum of well-seasoned and a more credible argumentation for traditional medicine.

S-N F.

9

Resignation of Titus Edzoa: The Demystification of a Mystic
April 25, 1997

The dramatic resignation from government of Public Health Minister, Dr. Titus Edzoa, last Sunday is just one more spoke thrust in the wheel of president Biya's anti-democratic train. The resignation (the third of its kind in the Biya era following the resignations in 1992 of Governor George Achu and cabinet member Garga Harman Adji just before the presidential election) comes on the trail of disquieting defections from the Biya camp by political capos such as Ayissi Mvodo, Genevieve Fouda, Delphine Tsanga, Simon-Pierre Tsoungui who hitherto were seen as part of the pillar propping the ethnic Beti oligarchy that has ruined the nation.

Indeed, Biya may soon find himself alone as the writing on the wall becomes clearer to many more of his dim-witted courtesans. Titus Edzoa has, indeed, read the writing on the wall and has jumped the boat before it sinks. However, for someone said to be an accomplished surgeon (he was Biya's personal physician), mystic and karate enthusiast, one cannot understand why he took fifteen years to realize the regime he was serving is-and has always been – a "tragic disappointment."

Hear him in his resignation statement: "Because of political conviction, I was from the beginning fought by a small influential clique within the regime by self-styled thinkers…" Which political conviction is he referring to after serving a despotic regime for fifteen years? Dr. Edzoa's resignation statement rings of so many falsehoods and hypocrisy that one has to doubt the righteousness of his indignation and castigation of the regime. In fact, his motives for resignation are far from altruistic as he wants people to believe.

Dr. Edzoa was not only the president's personal physician, but was the president guru in the Rosicrucian Mystical Order, personal aide and at one time the effective number 2 when he was Secretary-General at the Presidency – in effect the leader in this influential clique he aptly describes as "hypocritical and small-minded." He complains of repeated attempts to humiliate him but conveniently forgets that it was he, as Secretary-General at the presidency, who defiantly undermined and made several attempts to humiliate the then Head of Government, Prime Minister Achidi Achu by usurping the latter's powers.

Titus Edzoa did not only confiscate the Prime Minister's powers but also coveted his master's throne. He tried to play Alexander Haig but failed. On one of Biya's frequent and prolonged 'brief visits' abroad, Dr. Edzoa deceptively usurped the Head of State's prerogative by appointing a board chairman he wanted to impose on the air transport corporation, ADC. The scandal came on the heels of several incidents of impropriety including the award of a multi-billion francs contract for the dredging of the Douala estuary port to a company in which he had vested interest. He is alleged to have hatched a scheme to extort billions from public corporations under the pretext of fund-raising for the hosting of the OAU Summit last June.

Dr. Edzoa is even said to have had the cheek to invite the President, his spiritual novice, to visit his multi-million dollar moated castle snuggly situated in a lush wild life park on the south- western outskirts of Yaounde – a magnificently appointed castle, we are told, that would be the envy of the stingingly rich and spoiled stars of Beverly Hills.

The accumulated effect of this pompous grandeur earned him a presidential kick last September that plummeted him from the height of the Secretariat-General to the less coveted position of health minister. Bruce Lee, Cameroon version, has since been licking his wounds and plotting vengeance. And he chose the right time to strike – less than a month to parliamentary elections. That was a master chop at the solar plexus.

Dr. Edzoa's announcement that he would also run for the October presidential election only aggravated the festering ulcer President Biya must have developed after the recent defections from his bandwagon.

Asked on BBC on Tuesday to state why he expects the support of Cameroonian come presidential election, Titus Edzoa, in his characteristic procrastination, said he would explain that when the time comes. Same thing on CRTV Actualité Hebdo programme of March 16. Asked to throw light on the numerous deleterious acts in public office, he offered to explain when the time comes. When will that time be, Dr. Bruce Lee? What, indeed, is that record of public service that makes you presidential material? What are Edzoa's chances?

I put the question to an eminent opinion leader and you know his answer? He put the tips of his thumb and forefinger together, forming the eye piece of a telescope. Nought.

In denouncing the Biya regime, Dr. Edzoa has merely given room for the demystification of his mystic self.

S-N F.

35

10

Presidential Election: A Most Uneventful Event
October 20, 1997

Someone had predicted rather accurately that troop reinforcements in main opposition centres would have the effect of keeping away voters from the polling stations. That's exactly what happened in Victoria (Limbe).

After the official closing of polling stations on Sunday evening, one could still notice the heavy presence on the streets of mean-looking, gun-toting soldiers whose intimidating exercise could not be easily explained. On enquiry, it turned out that they were visibly angry about the near total boycott of the polling stations by the nonchalant electorate. They were out, I was told, to make sure that boycotters did not come out to rejoice about their victory (not stolen this time around). They were angry that the apathetic electorate had religiously adhered to the opposition call to stay at home during the voting. They were out to punish the recalcitrant voters who saw no use in the voting exercise, especially as the results in favour of the ruling party were a foregone conclusion.

For one full week, business in downtown Victoria came to a halt with barely a few tottering, pinched face soldiers patrolling the streets, disturbing the peace and bracing up to fight an unknown and unseen enemy – kind of shadow-boxing.

Captain Guerandi: Our Kabila in the making

Captain Guerandi Mbara is not a household name in Cameroon; not yet. A prominent spearhead of the April 6th 1984 failed coup d'état, Guerandi was one of the few rebels who escaped the country before it even dawned on everyone that the coup had failed. As they

37

say, there is "no failure like a failed coup." It can also be said that Guerandi has lived to fight another day.

From exile in Burkina Faso, Captain Guerandi published a memorandum titled: "Criminal government and the fomentation of civil war" (my translation) which appeared in L'Expression newspaper of October 6th. The 21/2 page document issued on the occasion of 20th May and especially addressed to members of the armed forced in a dismal account of President Biya's fifteen year of personal rule, mismanagement and depletion of the commonwealth. He describes Cameroon under Biya as a gun-powder keg that merely awaits ignition – a veritable time bomb.

He urged Biya to withdraw his candidature, an advice the tin-god did not take since he doesn't even read the papers and warned that should Biya not heed his advice, the Cameroonian people, in conformity with the universal rights of man, would resort to armed resistance.

The Kabilas are hardly heard of especially during their period of preparation for their 'salutary' (messianic?) mission. Guerandi had been gearing up for the past 13 years for the final show down. The eleventh hour has struck. It is just a matter of time to trade ballot for bullets.

Epitaph for Wilson the Philosopher

I have lost a few dear friends this year and since life under Biya's insensitive regime has made it almost impossible for one to give his dear ones a decent burial, I can only pay proper homage to them in this column:

Wilson Gwanyama, provincial pedagogic inspector of philosophy for the North West passed away last September after a brief illness. Though small in stature, he had the heart of a tiger. A committed revolutionary vanguard, Wilson sought for nothing but the truth. Another close friend remarked that had Wilson (a man who was hardly in ill-health) knew he was going to die when he did, he would have rigged himself with a bomb and taken Biya along with him. May his soul rest in peace.

S-N F.

11

SDF's Dilemma: To dine or not to dine
October 31, 1997

That the National Executive Committee meeting of the Social Democratic Front ended last weekend with no public statement comes as no surprise. To resolve the highly controversial item on the agenda viz whether its MPs should withdraw from the National Assembly and local councils, is not a piece of cake.

The taste of lucre and the possibilities of influence peddling are so tempting that the MPs and councillors would be hard put to forego the huge salaries and perks they now enjoy if asked to quite the dining table.

However, political analysts are rather surprised that the question of collaboration with the incumbent regime should now become a bone of contention when the SDF's policy of non-collaboration has been clearly defined and trumpeted. Boycotts, parliamentary walk-outs and refusal to join a proposed government of national union are all in line with this policy. Why then vacillate over the question of participation in parliament and local councils. The rather embarrassing and ineffectual symbolic presence of the SDF in these state institutions is in sharp contradiction of its policy.

If pragmatism dictates otherwise and considering the argument that continued collaboration in state institutions would go a long way to bolster the party's leverage in the conduct of public affairs (a feeble argument bearing in mind their insignificant number in parliament and the usurpation of powers in the local councils by the ruling CPDM party), then an extra-ordinary convention ought to be convened to deliberate and ratify that change in policy.

Some observers have suggested that it would have been premature for the National Executive to divulge any strategies after last weekend's meeting, especially as it came barely days after the proclamation of results of presidential election (boycotted by the parliamentary opposition) and less than a fortnight to the swearing-in of the incumbent president. Keeping matters dark, they believe, would keep the adversary perplexed and uncomfortable. But for how long and for what purpose, it is difficult to tell.

Who Takes the Lion's Share?

Looking at last week's results of the October 12 presidential election, it could be said, as one keen observer put it, that Biya had over played his hand. Cooked up figures giving Biya an over 90% score were a bitter reminder that Cameroon was virtually back to the authoritarian one-party polity. Some political eccentrics and cynics have even suggested that the disenchanted populace should now revert en masse to the ruling CPDM and recommence the fight for a share of the national cake from within.

Some believe such a move would neutralize the parochial and baseless conflict between indigenes and so-called settlers or strangers in certain parts of the country where the latter are perceived as anti-establishment.

With nearly every region boasting of over 90% score, one wonders who should now claim the lion's share of the national cake since such sharing has always been predicated not on sound economic principles, but on the farcical performance of political jokers who excel in arithmetical gymnastics and hat tricks. These political contortionists should be at each other's throat now, as they vie for vantage position in the 'banquet hall'.

In the meantime, Mr. Biya, the numerologist cum omenologist, the "Kateka" of the gambling house that the nation has become, gleefully dangles the carrot at the end of a stick and is tickling with laughter at the spectacle of political acrobats cutting capers to get a juicy morsel while he bides his time for the November 6 swearing-in just in keeping with the fetish of "l'homme du six novembre".

Speculation: Is Marafa Heading for Ports?

With political actors and clowns now warming up for the next round of the game of musical chairs, speculation is rife that Marafa Yaya, senior presidential aide might likely takeover the management of the National Ports Authority currently (mis)managed by Tchouta Moussa, who is said to have distinguished himself in political thuggery during past elections in his native Nde division. Poor Tchouta. After all the over zealousness and reckless spending of the corporation's funds to boost the CPDM campaign efforts, he may soon realize that his physical exertions and display of sweaty armpits during folkloric manifestations of political sycophancy could amount to nought.

Marafa's candidacy, I understand, is propped by a strong northern lobby who believe it's their turn, after the Bassa and the Bamileke, to dip into the juicy pot of Ports Authority. It is said that current transaction between a Japanese firm contracted to handle the maritime port terminal, are channelled directly to Marafa who equally played a prominent role in the CPDM campaigns.

Global Warming on the Mountain

The rate of deforestation on the slopes of Mount Cameroon could spell climatic disaster for inhabitants of the slopes of the mountain- an area cherished for its mild temperatures, flora and fauna.

I spent part of the last couple of nights slapping mosquitoes at a resort reputed for its well- kept lawns, flower gardens and hedges and endowed with a natural drainage that permits no ponding of rain water.

Natives and residents alike must be checked and reminded of their responsibilities towards the environment while a programme of reforestation should be put in place to restore the minimum level of forestation that was maintained under the federated state of West Cameroon.

12

From 'stolen victory' to 'moral victory': Euphemisms for emasculation or capitulation?

Monday, November 03, 1997

When victory is qualified, it is no longer victory. The tendency by the leading opposition parties to delude their followers with dubious slogans aimed at camouflaging strategic weaknesses and failure ought to be critically re-examined.

So far, the main opposition parties, SDF, UNDP and CDU, have since the beginning of multi-party elections in 1992, failed to satisfactorily explain the rather inconsistent policy to boycott certain elections on the grounds that the rules of the game were unfair and at other times, participating in other elections despite unfair rules.

So far the main opposition parties, described as radical, and demonstrably in control of three quarters of the electorate, have not explained why they had failed to come up with that single candidate to face the incumbent in the October 12 election, bearing in mind that since 1992, activists for change have been unanimous that the single candidate strategy seemed the most viable alternative to violent change. Could it be said that the collective good was sacrificed for personal aggrandisement?

So far, the radical opposition has failed to explain whether election boycotts were conducted for the mere sake of boycott or whether they were a means to an end, or an end in itself?

The tactic, especially by the Social Democratic Front, SDF of wait- and- see, that is giving the impression during periods of political impasse of waiting for an imminent miracle, was crafted to give a false sense of hope and great expectation that seems to have crashed on the dilemma of 'to dine or not to dine.'

The SDF's difficulty in deciding whether to withdraw from parliament was compounded by their decision to enter in the first place and, as one observer has noted, Chairman Fru Ndi himself forms part of the difficulty since he is a beneficiary, we are told, of a monthly contribution by SDF MPs. Critics see the SDF entry into parliament not merely as compromise but a surrender, and any attempts to transform a boycott into a victory is sheer papering over the cracks because you cannot win or lose without competing.

The SDF, whose creation and the sacrifices incurred by that creation, was conceived and nurtured by a burning Anglophone desire and determination to restore the sovereignty of Southern Cameroons departed from its intrinsic quest to embrace a nebulous notion of a 'national mission' which has not only deviated and demobilised the momentum of the Southern Cameroons struggle, but has also dissipated and squandered the resources of Francophone Cameroon which deviously supported it with a hidden agenda to eventually usurp Ambazonian (Anglophone) power.

If there is still any gas left in the Chairman's political tank, observes a Free West Cameroon Movement activist, he should be better advised to "take up the Southern Cameroons [Ambazonia] cause if he intends to have any political relevance in the near future."

S-N F.

13

Bakassi Blues: Random Notes
Friday April 10, 1998

Besides a battery of treaties and events within the realm of international law cited to justify its claim over the disputed Bakassi Peninsula, the Yaoundé government mentions the UN supervised February 11, 1961 plebiscite in which the Southern Cameroons decided to gain independence by joining French Cameroon. This indeed is an unavoidable acknowledgment that the disputed territory belongs to Southern Cameroons. And to no one else.

After the recent border conflict erupted in Bakassi in December 1993, Nigerian Nobel laureate, Whole Soyinka suggested the holding of a referendum in the peninsula to resolve the ownership dispute. Wole however forgot that the plight of Bakassi is a microcosm of the plight of the Southern Cameroons resulting from the Yaoundé policy of marginalization, economic plunder and moral degradation. Not only Bakassi but the entire Southern Cameroons would have to take part in such a referendum as the case may be.

It is quite instructive to note the change of tone in the Yaoundé government spokesman's recent pronouncements on the recent wave of border clashes. About five years ago, when the conflict erupted, jingoistic declarations indicated there was nothing to fear about Nigeria's giant size and population- the military triumph of David over Goliath was a question of the quality of men and weapons.

Today, the spokesman sees Nigeria as a formidable power and unbeatable foe with a large and war-tested army capable of overrunning the territory. What happened to the quality of men and weapons? Somehow, by some ironical twist of fate, the one and most unlikely character who knows something about that quality is none other than Nigeria's military ruler, General Sani Abacha, who, as Nigeria's number two after General Babangida, visited Cameroon less than ten years ago and inspected the country's strategic military installations under the auspices of bilateral cooperation. Few observers did grasp the implications of the visit at the time.

It is also worth noting that in 1986, the journal of Nigeria's Defence Academy Studies in its first issue carried no less than two articles on the military implications and deployment routes of the Bakassi Peninsula occasioned by "a possible emergency along the Nigeria-Cameroon border". This is a clear example of preventive policy-making as opposed to Cameroon's corrective policy making strategy.

It took Cameroon twelve years between the Lake Nyos gas disaster and the Nsam petrol explosion to realize the need for a permanent structure to handle national disasters. Always selling after the market.

At a rally in Bafoussam about a fortnight ago, opposition SDF Chairman, John Fru Ndi, revealed that the seven Cameroonian soldiers who were shot dead recently in the Bakassi Peninsula were not victims of Nigerian incursions. They were shot by a desperately hungry and frustrated comrade-in-arms, according to Fru Ndi. This revelation is spine-chilling and a reflection of an unmistakable decline in morale. So we now have a discouraging situation where the quality of men means and morale- the three most crucial factors in any military campaign- is doubtful.

If this deplorable situation persists, then the Yaoundé government, in the event of an unfavourable verdict at The Hague, would have to resort to what it should have sought in the first place – a bilateral arrangement. Whatever approach it takes, Yaoundé would have a hard time obtaining a durable solution to the Bakassi dispute without resolving the Southern Cameroons question.

Anti-Corruption Campaign: An Exercise in Shadow Boxing

No well-meaning and right – thinking person would affirm that the current noisome media campaign against corruption, bribery and embezzlement is the sensible way to go about checking and eradicating this triple-headed evil.

Dr. Adamu Ndam Njoya, leader of the opposition Cameroon Democratic Union told Cameroon Calling: we have laws against corruption, bribery and those laws should be implemented. Period.

If all the big noise about corruption is intended to distract international finance circles who insist on accountability as a precondition for further financial assistance, then the government ought to invent another gimmick because this one won't wash.

S-N F.

14

Fun of Fons: A Cautionary Word about Fondoms
July 06 1998

Informal debates about the relevance of traditional rulership in the Grassfield province of the Southern Cameroons has gained much currency especially following the recent creation of the North-West Fons' Union, a re-emergence of a previously split grouping of sub chiefs, chiefs, chieftains, warlords and genuine Fons. No one is contesting the desirability for traditional rulers to be symbols of dignity, unity and justice, but the fact that most of them have become actively involved in partisan politics since the restoration of multi-partism at the beginning of this decade has made it impossible for them to fulfil their ordained mission, thereby encouraging discord amongst their subjects. Before and after the one party system , tribal leaders were and continue to be officially designated by francophones as 'auxiliaries of the administration- the state' and whereas the Southern Cameroons had endowed the institution of traditional leadership with a dignified consultative legislative chamber known as the House of Chiefs, the integrity and pride of this institution has steadily eroded in Anglophone Cameroon since the Southern Cameroons was hoodwinked in to an unholy marriage with French Cameroon. The process of undermining the role and dignity of this institution reached its peak in 1983 when President Biya, a few months-old novice in power, was conferred the incongruous title of Fon of Fons by some gullible, attention- seeking traditional leaders of the Grassfield. Was it an act calculated to make fun of the institution of Fon-doms? This act of picking up crowns from the gutter or is it casting pearls to swines, or more appropriately, elevating humpty dumpty to the throne; this gesture was viewed by serious-minded citizens as a buffoonery at best and an abomination at worst. And ever since that act of desecration, every Tom, Dick and Harry who wears a red feather on his raffia skull cap began parading around with the self-declared title of Fon. Who in God's name is a Fon? Ethnologically speaking, every village head in the Grass field and its immediate ethnographic environs was invariably addressed as *FO, Nfon, Nfor, Mvon,* but with the coming of colonial administration in the late 19th century, the title Fon and the geographical entity recognized as a Fon-dom assumed a more precise definition referring strictly to kingdoms (not villages or clans) which the colonialist met in place, viz; the Fondoms of Nso, Kom, Bafut and Bali-Nyongha. You may dismiss this as a piece of "ancient" history. Fair enough. But we have no right to distort that history. The arrogation of titles has led to harmful trends such as self-aggrandizement of petty rulers, territorial ambitions of errand-chieftains of the regime, and one of the most recent being a noisome suggestion by pro CPDM plotters that Santa, an asyphalus chief less agglomeration, described by ethnographers as a "no man's land" could attain the status of an administrative division by an intriguing political algebra that would miraculously subsume the Fon-dom of Bali-Nyongha as part of Santa. This is more than a mouthful of Santa black beans to swallow. This kind of political chicanery is certainly informed by a shameful precedent whereby several years ago, Mbengwi, the chief town of Momo division, after failing to meet the qualifications to become a SONEL centre such as population density and number of electricity consumers, adumbrated a political formula which automatically transformed Bali Nyongha into a part of Mbengwi in order to win its bid. These reckless and irrational consequences of aggrandizement by petty entities and nonentities must be checked, and soon enough, if we are to stop this phenomenon of making fun of Fons or is it Fon of Fons?

S-N F.

52

15

Give Peter Acham a Chance
August 24 1998

It appears the general euphoria that greeted Mr. Acham's appointment as Governor of the South-West Province late last month is rapidly turning sour for no apparent reason other than the resurgence of a mischievous, parochial, and sectarian sentiment which was thought to have been laid to rest following his appointment.

It is still not clear how and why the impressive attendance of North-West traditional rulers at Mr. Acham's installation has been interpreted by certain quarters as an affront. These Fons and Chiefs might have stolen the show but they did not steal away the Governor whose prime duty is to cater for the welfare of everybody within his jurisdiction irrespective of tribe, nationality, gender and creed.

It would seem that every Peter who rises to prominence automatically becomes the target for mudslinging even when he has not had a chance to prove his mettle.

This observation is informed by allegations that the newly appointed Governor was given a reception in Buea by the opposition SDF party Chairman John Fru Ndi. Assuming that the allegations were founded, what, one may ask, is wrong with that?

Of course it is quite clear that the propagators of these allegations intend to portray the Governor as a sympathizer of the opposition and to draw a parallel with another kinsman of his, former Governor George Achu (on self-exile) who blew the whistle on the CPDM regime for setting up a diabolical machinery that massively rigged the 1992 presidential election.

If the CDM regime and its mudslinging agents are sincere about its recently minted policy of "democracy of appeasement" which dictates that some kind of dialogue or rapprochement is established with the opposition parties, then it should encourage rather than decry any social function of conviviality that brings both sides together.

Multiparty politics is primarily at ensuring political alternation by providing choices open to the electorate. It is not aimed at engendering enmity and intolerance.

Appointments in Cameroon are usually not based on merit but when someone is perceived by members of the public, irrespective of their political creed, to have merited an appointment, it would be simply unfair to expect his kinsmen to remain indifferent because of political differences.

Unlike his predecessor, Governor Acham has promised to make every Cameroonian residing in the South-West Province to feel at home; a highly commendable pursuit which ought to be a chance to succeed, not thwarted by petty sentiments.

Retired Governor Peter Oben Makes Peace with his Maker

The man who is widely credited with setting up a neo-Nazist rule in the South-West Province and who was relieved of his duty in the recent gubernatorial reshuffle, former Governor Peter Oben Ashu attended Church service a week ago at his Bokwaongo Parish accompanied by his family. Reports say he put on cheerful appearance as he greeted fellow parishioners after the service.

In conclave with the Parish Council, Peter the Hitler explained his reign of terror as human weakness. He is said to have confessed that he had acted the way he did because his paymasters expected that of him. He was merely pleasing his political puppet masters in order to stay in office. In a remorseful tone that amounted to a mea culpa, *Massa* Peter pleaded for understanding and the human milk of forgiveness.

Such antics can pass muster in a parish context but certainly not in tribunal for crimes against humanity. Violation of human rights cannot any longer be justified on grounds of blind obedience of hierarchy even if one were a military Governor or a mercenary. That argument had long been buried at the Nuremburg trials.

However it is a commendable act when humans express contrition for crimes against humanity, especially when they have been stripped of the claws that made them predators. So the question still lingering in the air is: Would Peter Oben Ashu behave differently if he were to be appointed governor again at some point in future? That would depend on whether his acts of terror were compulsive or congenital.

S-N F.

16

Biya at Non-Aligned Summit: A Regurgitation of Pious Platitudes
Monday, September 14, 1998

The last summit of non – aligned states in Durban, South Africa, ended without anyone seeing the man doing his stage act. Even though he was elected one of the vice-presidents of the conference and also gave a speech, I watched the tube closely and did not see Mr. Paul Biya doing his thing. Not on CNN, neither on TV5 nor CFI. I doubt if he came on our local CRTV during the course of the summit.

The cameras failed to capture the man; not with such charismatic characters around like Mandela, Mugabe, Kofi Annan and enigmatic ones like Kabila who was not even expected. Our man was simply dwarfed. Effaced, indeed!

According to Radio Cameroon, the President mounted the rostrum and throatily sermonised on the need for the re-orientation of the non-aligned movement and the strengthening of stability, security and development. A perfect case of regurgitation. No originality. So far, so good, considering the man's usual insipid style. Then, soon after, he began wobbling when he identified "the resurgence of nationalism' as one of the issues to be tackled by a 'born again' non-aligned movement.

One could not tell from the news report whether or not President Biya identified the cases of this resurgence and if he suggested ways to tackle the phenomenon. One only hopes that when he mentioned the resurgence of nationalism(s) he was not only thinking of Kosovo, Cherchnya, Erythea, Casamance, the Sahrawi, Anjouan etc. We hope he was also seriously thinking of the Southern Cameroons question which stands right at this own doorstep, but which he has frequently snubbed, going even as far as declaring some time ago at the Elysee Palace in Paris (his favourite location for making important national pronouncements) that there is no Anglophone [Southern Cameroons] problem in his country because he had not noticed any public agitation related to any such problem. If my memory is correct, he made the statement in early 1992. Five years later, hundreds of Anglophones were arrested and detained on cooked up charges of involvement in armed terrorism against military installations. More than 50 are still languishing in jail, while some have died and none had been brought to trial so far. Since the regime had not perceived "public agitation", it had to fabricate and execute terrorist attacks in the Anglophone Northwest province to justify a tighter military occupation of the area.

The resurgence of nationalism can mainly be attributed to the hegemonic power that certain groups of leaders from certain ethnic groups have exercised with 'divine' mandate over the rest of the majority of a given national territory. This hegemonism, as the case of Cameroon, is most repugnant in a situation where a previously autonomous or sovereign entity is being lorded over (either by default, force or fraud) by a consensual partner or an invader.

Chairman, Look Out!!!

The Minister of Transport has issued a communiqué reiterating regulations governing the matriculation of automobiles (see Cameroon Tribune, August 27, 1998).

The communiqué would have appeared perfunctory were it not for the fact that it prohibits personalised vehicle number plates because this is not provided for by the regulation in force.

There can be no doubt in anyone's mind as to whom this prohibition is directed. The communiqué enjoins law enforcement and security agents to ensure the application of the regulation by organizing joint traffic controls as from August 31st.

Opposition SDF Chairman, J.F. Ndi, is the only individual in Cameroon I know of so far who has a personalized number plate on one of his Turbo-engine luxury jeeps acquired when he honoured an invitation to Bill Clinton's first inauguration is the US in 1993. Not long ago, we learnt that local administrators in his home base, Bamenda, had threatened to impound the vehicle in question if the number plate were not normalized. One of the Chairman's aides argued that the said vehicle was duly registered.

John Fru Ndi has been going about with his personalized number plate for more than 5 years and the recent ministerial communiqué explicitly forbidding name plates, thought timely, could be a camouflage for sinister motives. Fru Ndi like every other citizen is not above the law. Granted. However, if we agree that laws and regulations are dynamic not static, what then has prevented the authorities from providing for customized number plates. This could help generate sorely needed revenue for the national treasury.

What I suspect is that the regime is again calculating to take advantage of the current vulnerability of the SDF to spring a humiliating surprise on the Chairman, especially if and when, the party holds its long overdue Convention in Yaounde.

Local authorities in Bamenda may not dare to impound the Turbo in their jurisdiction; but, in Yaounde, anything is possible. We all remember the assassination attempt on the Chairman in downtown Yaounde by the police Commissioner for Yaounde Central and his cohorts a few years ago.

This and other circumstances raise doubts as to the wisdom of the SDF decision to hold its Convention in Yaoundé besides the high possibility of infiltration and destabilization by the regime's political thugs.

For 5 years the regime has condoned the Chairman's personalized number plate. If it is flexing its muscles now, it can only be because it now perceives the SDF to be in a position of weakness. So, Chairman, be on the watch – out!

S-N F.

17

Epitaph for Ebssiy
Monday, October 12, 1998

Here lies Ebssiy Ngum who stood for the right. A heroic chronicler, he was let down in the prime of life by friends and foes and kith and kin alike

The above epitaph pales against one proclaimed by the deceased news anchor and ace commentator, Ebssiy Ngum, sometimes In June 1986 to mark the death of the Sunday English- language news commentary programme, Cameroon Report, over the national radio.

When Ebssiy, the coordinator of Cameroon Report, solemnly, announced the mischievous banning of the programme through the agency is bound to persist hardly did he realize at the time that he had sparked the fuse of the political time bomb that finally exploded in the fiery circumstances surrounding the pro-democracy activism and the restoration of multipartism at the beginning of this decade.

For historical record and the sake of posterity, it is most timely to reconstruct events that constitute what I now refer to as the Monkey File.

The June 1986 budgetary session of parliament had just got off the ground when the Honourable Deputy of Ndian, Mr. Lobe Nwalipenja, during the Information Minister's defence of his annual budget, asked the Minister why he thought parliament should approve allocations for a department whose journalists had been attacking public officials and parliamentarians. In a fit of embarrassment and in a bid to please the National Assembly, the Information Minister hastily issued informal instructions which filtered down the `hierarchy and were finally interpreted to mean the death of Cameroon Report. A roughly scribbled service note in the newsroom merely announced the suspension of the programme, but no one was fooled. The programme had been spiked to death and despite its resuscitation and re-baptisms, it has not been and can hardly be the same again.

The background to this chicanery is politically instructive. In a bid to give a semblance of open democracy, President Paul Biya, Chairman of the one and only CPDM party, introduced the idea of at least two contestants for the party section elections. Mr. Nwalipenja who, like his counterparts throughout the nation had been used to being elected by unanimous acclamation, was floored by a political unknown in his Ndian constituency. Instead of taking his humiliation in stride, the Honourable gentleman decided to take it out on the media, the Cameroon Report team in particular, as if he had expected them to announce a victory in his favour. This was a gentleman who had been denounced by his constituency for his ineptitude and hopeless record of political husbandry, who decided to take revenge on the media instead of learning from his political errors.

One Saturday in the newsroom, the Cameroon Report team had assembled with all enthusiasm to tailor and package the Sunday morning programme when they learned, to their utter shock and dismay of the suspension of the programme. "We shall not take this lying down!!" Everyone was indignant and in an emergency meeting it was resolved that since Cameroon Report had been suspended, we were going to pursue our pro-democracy struggle through the revival of daily news talks at the tail end of the evening newscast. Each member of the team either choose or was assigned a topic in an all-encompassing democracy crusade with the conviction that President Biya was indeed serious about opening up the suffocating political atmosphere.

That done, the last point was who will bell the cat? The crusade was to start the following Monday and it was agreed that the head of the English- language news desk, George Tanni, was to sound the bugle for battle and fire the first salvo to announce the new battle for democracy. He reneged.

Come Tuesday, my turn. The choice was either to take the bull by the horn or betray the collective conscience and professional integrity of Cameroon Report. I chose the former. My theme, because there was no script whatsoever except Ebssiy's epitaph, was "The Enemies of Democracy" in which I castigated anti-democratic elements describing same as parliamentary hand-clappers and a certain species of primates i.e. Monkeys. How else could they be described if Ebssiy's description of their act as buffoonery were right? That Tuesday's evening newscast was ably anchored by Jonnie McViban. And so less than 72 hours later, Ebssiy, Johnnie and I found ourselves in police custody for the beginning of an ordeal stretching from June to October, making us the V.I.P. guests of the First district, Mokolo and Central police precincts as well as the Kondengui maximum security prison.

The rest is history. We had earned the notoriety of being the first state employed journalists of be held in detention on a politically motivated charge to wit: contempt of authority. Ebssiy and Jonnie were victims of the conspiracy theory which in Cameroon means that it is inconceivable for an individual to engage in what is perceived as subversion without the complicity and backing of an underground movement.

Ebssiy and Johnnie's understanding of the situation helped a great deal to mitigate the occasional pangs of guilt I felt for having been the agency of their trial and tribulations. They had taken the whole event with equanimity despite their relative status of novices in the profession. They braved the baptism of fire like the true crusaders of yore. At the end of the ordeal, they had matured.

Going through a similar ordeal was Barrister Gorji Dinka in the nearby political prison at the BMM, for championing the Southern Cameroons (Anglophone) quest for independence. Two years or so later, human rights activist, Albert Mukong who was later to become the brain behind the movement to restore multipartism, was jailed for exposing Biya's corrupt system. Then in 1989, it was the Yondo Black affair, then the bloody launch of the Social Democratic Front in Bamenda etc. etc.

The next is history. Ebssiy's legacy lies in the turbulent circumstances surrounding the political renaissance of this decade. It is merely a curious twist of fate that led to his becoming the moderate moderator of what was once the voice of the people and the one and only alternative channel of social expression to the perverse one party system prior to 1990, to wit: Cameroon Calling (former Cameroon Report)

May the memory of this harmless monument of Cameroon journalism remain evergreen. Rest in Peace.

S-N F.

18

The Epitaph: A Milestone on the Hard Road to Democracy
Monday, October 26 1998

It is incumbent on me to make available to our readers the full text of the epitaph proclaiming the death of "Cameroon Report" as read by the coordinator over Radio Cameroon on June 22 1986 by the recently deceased senior Journalist, Ebssiy Ngum. It reads:

"Here lies a programme in peace, not in pieces; it served the wind of change selflessly, yet it died. But it learned something: the forces against democracy are apparently stronger than the forces for democracy. The forces against democracy are more committed than the forces for change. And the buffoonery keeps over flowing."

Last week, I made a sketchy attempt to demonstrate that Ebssi Ngum's legacy could be summed up in the above epitaph and the chain of events it triggered along the rough path of Cameroon's quest for democracy and freedom.

It is with mild disappointment that I read an interview granted recently in Le Messager (Oct. 12, 1998) by SDF parliamentary Chief Whip, Barrister Mbah Ndam, in which he claimed that it is thanks to pro-democracy street demonstrations organized in the recent past by the SDF to obtain the limited liberty Cameroon enjoys today, which now permits journalists to talk. For anyone to assert that the opposition parties brought about freedom of expression and the press in Cameroon is an attempt to distort historical facts. It is putting the cart before the horse. It is false.

Long before the 1986 Cameroon Report incident and its ramifications which I dubbed last week as the Monkey File, there had been yet another highly inflammable Cameroon Report panel discussion in which Anglophone politicians including Honourable S.T. Muna, John Ngu Foncha, E.T Egbe, V.E Mukete, and the late

Professor Emeritus, Bernard Fonlon were taken to task for the marginalization and plunder of Southern Cameroons (Anglophone) by the Francophone hegemony. That was in November 1982, barely a week after the resignation of Cameroon's first dictator, Ahmadou Ahidjo. What we can now conveniently call the Ahidjo Tapes (actually broadcast over a special edition of Luncheon Date), was titled " Tribute to Ahmadou Ahidjo" and the programme earned some of us including the coordinator, George Ngwa (now journalism lecturer at Buea University), two weeks of excoriating and intimidating inquisition at the lake-side location of the political police, Cameroon's version of the Gestapo, known at the time as SEDOC under the bull-doggish command of the terror-inspiring Jean Forchive (now of late).

It may sound ironical that the fight for freedom of expression was pioneered and championed by a self-appointed segment of the Anglophone official media, not even the private press. This can be explained by the fact that Anglophones were and still are endowed with a more liberal political culture than Francophones and that those of the official media, especially the radio, did not only avail themselves of a certain measure of job security at the time, but had an enviable access to a much larger audience at a time when government had monopoly over the broadcast media. The spirit of Cameroon Report, created in 1972 with pioneer coordinator Bob Forbin (now editor of the Herald newspaper), can be traced back to the 1960's in Anglophone radio programmes such as Where are We? And the critical Ako Aya columns of the late editor of Cameroon Outlook tabloid, Tataw Obenson.

You can now readily see why Barrister Mbah Ndam's claim that the limited freedom of the press enjoyed in Cameroon today was the result of street demonstrations masterminded by the opposition is misleading. The fight for freedom of expression (including street marches) started two-and-a half decades before the reinstitution of multipartism in 1992; long before the civil rights demonstrations and stay-at-home strikes organized by the opposition parties at the dawn of this decade.

Credit for the freedom of expression crusade cannot be entirely limited to the self-appointed Cameroon Report institution. By the mid-1990s, a number of fearless individuals such as Charly Ndi Chia and his editor, now Barrister Bonou Mo Chungong of the defunct Cameroon Times, as well as Richard Nyamboli with his Thinking Aloud column of the state-owned Cameroon Tribune joined the crusade.

It must be emphatically stated that all these crusades were being waged when a critical segment of the Anglophone media constituted the only "'opposition party' in Cameroon. And it is thanks to the valiant spirit of this media crusade that the renascent opposition parties were conceived and delivered.

Pius Njawe: Free At Last?

Pius Njawe, the publisher and editor-in-chief of *Le Messager* who was serving a commuted one year jail sentence on trumped-up charges of "spreading false information" has regained his liberty following a presidential clemency granted him on October 9.

Mr. Njawe, a well-known activist whose clashes with the regime began in 1991 when he published an article by another activists and banker, Celestin Monga castigating President Biya's political ineptitude and describing parliamentarians as "illiterates," has denied having applied for the clemency which came about two months before the expiration of his jail term.

The circumstances surrounding the clemency provide further evidence of disinformation which has become a hall mark of the regime's media policy since the renascent struggle for democracy at the start of this decade. The presidential decree sanctioning the clemency purports that the pardon was granted at the request of the convict who, it adds, was expected to be released in May 1999; an indication that he still had seven more months to serve in prison.

Njawe was jailed last December for reporting that President Biya might have suffered an acute cardiac malfunction while presiding over the national challenge cup final at the Ahmadou Ahidjo stadium.

The idea of the regime's propaganda machinery always trying to portray the president as a superman – immune to disease – has resulted in robbing the man of the human qualities it takes to endear him to the people.

It cannot be said with certainty that Mr. Biya granted Njawe clemency because of the thousands of petitions from all corners of the globe demanding his release. If that were so, we would equally have expected Biya to release the more than 60 Anglophones languishing in Francophone jails on mere suspicion of terrorist activities believed to have actually been perpetrated by hired thugs of the regime. No formal charge has so far been proffered against these Anglophones and whether they will ever be brought to trial is any one's guess. Mr. Biya's unpredictable and fake gesture of magnanimity in the Njawe case might just as well be a camouflage of a hidden agenda, the ramifications of which are bound to unfold as time goes on.

S-N F.

19

'Pa Foncha was a Freedom Fighter'
Monday, April 26, 1999

Dr. J.N. Foncha popularly known as" Little John" died at the ripe old age of 83 having abandoned his old political robes in the spirit of a true prophet of the Southern Cameroons renaissance.

In June 1990, after watching with grudging acquiescence for close to three decades the political emasculation and economic subjugation of his people, Foncha, prompted by the brutal killing of six innocent civilians during the launching of the SDF on May 26th 1990 wrote his letter of resignation from the CPDM and probably bequeathed to us the most eloquent testimony of his re-unification mission:

""…The Anglophone Cameroonians whom I brought into the union have been ridiculed and referred to as 'les Biafrais' … 'les Enemis Dans la Maison' … 'les Traitres' etc. and the constitutional provisions which protected this Anglophone minority have been suppressed, their voices drowned while the rule of the gun has replaced the dialogue which the Anglophones cherish very much.it was understood at the time of unification that '…there would be no arrogant and selfish majority and a suffering and cringing minority.'" But alas! That vision has been completely distorted, reviled and almost transformed into a nightmarish experience for the Anglophone Cameroonians.

After having ensured the political subjugation of the people of Southern Cameroons, the arrogant and selfish Francophone majority proceeded with the economic spoliation of their territory, closure of corporations like WCDA, the Produce Marketing Board, the Victoria/Tiko Ports etc. and today with the sale of the Cameroon development Corporation (CDC) looming in the horizon, the scales have begun to fall. The deliberate exclusion of Southern Cameroonians from certain government positions such as Minister of

Finance, Defence or Secretary General at the Presidency (even Ephraim Inoni who has been ASG for almost a decade now cannot tell us he is doing fine) is a constant reminder to Anglophones that they don't belong.

We have had occasion before to warn the Anglophones about the magical spell that held the Jews in total disbelief about Hitler's diabolical intentions until the holocaust finally descended on them like a plague from the skies. We are not prophets of doom but the reality is there for everybody to see; the government of La République with the backing of France has drawn up a master plan for the gradual and systematic assimilation of Anglophones that would naturally culminate with the disappearance of their distinct society. Is it an accident of history that the upper echelons of government, the civil service, the military, the diplomatic corps and civil society in short? Consider the following:

- 2 out of 58 SDO's are Anglophones
- Ambassadors to big English speaking countries like Nigeria. Britain and USA are all Francophone
- Do you know of any Anglophone businessman of national stature?

Our francophone brothers would simply like us to believe that they are even helping us to get along as if we represented an economic burden to the nation whereas the facts prove the contrary. Charles Assale, former Premier of East Cameroon declared recently that he used to carry cash to Buea from Yaounde to give late Pa Foncha since the West Cameroon Government was virtually crippled financially. However, as M. Vewesse, President of the Fako Worker's Union pointed out in his timely rejoinder (The Post...) the West Cameroon Government with an annual revenue of 2 billion francs was able to meet up with all its commitments including pension benefits, farmers' produce, subventions for school etc. etc. Today for example, we know the colossal sum of one billion francs leaves the Buea treasury every week for Yaounde.

The fact that Foncha, father of unification, became one of the frontline leaders opposed to it before his death is such a central element in any assessment of the man's political career that no amount of political manipulation can minimize the unbridgeable gap that existed between the elderly politician and the authorities of La République du Cameroun. So disgusted was he that in one of his last interviews, he bemoaned the fate of the Bamenda 57 who have been held incommunicado in Yaounde since the so-called terrorist attacks in North West Province (some have even died) and simply concluded by saying that things were being done as if there was no government. Just as if they were waiting for him to die, the detainees were hurriedly arraigned before a military tribunal on the 15th of April for what would obviously turn out to be a Kangaroo trial.

Right to his last days, Pa Foncha remained a lover of peace and a freedom fighter. Now that he is gone, it is time for all of us to seriously reflect on what he stood for and rededicate ourselves to the pursuit of those ideals of peace, freedom, social justice and self-determination.

It is quite significant that Pa Foncha's death coincides with severe eruptions of Mount Cameroon which, as we predicted, has manifested its disapprobation of the persistent maltreatment of Anglophones and heralded a new era that has laid to rest once and for all the dream of re-unification.

S-N F. for the **Free West Cameroon Movement**

20

Journalism, Watchdogism and Alarmism
Monday , May 24, 1999

Mola Luma is a peaceful middle-aged farmer, resident in the Bokwaongo neighbourhood of Buea. He grows pigs, goats and fowls, and for the sake of division of labour, he employs a night watchman to look after his cartel. One night in the heart of the dry season, a fire broke out in his back-yard and gradually began to consume his investment. His watchman, Mr. Mumu Ngombe, stood transfixed as the raging inferno leapt unto his "caraboat" house and proceeded to do damage. The Lord was merciful and Mola Luma was divinely jolted from his slumber and immediately embarked on damage control.

After dousing the flames, Mola queried his watchman why he did not raise an alarm. Mumu Ngombe, replied, rather astonishingly that: *"Oga, this thing happen for night and a bi di wait say for morning time, you go give me permission for raise alarm."* The back drop of Mumu's attitude was conditioned by a robotic relationship with his employer, whereby it is forbidden for a subaltern, menial or slave to cry, without seeking permission from his boss or oppressor as the case maybe.

It is with unmitigated consternation that I was made aware of the fact that a trusted watchdog, Mr. Zachary Nkuo of Radio Buea, like all residents on the foot of the Buea Mountain, has been queried, bullied, intimidated and chastised for having alerted the authorities that there was "danger for Cameroon," that the bowel of the earth was rumbling, that the earth was quaking. It is a month now since the earthquake yet no one in authority has had the decency, honesty and sheer guts to thank Zachary for having fulfilled his most divine mission as the watchdog of society; a conscious and conscientious professional of a quarter century experience, who, with a sense of dedication, alerted the nation with promptitude that the "Chariot of

God" was crashing not at Mvomeka, but in Fako; that the ancestral powers, the intermediaries of the God- head, have stomached enough of the trash and decadence, the brutal obliteration of a segment of the universe called Cameroon.

Mr. Zachary Nkuo was not decorated, given due recognition for having incarnated and courageously staked his neck for the collective good and protection of humanity.

It is with outrage and a sense of righteous indignation, disgust and distaste that we learn that an errand boy descended from Yaounde, to reprimand Zachary Nkuo, for having done nothing else but his job.

S-N F.

21

BOBA Today
Special Cameroon Protestant College, Bali (C P C) Golden Jubilee Magazine 1949-1999
Memory Lane: Tribute to Reverend Gordon

He stood above average height. Five feet seven or there about. He wore thick white cotton socks, black leather shoes, grey tuck less trousers and white short-sleeved shirts. Two permanent crimson spots marked both sides of the bridge of his nose that inevitably supported his heavy pair of dark rimmed glasses.

Reverend Gilbert Gordon sported dark curly receding hair and had a broad grin for everyone. He hardly scowled. On his elbow (I can't remember which) were two bluish wart like growths sustained in the Korean War where he fulfilled his military service obligations.

Rev. Gordon, nicknamed _Nfundis_i or _Nfun_ for short (after a holy character in _Cry, the Beloved Country),_ taught English language and Literature, Religious Knowledge, and Music. A master librarian, he selected assistants, improved the library cataloguing by introducing the Dewey Decimal system, repaired damaged books, and through his agency, increased the library stock by thousands of volumes from his native Oregon and his American Baptist connections.

His language teaching skills had a tremendous impact on my generation. Right from the first form, we were introduced to phonetics, pronunciation and intonation. He introduced what was called the bibliographic entry which required every student to keep a record and summary of all extracurricular books read during the term and you would be stupid to think you could fool the _Nfun_ who had the uncanny ability to detect falsehood. It was believed he had read all the volumes in the library, so it was useless trying to fool him. It was not a question of whether you were art or science inclined. As a matter of fact some of the most formidable *bibliovores* I competed with ended up in the medical field such as Dr. Peter Ndumbe now Dean of the Faculty of Medicine, University of Yaounde 1 and Dr. Christopher Anyangwe, Alpha Clinic Bamenda.

While everyone acknowledged that he accomplished his conventional teaching duties admirably, Rev. Gordon's most memorable impact, in my opinion, was in the area of extracurricular training and general knowledge. His approach was the quintessence of the liberal arts of the American tradition.

He taught speed-reading as we all strove to achieve the 1,500-word per minute rate. He advanced the teaching of music by moving from the tonic solfa to staff notation and the code phrase-: Every Good Boy Deserves Food-helped us remember the keys of E, G, B, D and F represented by the horizontal lines on a musical chart. We practiced on the organ, recorders and flutes, the violin, and a pixiphone- a portable vibraphone i.e. a miniature xylophone with metal instead of wooden bars. He took the pains to manufacture his own harpsichord which was accessible only to his best students and never left the confines of his living room; a living room which was virtually an extension of the library with piles and piles of books sprawling all over the floor and his dinning cum writing table.

His home was the hallmark of bachelorhood stacked with a variety of objects of academic and artistic curiosity. The air was redolent with the musty smell of books, pelican paste for book binding and the enticing fragrance of freshly baked pastries that issued from his kitchen.

As chaplain of the college, we very much enjoyed his conduct of evening devotion as we learnt new hymns from the Baptist song book which provided songs that were a departure from the standard fare such as "Let Us Break Bread Together on Our Knees."

Rev. Gordon's liberal and gentle ways greatly influenced our later approach to studies and life. His underlying philosophy was broadmindedness. "Stop biting!" he would admonish, raising his bushy eyebrows every time he came across students quarrelling or making noise. Admonishment was his style. He admonished and counselled erring students and only punished in extreme cases. He never bore a grudge, was never angry, nor vindictive. He was a shining example of tolerance. Even when one student was dismissed for indiscipline, Reverend Gordon made him a present of an old church organ and encouraged him to go through the GCE examination which was just round the corner. That student became a pop musician who later composed, arranged and played the guitar and keyboard on the highly acclaimed tune, "Fuel for Love". As destiny would have it, he is today a preacher with a Christian revivalist persuasion in Nigeria. His name is "Ginger"Forcha.

Reverend Gordon helped us produce and direct Shakespeare's Richard II and during rehearsals and staging which went beyond the confines of the college campus, he exercised patience with the recalcitrant backstage director, me and a distracted prompter Sunday Enoh alias Bronco and other dodgers.

Reverend Gordon was also an enthusiast of linguistics and he spent the little spare time he had, codifying the Wimbum dialect of Donga Mantung Division.

His contribution to the academic, spiritual and social life of everyone he came across is unforgettable. He will forever remain a model for those of my generation.

S-N F.

22

Liberalisation of audio-visual media:
A grudging step towards plural democracy
Monday, April 17, 2000

The Prime Ministerial Order early this month outlining conditions of the procedure for the acquisition of a license to operate private radio, television and cable TV, marks one more grudging step for Cameroon's democratization process. The Enabling Act, coming ten years after parliament had passed a law to liberalise the sector, has been greeted with mixed feelings as it is widely believed that government's decision to implement the law was prompted by external pressure and an internal fait accompli as several Francophone private radio stations had begun airing programmes more than one year ago.

The political timing of the decree, coming shortly after an ominous cabinet reshuffle, and which incidentally saw the emergence of the smooth academic don and media guru, Professor Fame Ndongo as Communication Minister and his prompt and unmistakable appointment as Board Chairman of CRTV (a post that has been left vacant for more than a decade), was obviously calculated to beam a sharp signal on the exciting, albeit precarious bend Cameroon's media train is about to take on the millennium communication super-highway.

Professor Fame Ndongo may appear to some as a demagogue, but he has sound credentials which arguably make him one of the best suited for the communication portfolio. Like the late Henri Bandolo, he is well respected in media circles and widely regarded as the architect and social engineer of the present media landscape in Cameroon.

After serving with the state owned daily newspaper Cameroon Tribune for several years, he became Head of the Advanced School of Mass Communication, ASMAC -a position he held cumulatively with that of Communication Adviser at the Presidency. Prior to his ministerial appointment, he was Rector of Yaoundé University I.

His credentials are not in doubt, neither is his puppet mastery of the strings of media manipulation nor his penetration of the arcane world of semiology and the corridor it offer into the shady recesses of nebulous. Fame Ndongo's avowed intention to level the media play ground and to offer both the public and private media an equal opportunity to excel is, however, questionable, given that he is board chairman of the state- owned CRTV. Some observers are sceptical about his ability to exercise impartiality. He is a traditional ruler from one of the Bulu villages around Ebolowa and has recently emerged as the facto leader of the Beti elite, a son of the soil – so to speak. These fears are however counter balanced by his personal commitment to academic and professional excellence and the remarkable influence he has wielded in the mass communication sector over the past two decades.

From State Monopoly to State Predominance

In which case, professor Fame Ndongo cannot be entirely innocent about the spirit and the dark and inexplicit areas of the decree to de-emphasise government control over the audio-visual media of mass communication – because that is exactly what it is: government's undeclared ambition to retain relative monopoly has been surreptitiously demonstrated by the preclusion of Private Nationwide Radio Broadcast which remains a state monopoly. (See Art. 15)

You don't have to be a media guru to understand that control of nationwide radio is effective control of the electronic media. No further comments.

Statute of Enterprise

The arbitrary manner in which the exorbitant licensing fee was arrived at is a matter for revenue and tax collectors to analyse, but political economists, especially those of the free market persuasion, can readily discern the ulterior motive behind the provision which prohibits an individual or a corporate body from holding shares in more than one audio-visual establishment. This measure, ostensibly, is intended to pre-empt private electronic media ownership in the hands of a few money –bags. Conversely, it ensures that government preponderance is not challenged: blocking the likely emergence of a new monopoly to protect the old one; the resurrection of political 'fossils' in the recent cabinet reshuffle is quite revealing!

Furthermore, the statute of enterprise appears to be silent about the economic status of non-commercial applicants of license. Under what regime do they fall since all applicants are required to furnish a business registration number? Political economy dictates that a non-commercial understanding of public interest ought to be classified under the cooperative status of organisations entrusted with services of common interest – a la rigueur, they are non-profit, non-governmental organizations.

A week ago on the TV current affairs programme – Actualité Hebdo – Professor Fame Ndongo sweetened his brilliant performance with promises to negotiate tax exonerations and preferential tariffs for media establishments as a whole. But one would have expected conditions and procedure of granting such advantages to be formerly incorporated into law with the unequivocal understanding that such advantages shall not serve as a means of economic pressure for partisan ends, but as a matter of serving the public interest.

Statute of content

The decree's statute of content (cahier des charges), innocuous as it may seem, prohibits messages that could discredit the state. Since the state, the government and the ruling party are considered one and indivisible (an irreproachable trinity in Cameroon) it requires no clairvoyance to expect how that provision will be interpreted and implemented by the running dogs of 'advanced' democracy.

The ambiguous attempt to address the issue of pornographic content on radio and TV is a shameful record of a pervasive culture of hypocrisy and the negation of religious values. The statute should have clearly prohibited pornography from our air waves because pornography - cryptographic or not -is pornography. No further comments.

Another foggy area of the statute of content pertains to the rather tedious hair-splitting over the notion of patronage and sponsoring of programmes. Unless the statutes clarity what is commercial and what is not, the social engineers of the decree would have to go to parliament again and explain to the nation what has been happening to the monthly stoppages amounting to billions of francs paid by Cameroonian taxpayers as TV dues -'*redevance*'. Until such an official extortion of the taxpayer is accounted for, or else an arrangement that should ensure the rational redistribution of such funds for the promotion of the public interest is arrived at, citizens may begin to question their obligation to comply with the levy.

The statute of content defining the obligations of the audio-visual medial to protect the interest of society, recommends sanctions in case of default, but fails to provide for recourse or procedure of redress, unless we assume that such redress remains within the domain of the law courts.

One uncomfortable feeling about the audio-visual statutes is that government has given liberalization with the right hand and simultaneously withdrawn same with the left hand.

There is absolutely no reason to have created such an impression if our political craftsmen had merely realized that the new decree merely marks a toddling step in our misdirected approach to plural democracy, even though the political scouts have missed yet another chance to learn from the mistakes of advanced industrial nations, who, themselves as inventors, are now grappling with the intractable dangers of violence, abuse and indignity in media content.

Cameroon would have taken a lead in this respect by crafting a media statute that would have gone beyond the hardware issues to elaborate on the quality of broadcast content. Such a leadership would have significantly reversed other negative practices, corruption not being the least.

Government's comfort, at the local level, is its undeniable advance in the installation and control over audio-visual hardware, but he advantage has been severely compromised by its glorification of mediocre professional standards, due to a very noticeable erosion of authoritativeness and credibility in the conception, production and delivery of media content.

The arbitrariness and suspected nepotism and favouritism in the choice of on-the-air broadcast performers with a tiny index of the vulnerability of state-owned media in Cameroon.

The new drum major of Cameroon's mass communication knows all these and it is up to him to match words with action if he intends to go down in history as a most eligible and effective social engineer to usher the nation into the marvellous new world of global communication.

S-N F.

23

BBC/CRTV and the Anglophone Problem

September 28, 2001

Last week, the BBC World Service broadcast a panel discussion on the status of the English and French languages in Cameroon. The radio programme "Talk about Africa" was jointly produced by the British Broadcasting Corporation, BBC and the Cameroon Radio and Television, CRTV. Media consultant and current Affaires analyst, **Sam-Nuvala Fonkem** *considers the manner in which the issue of bilingualism in Cameroon was handled as superficial and the timing of the programme as suspect.*

With Southern Cameroonians (Anglophones) gearing up to remember their independence day on October 1, the timing and choice of subject of the BBC programme can be viewed as suspiciously calculated to hoodwink international public opinion and a cheap propaganda gimmick.

The programme was a shameless showcase of chicanery and clumsy attempt to divert attention from the actual focus of the Southern Cameroons Question that has been dishonestly reduced to a linguistic minority issue; a pathetic simplification of a very grievous political question consisting of the annexation and subjugation, by political fraud and subterfuge, of English- speaking Cameroons by French Cameroon.

The very fact that CRTV (whose top management is francophone and is headed by a Francophone Director-General) was a co-producer of the programme in question smacks of a political conspiracy. In this conspiracy, the BBC can be seen as an unscrupulous seducer willing to lean over backwards to please a whore-mongering regime in a tragic-comical show of gratitude for allowing it to plant an FM relay station in French Cameroon. And the misuse of ace Anglophone commentator, Adamu Musa to moderate the panel discussion in order to give it a semblance of credibility, was sheer window dressing.

The BBC may not be responsible for the content of the programme, but it is certainly guilty by airing it, thereby compromising its widely acclaimed standards of balance and objectivity. If the BBC seriously wanted to give a true picture of the plight of the Anglophones in Cameroon, it is unfortunate that is merely succeeded in insulting the intelligence of all full-blooded Southern Cameroonians. By highlighting the minimization of the English language in Cameroon as if it were the fundamental cause of the Southern Cameroons deep-seated discontent, the programme was an outright provocation.

From a credibility standpoint, the programme fell flat on its face. All the panellists, except one, Professor Bole Butake, who refused to be *lapiroed*, that is compromised, hold their positions at the pleasure of the regime. Mr. Butake was the only one who came close to identifying the crux of the matter by stating the simple truth that the French language owes its dominant position in Cameroon not necessarily because of the bigger francophone population but because it is the language of power and authority in Cameroon, and one may as well add that it is the language of the 'conqueror', the annexationist and the oppressor.

It is the language of authority to the extent that even Anglophone officials who want to be in the good book of their Francophone masters speak to their own kith and kin in French. Even though the 1996 constitution puts the two official languages at par, that parity is merely on paper. The minimization of the English language, since Reunification in 1961, is merely a superficial manifestation of the marginalization of the Anglophone in Cameroon.

It is very surprising and disappointing that even when the moderator of the panel discussion asked to know whether qualified Southern Cameroonians have been denied appointment to high office because they were Anglophones, one panellist replied that there was no such scenario. Good grief!! No panellist bothered to recall that of the 58 senior District Officers in Cameroon, only 7, up from the previous 3, were Anglophones; that only one Anglophone minister has a portfolio; that only one army general out of 15, is Anglophone; that no Anglophone has ever been appointed Ambassador to English speaking capitals like London Washington, Abuja or Pretoria.

It did not occur to the panellists that no Anglophone has ever headed the ministries of Defence, Finance, Territorial Administration, Foreign Affairs or the Economy. Is it that Anglophones are not qualified? Attempts, especially by Francophones to project the Anglophone question as a linguistic problem is a mere exercise in dissimulation. The fact that the programme and its French equivalent broadcast on BBC World Service has been rebroadcast, over and over again, indicates that the regime is out for a disinformation campaign to water down the Southern Cameroons Question.

In fact, a repeat of the French version last Saturday referred to Anglophone grievances as "les revendications ethniques" That was sheer intellectual dishonesty! To project the English speaking Southern Cameroons as an ethnic group is not only an illustration of ignorance and stupidity, but worse, a desperate attempt to tribalise a serious issue of nationalism.

The current frantic attempt by the Francophone-led government to downplay the Anglophone issue calls for an urgent need to refocus the Southern Cameroons Question. And that question is political and territorial, bearing on the right of a given people to self-determination.

S-N F.

24

Restating the Southern Cameroons Question
Monday October 1, 2001

The political destiny of the Southern Cameroons took the wrong course on October 16, 1959 when the UN adopted resolution called for arrangements for a plebiscite to be held in order to decide on two questions that would determine the fate of the Trust territory:

A) Do you want to achieve independence by joining the independent federation of Nigeria? Or

B) Do you wish to achieve independence by joining the independent Republic of Cameroon?

It is worth nothing that there was no third option for the territory to achieve complete independence, because in the view of the administering authority- Britain, the United Nations had clearly ruled out a period of continued trusteeship as soon as Nigeria and the Republic of Cameroon gained independence in 1960.

The terms of the UN Trust gave Britain the responsibility "to bring the inhabitants of the territory to full self-government or independence by enabling or encouraging them to play progressively more important parts in every branch of public life until they are competent to assume full control." By depriving the inhabitants of Southern Cameroons of the option of full independence, Britain and the UN severely distorted the evolution; a course plagued by betrayal on the part of Britain and negligence of the UN.

As some experts have pointed out, the UN, by hinging the fate of Southern Cameroons on either joining Nigeria or French Cameroon, was giving the impression that some trust territories were more important than others whereas the Southern Cameroons was larger both in area and population than many other British dependencies such as Honduras and Fiji. Britain's tendency to undermine the status of the Southern Cameroons dates back to 1922 when it came under the mandate of the League of Nations and was administered by Britain as an appendage of its colony, Nigeria.

A perilous Reunification

The plebiscite took place on February 11, 1961 and the Southern Cameroons, deprived of the option of attaining full independence, voted in favour of joining French Cameroon, which had gained independence a year earlier, on January 1. According to the terms laid down by the UN, it was agreed that in the event of a vote in favour of joining French Cameroon, arrangement would be worked out by a constitutional conference of representative delegations of equal status from *La République du Cameroun* and Southern Cameroons, for the unification of the two parties in a Federal United Cameroon republic. Both sides had agreed it was to be a federation of TWO EQUAL STATES. But when the constitutional conference took place in Foumban, in June 1961, neither the UN nor the British was present, whereas Ahmadou Ahidjo, the leader of French Cameroon was surrounded by French advisers.

Despite the flaws of the federal constitution, it at least provided a minimum basis for the self-governing status of the Southern Cameroons. On October 1, 1961, the federal republic was proclaimed and on that same day, and as if they could not tarry a minute longer to see the mess they had fabricated, the British Commissioner for Southern Cameroons, J O Field and his colonial entourage, packed out of the country. That same day Ahidjo proclaimed a decree carving out the federation into six regions, with the federated state of West Cameroon, as Southern Cameroons came to be known, being one of them. Contrary to the letter and spirit federalism, local administration was placed under the federal government and a Federal Inspector of Administration, who was answerable to President Ahidjo, was appointed to West Cameroon. The said Federal inspector usurped the prerogatives of the Prime Minister of Southern Cameroons, flying the national flag on his official car and being escorted by sirens and a motorcade in the most cocky and provocative manner.

Monopartism and Unitary State

Whereas Ahidjo had succeeded by coercion to institute a one party polity in East(French) Cameroon in the late 1950s, West Cameroon still enjoyed multi-partism and a good measure of civil liberties. However Ahidjo coerced West Cameroon leaders to dissolve their parties and join his *Union Camerounaise* to form the Cameroon National Union, CNU, in September 1966.A de facto one –party polity was established and this was merely a prelude to the dismantling of the federal system of government in favour of a unitary state in 1972. The institution of the unitary state was in violation of the entrenched clauses of the 1961 constitution which stated clearly that any attempt to change the federal structure of the country was unacceptable.

Ahidjo made the world understand that he was motivated by the desire to promote the integration of the nation, but in reality he wanted to accelerate the assimilation of West Cameroon, which, it was discovered, was endowed with lucrative petroleum reserves.

The death of the federation was stage-managed in the most high-handed and dictatorial manner. In an article written in 1972 titled "Mercenaries Rule Cameroon" and published in his Conversational Autobiography by Patron Publishing House, Bamenda (July 2001),Ndeh Ntumazah, leader of the defunct One Kamerun Party, recounts that on May 8, 1972, Ahidjo went to the federal parliament and informed the deputies of his decision to dissolve the four parliaments of the federation namely, the federal parliament, the two parliaments of the federated states and the West Cameroon House of Chiefs, for economic reasons. All members of the four parliaments were advised to go on a long vacation during which time fresh elections for a new unitary parliament would be held and a referendum to ascertain the wishes of the people on a new draft constitution was to be organized. Without seeing the draft

91

constitution, let alone discussing it, the parliamentarians gave their chiefs a standing ovation and left for their homes.

The next day Ahidjo abrogated the 1961 federal constitution by decree and attached to it a draft constitution to be submitted to a referendum on May 20. The post of vice president, which according to the 1961 constitution was held by a West Cameroonian, Hon. S.T Muna, was scrapped. Voters in the referendum were called upon to answer "yes" or 'no' to the following question:

"Do you approve, with a view to consolidating National Unity and accelerating the economic, social and cultural development of the nation, the draft constitution submitted to the people of Cameroon by the president of the federal republic of Cameroon and instituting a republic, one and indivisible, to be styled in the United Republic of Cameroon?"

The question, which one writer has described as a choice between oui and 'yes', does not explicitly mention the institution of a unitary state. While constitutional experts would agree without exception that this was a clear case of political brigandage, Ntumazah raises a number of questions that underline the illegality and nullity of the May 20 referendum and the ensuing unitary state thereof: who was the president of republic when the decree of May 9 became law? The president and vice president were elected on a single ticket, and if the election of the vice president had become invalid, what right had the other candidate to pretend he was still president? Can the president claim that as head of an electoral list (for president and vice president) he had the power to terminate the office of his partner and still claim that he had a mandate to remain president? Why was the decision to annul the constitution taken by decree? Did the annulled constitution empower the president to end the life of the constitution itself and draft another without the participation and consent of parliament?

If I have paraphrased Ntumazah to this extend, it is simply because of his instructive and pertinent expose of a terrible political fraud which completely robbed the Southern Cameroons of its birth right. It suffices to add that whereas the 1961 plebiscite gave an

92

allowance of nine months for political sensitization, the May 20 referendum, cynically dubbed the 'peaceful revolution' by Ahidjo, gave merely ten days for sensitizing a population whose overwhelming majority resided , then as now , in enclaves that were not easily accessible. This was because of the deplorable road network. Whereas the plebiscite concerned exclusively the inhabitants of Southern Cameroons, the May 20 referendum included francophones who had never had any experience in democratic balloting and had long been cowered under the yoke of Ahidjo's dictatorship. The result of the referendum – a 99.97 percent 'yes' vote- was not a surprise.

Ndeh Ntumazah also reveals that in an attempt to counter Ahidjo's tyrannical designs, former vice president John Ngu Foncha, whose KNDP party advocated joining French Cameroon and who had been sacked by Ahidjo in 1970,AugustinJua, Vice President of KNDP who had been sacked as Premier of West Cameroon in 1968, and Chief Victor Mukete, then chairman of the Cameroon Development Corporation, got together to form a front. Their move was betrayed and Ahidjo arrested the trio and hundreds of other West Cameroonians and detained them in Bamenda. However the leaders were released soon after with a stern warning to go and join the campaigns for the referendum.

S-N F.

25

From Unitary State to Annexation
Friday October 5, 2001

On the occasion of May 20 celebrations this year, the English-language tabloid newspaper, The Herald, conducted a man-in-the street random opinion sampling, which reflects the tenuous state of Cameroon's unity and stability. One respondent had this to say:

> *"In the real sense of unity, there should be no discrimination in the country. But this is not the case in Cameroon where Francophones lord it over their Anglophone counterparts. This is unacceptable."* Yet another respondent had this to say:
>
> *"We realize the pompous slogan of unity is not translated in reality into our daily lives when you look at the two cultural divides; one [French Cameroun] dominates the other and this situation invariably lays bare any claims to unity. Why did they change the name of the country from United Republic to La République?"*

Barely 14 months after succeeding Ahidjo in November 1982, President Paul Biya convened an extraordinary session of parliament to rubber stamp constitutional amendments to change the appellation of the country to the Republic of Cameroon, the name French Cameroon assumed at independence in 1960.

If Ahidjo had killed the federation in 1972, Biya merely nailed the coffin in June 1984, thus accomplishing French Cameroon's agenda of annexation and assimilation, even though the legal implication of the act simply meant that one component, La République du Cameroun, having reverted to its political identity prior to unification had seceded from the union; this is the legal opinion of Barrister Gorgi Dinka Q.C (in exile for the past decade and half) who, in the face of Biya's constitutional aberration, sounded the trumpet of battle in 1985 for the restoration of Southern Cameroons' sovereignty. And when he was arrested and incarcerated, the Free West Cameroon Movement took up the battle cry to reawaken the conscience of Southern Cameroons' nationalism. Thereafter the Cameroon Anglophone Movement, CAM, later known as the Southern Cameroons Restoration Movement, joined the nationalist conscientisation movement, which cumulated with the formation of the umbrella organization, the Southern Cameroons National Council, SCNC, in Buea in April 1993.

Origin of Southern Cameroons Nationalism

The seed of Southern Cameroons nationalism can be said to have been planted in 1916 when British troops, along with local conscripts ousted the Germans in the battle of Nsanakang (Mamfe) as part of World War I campaign to curb Germany's expansionist onslaught. That seed germinated in 1939 with the formation of the Cameroon Welfare Union, CWU, whose Lagos branch began agitating within Nigeria's political circles for a separate representation of the Southern Cameroons in the Lagos Legislative Council. The CWU evolved in 1954 to the Cameroon Youth League, and soon after to the Cameroon National Federation, which succeeded in raising political awareness amongst its members and obtaining a separate legislature for Southern Cameroons in 1954.

From then until 1961, the Southern Cameroons was self-governing with a National Assembly separate from Nigeria, a Council of Ministers and a House of Chiefs.

This state of affairs was quite consistent with the aspirations of the people of Southern Cameroons and its political formations namely; the Cameroon People's National Convention, CPNC, led by EML Endeley, the Kamerun People's Party, KKP, led by PM Kale and the Kamerun National Democratic Party, KNDP, led by J.N. Foncha.

The primary objective was Southern Cameroons' sovereignty. For anyone to think, let alone suggest, that 85 years of Southern

Cameroons' political consciousness and 62 years of experience in political organization should simply be sacrificed on the Francophone altar of tyranny, is sheer denial of the facts and reality of Southern Cameroons' right to pursue its course of self-determination, which was thwarted in 1961.

The Francophone-led regime should now understand that the Southern Cameroons is no longer concerned with trivialities like the minimization of the English language in Cameroon, nor is it bothered about power sharing with French Cameroon.

Southern Cameroonians now demand a halt to the economic plunder of their fatherland and the withdrawal of the forces of occupation, and the surrogates of the alien administration implanted by La République du Cameroun! Failure to resolve the Southern Cameroons Question peacefully can only give rise to undesirable but inevitable action to terminate the excessive plunder, subjugation and underdevelopment of the territory, whose patience and apparent docility are legendary but not inelastic.

S-N F.

26

The Anatomy of Terrorism
October 8 2001

The despicable destruction of the New York World Trade Centre and the Pentagon in Washington and the loss of thousands of lives bring to sharp focus the issue of violence and terrorism as a political weapon. Terrorism as practised by revolutionary groups is an instrument of international public relation albeit deplorable. Some experts of the phenomenon have described terrorism as theatre. It is aimed at the people watching not at the actual victims.

One of the most spectacular and shocking terrorist attacks was the one meted out on Israeli athletes at the 1972 Munich Olympic Games, by the Palestinian Black September group. One Arab was quoted as saying "we recognize that sport is the modern religion of the western world. We know that the people of England and America would switch their television sets from any programme about the plight of the Palestinians, if there was a sporting event on another channel. So we decided to use the Olympics, the most sacred ceremony of this religion, to make the world pay attention to us. We offered human sacrifices to your gods of sport and they and they answered our prayers. From Munich onwards nobody could ignore the Palestinians and their cause ".

The purpose of terrorism is to gain attention by shocking public opinion. At our local level in the 1950's, the UPC bands of terrorists led by Momo Paul, Singap, Tagatsi Alexandre and Ndeh Ntumazah, perpetrated nightly raids on chiefdoms that were unsympathetic to their cause, Roman Catholic Missions and towns in the Bamileke region. David Gardinier wrote that in lightning raids, they slaughtered everyone in sight.

With regard to the terrorist attacks in the US, it is quite significant and unusual that no group has claimed responsibility for the carnage.

Even the prime suspect believed to have masterminded it, Osama bin Laden, has not said much concerning the bombings. Yet the US government has sworn to get him dead or alive with a 5-million dollar prize posted on him.

Even though Palestinian and other anti-American groups are rejoicing over the suicide operations, it cannot be said with certainty that those who carried out the attacks were necessarily representing any Palestinian group. The sheer magnitude of the operation seems to suggest that the perpetrators were advocates of a world revolution aimed at destroying imperialism as symbolized by America. The unprecedented scale of the operations also suggests that the terrorist had a tremendous ground support from a vast network of dissidents, all of whom cannot be said to be Palestinians or Arabs. And this is where American president George Bush has miscalculated by focusing on Osama bin Laden and his associates.

By declaring a crusade against terrorism, George Bush is implying a holy war and a holy war or jihad as the Muslims call it, is usually very emotive and blind. And that is why several world leaders have advised President Bush to exercise caution. For one thing, the capture and execution of Osama bin Laden would only provoke a series of even more spectacular acts of terrorism. It is, however, understandable that the families and friends of the victims would like to have vengeance and soon.

William O. Beeman, writing for the Pacific News Agency in Providence, Rhode Island remarks that "the American State Department has theorized that if the people of a rogue nation experience enough sufferings, they will overthrow their rulers or compel them to adopt more sensible behaviour. The terrorist actions in New York and Washington are a clear and ironic implementation of this policy against the United States." He describes Osama bin Laden as a true ideologue who believes his mission is sacred. The structure of his organization is essentially tribal or cellular and his followers are as fervent and intense in their belief as he is. They carry out their actions because they believe in the righteousness of their cause, not because of Osama bin Laden's orders or approval.

The devastating tragedy in America comes after recent failures to chart a new world order in several international forums, notably the World Trade Organization and the International Conference on racism in Durban, South Africa, which failed to put a racist label on Zionism and to persuade European countries to apologize for their African slave trade and to pay reparations to Africa for the devastating effects of slavery. The intransigence of western imperialists cannot be ignored as a factor that could have sparked the conflagration in New York and Washington.

While America feels righteous indignation at the attacks, it should also remember that he who goes to equity must come with clean hands. But America is also guilty of attacks on Iraq and Bosnia, which border on terrorism. Even though their attacks were aimed at military targets, significant civilian casualties were registered.

The response of the American government should be aimed at getting the actual culprits rather than an all-out attack on Afghanistan or any Arab country. Such a response would split world opinion because it is said that one man's terrorist is another man's freedom fighter. America will have to modify its relationship with Israel, the Islamic states and the Third World countries in general.

One lesson America ought to draw from the attacks is that technological sophistication and Star Wars defence system, at the expense of the human factor, do not guarantee invincibility and that its arrogant position as the world's sole super power has not endeared it to the less fortunate and impoverished strata of the globe.

S-N F.

101

27

Terrorism and War: The Ugly Equation
Friday October 19 2001

On the dawn of the September 11 terrorist attack on the United States, American President George Bush declared a crusade against the culprits and terrorism in general. His battle cry can well be understood within the context of the human thirst for vengeance in the wake of the massacre of nearly 6000 civilians of various nationalities at the World Trade Centre in New York and the Pentagon.

While other world leaders were urging President Bush to exercise restraint, he modified his battle cry for a crusade (which a Christian holy war against Islam) and termed it a war against terror, most especially against Afghanistan for providing training ground for terrorists as well as a hideout for the prime suspect of the massacre, Osama bin Laden and his group.

Barely one month after the atrocities, Mr. Bush launched air strikes against Afghanistan and changed the slogan "war against terrorism " to "strike against terror". Within two days of the air strikes targeted at military installations controlled by the Taliban government, dozens of civilian deaths were recorded. America and its European allies launched the attacks knowing very well that civilian would inevitably be destroyed and no amount of euphemisms such as "collateral damage" can obliterate the fact that these are human lives squandered by a kind of terrorism whose only difference with that of Mr. bin Laden's is that it carries the official government approval.

America's linguistic acrobatics with the words 'crusade, war and strike' have failed to convince the world that they mean different things. The language camouflage employed by the U.S. and its allies, especially Britain, cannot hide the fact that by launching an armed war against terrorism, they have resorted to the use of the same techniques employed by the likes of bin Laden whose ideology is to bring the downfall of Western imperialism that is dominating the world by economic dictatorship; a dictatorship that has impoverished more than 95% of the world's population and rendered them destitute and dependent on Western hand-outs.

Euphemisms and Oxymorons

The phrase 'war against terrorism' is an oxymoron, a paradox of the highest order. Using terror with the excuse that it is aimed at eradicating terrorism cannot amount to a moral justification for terrorism, no matter how religiously one invokes the imperatives of national emergency, defence etc.

The paradox of war against terrorism reminds one of a similar oxymoron coined by Western powers in the 1970s to justify their monopoly over the development of nuclear weaponry to the effect that they were amassing "nuclear weapons for peaceful purposes." Thus when the nuclear arms race was becoming highly competitive, the U.S. and its European allies of the North Atlantic Treaty Organisation NATO that had developed or acquired substantial stockpiles of nuclear arms decided to consolidate their exclusive club by instituting the Strategic Arms Limitation Talks SALT in order to prevent other middle powers from acquiring the technology. This situation gave rise to a new political evangelism known as the Nuclear Non-Proliferation Treaty propagated by the Grand Master of shuttle diplomacy, American Secretary of State Henry Kissinger.

The doctrine behind non-proliferation was that those up comers aspiring to join the nuclear club could not be trusted to handle such sophisticated weaponry. In fact they were irresponsible and could not vouch for their moral integrity. As such the Western claim over nuclear monopoly was predicated on a presumptuous moral superiority of western imperialism.

In waging a war against Afghanistan with a promise to do same to other nations or groups that sympathise with Afghanistan or nations which fail to join the American-led crusade, the U.S has summoned the notion of provocation and righteous indignation to its defence. But at whom is righteous anger directed?

The perpetrators of the September 11 attacks died in their suicide mission. Instead of arresting suspected accomplices and bringing them to justice, the U.S. prefers to embark on a scorched earth policy. Critics have demonstrated beyond reasonable doubt that America's feeling of moral (like racial) superiority is chiefly responsible for President Bush's arrogant and biased attitude to the Israeli-Palestinian conflict as well as major issues of international concern such as global warming, compensation to Africa for the evils of slavery and the need to establish a more equitable world economic order.

In a bid to make the reprehensible war against Afghanistan less reprehensible, Washington and its allies have insisted that it is not a war against Islam and that they would exercise to limit civilian casualties that is if the civilian death toll came up to say 5000, it should be regarded as an achievement, less evil and less brutal than the September 11 death toll of about 6000. The Afghan casualty can easily be written off as a collateral damage, an expendable factor in the calculus of official terrorism just because it was unintentional and impersonal.

The whole idea that the value of human life can arithmetically be qualified smacks of moral perversion. If one is inclined to give arithmetical value to human life then it can be said, to the credit of the bin Ladens, that the total number of casualties caused by terrorism during the last century does not amount to a fraction of the civilian death toll recorded in the Second World War alone, caused by western air strikes. It did not matter to the bombers whether the German people approved of Hitler's campaign or not. As long as he was "kraut", he was not on our side and if he was not on our side, he was against us.

105

Violence as a means of social communication

Whether it is conventional warfare or terrorism, the bottom line, the two occupations could not at any given time resort to blind cold-blooded murder. The highest common factor is their function as a means to make political statements. They are a means of political expression equally favoured by nationalist movements that alternatively use guerrilla war tactics and terrorism to achieve their objectives. The equation between war and terrorism is balanced on ideology and its attendant inflexibility. Whether you are a partisan of war or terrorism, the difference is immaterial.

An authoritative social scientist and writer on the phenomenon, Jan Schreiber has made the compelling observation that "as soon as the partisan reaches a stage where he can either deny the innocence of anyone who is not on his side or assert that such innocence is irrelevant to the overriding issue, which is his own side's final triumph, then he is in a psychological position to commit a terrorist act." To borrow from yet another eminent social scientist, Marshall McLuhan, the medium (in this case –political violence) is the message irrespective of the sender of the message. The message is: "We have been propelled beyond the threshold of tolerance; our backs are on the wall."

One critical lesson of the September 11 suicide attacks is that in the business of political violence, might and numbers could be incrementally proprrtionate4 to vulnerability; that might and numbers are not critical factors in determining the impact of political violence; that to undermine an adversary's capacity to inflict irreparable damage because that adversary is a minority is to indulge in self-deception.

A child who decides to keep his parents awake all night shall himself know no sleep. If the U.S. and its NATO allies are determined that the rest of the rest of the world will not sleep until they have extracted their pound of flesh, then they too shall know no sleep.

S-N F.

28

Poem by Sam-Nuvala Fonkem
Friday October 26, 2001

Drumbeats
(For 1ˢᵗ October Martyrs)

They were marching, singing
Sweet Songs of Freedom
They were marching, brandishing
Fresh Green stalks of peace
Tender Stalks of the peace plant
Sacred Symbols of peace

Presently
Gun-bearing gorillas of law and disorder
Erupted and disrupted
The sweet songs of freedom
As man not gorilla
Became endangered specie

The plunder ended in thunder
When Boniface, Amidou, Terence
Lay wasted in Blood
Sacrificed on tender cushions of green

Fresh stalks of peace
Sacred symbols of the force of argument,
Futile shields to fight
Satanic forces of fascism,
The argument of force
The policy of pirates

Perpetrators of plunder and tyranny.

They were marching, singing
Sweet songs of Freedom
For beloved Ambazonia
Their fatherland
Perpetually pillaged by alien primates
Unleashed from sinister cages
Based in Satan's private principality

S-N F.

29

CDC and the Privatization Palaver (I)
Friday November 2, 2001

In the late 1980's, the Cameroon Government drew up a programme of economic privatization based on three parameters namely; to relinquish control over state-owned enterprises that were:

a) No longer functional

b) Functional but unprofitable

c) Potentially profitable but poorly managed.

Ever since the mid-1990s, government has embarked on a rather promiscuous privatization scheme predicated on a policy of non-intervention by government in the economic sector to the extent that strategic public infrastructures and utilities like potable water, energy, transport and communication, and agro-industry have been privatized or are in the process of being privatized.

This policy of indiscriminate privatization for the sake of privatization, which is actively promoted by international organizations such as the World Bank, has been pursued in the mistaken belief that it is the sole qualification for joining the free market economy and by extension, the democratic club. Experts have observed that failure to accompany economic reforms with democratic governance constitutes a serious handicap to the development of a free market economy.

Mr. John D. Sullivan, Director of the Centre for International Private Enterprise has drawn the conclusion that based on the experiences of the 1980's and 1990's, "there is no truth to the belief that markets will spontaneously emerge if government stops intervening in the economy." He recommends that business must do its part to eliminating the corruption that is devastating to economic growth and poverty reduction.

The fact that Cameroon has been governed uninterrupted by a notorious kleptocracy for nearly two decades and championed the league of the world's most corrupt nation; the fact that the government has adamantly refused to set up an independent and credible electoral machinery that would ensure free and fair elections; the fact that the country has plunged from the middle income bracket in the early 1980's to the bottom league of highly indebted poor countries (HIPC) in recent times, coupled with the arrogance with which the regime has displayed its ineptitude in matters of good governance as if it were a badge of honour – all these facts and many more make a mockery of any claim to democracy.

All the noise about privatization just because the regime wants to be seen to be in fashion amounts to mere cant and humbug. We are still light years away from a free market economy whose primary objective is to foster economic growth, provide equal opportunity and ensure a better standard of living.

Any privatization scheme that is not selective, ignores public opinion, fails to consider the interest of affected communities and is identified as a sell out to foreign capitalist consortiums for the purpose of the stark naked exploitation is bound to provoke antipathy and is equally doomed to fail.

The Case of CDC

Now that the Yaounde government has embarked on a wild auctioning spree of the nation's patrimony, it is appropriate to signal a warning with regard to the imminent privatization of the Cameroon Development Corporation, CDC, established by Nigerian Ordinance in 1947 in the Southern Cameroons.

The creation of the CDC was guided by the political philosophy that "the transference of large areas of land to the control of an organization located outside the territory would be bound ... to attract to the controlling body... the suspicion that it was in some way exploiting for outside interest the territory in which it was

110

operating and thus prejudice the profit of cooperation with local interests which would be vital for the success of any scheme".

This view was expressed in a report by the Colonial Development Corporation of Britain, which suggested that indigenous public opinion be given the opportunity of commenting on, and influencing corporate policy. The opposition labour backbencher, Mr. Creech Jones who led an investigation team to British West African territories concluded the report by stating that "trusteeship [of which the Southern Cameroons was a member] is cant and humbug unless it is implemented in constructive terms of development and social targets, and unless that development is for and in the interest of African people."

It can readily be understood why the original mission of the CDC stated that: "In so far as it is consistent with the promotion of the common benefit of the inhabitants of the Southern Cameroons, the corporation is also required to provide for the religious, educational and general social welfare of persons employed by it by means of building, establishing or supporting housing, factories, churches, hospital, dispensaries, schools, etc."

The three cardinal preoccupations that influenced the raison d'être of the CDC include the consent and cooperation, the development and the welfare of the indigenous population of the Southern Cameroons.

Could the CDC be said to have fulfilled the above objectives since the Southern Cameroons joined French Cameroon in a federation in 1961; a federation that was fraudulently dismantled in 1972 by French Cameroon?

The impending privatization of the CDC would fatally result in the transfer of CDC into the greedy hands of Western capitalist monopoly whose religion of profit making would only spell disaster for the development and welfare of the local population so affected and make nonsense of the principle of economic derivation, which wisely commands that an equitable quota of the financial proceeds derived from the natural wealth of a given region be exclusively set aside for the benefit of the inhabitants of the area.

Socio –Cultural Ramification

There are many reasons why the Yaounde government should proceed cautiously with its CDC programme of privatization. First of all, in what appears to be an attempt to allay the fears and concern of the indigenous population, the CDC General Manger has recently been propagating a false consolation that after all CDC land is not being sold, CDC is not only found in Victoria division ... therefore the Bakweri people – the indigenous owners of the land and the inhabitants of Southern Cameroons – have no cause to complain about privatization. It beats the imagination how the privatization of CDC and its hundreds of thousands of hectares of oil palm, banana, rubber, tea plantations would not necessarily alienate the land for as long as it lasts.

If the Yaounde government decided to subsequently expand CDC operations to French Cameroon, it is of no consequence to the inalienable rights of the owners of the original CDC lands.

S-N F.

30

CDC And the Privatisation Palaver (II)
Monday November 5, 2001

Land in Africa is communal property and there is no such thing as 'no man's land' whether or not such land is actively occupied. African traditional wisdom commended the reservation of undeveloped land for the purpose of grazing livestock and to provide fuel and raw material for building, carving, weaving textile, medicinal plants etc. and above all, for posterity. The introduction of a capitalist mode of production brought about a painful social revolution and injected an imponderable element into the social fabric of the indigenous communities.

The Bakweri people, who have been unfairly regarded as lukewarm (lazy), have a traumatic story to tell. The venerable Southern Cameroons statesman and Speaker of the House of Assembly, Rt. Honourable P.M. Kale, in his youthful days as Secretary of the Cameroon Youth League he co-founded in Lagos with Southern Cameroons' first Prime Minister, EML Endeley in 1940, dispatched a petition to the colonial office depicting the plight of the indigenous population when Germany confiscated their land.

"[Indigenes] who refused to work for the Germans were expelled from the fertile plains to try farming for themselves on the rocky slopes about 6000 to 8000 feet above sea level. No economic crops can thrive well at such heights except probably coffee. All the former native food stuffs, which were yams of all species, gourds of all species etc. cannot in any case do well at such heights." The 1946 petition, written on behalf of the chiefs, was renewed the following year, reiterating demands for the restitution [at least] of all unoccupied land ceded to missionary bodies. Extracts of the petition published by George Padmore (Africa: Britain's Third Empire, 1950) noted that "As a last resort to eke out a living, we fell on planting foreign foodstuff which is coco-yam. But unfortunately this is not suitable foodstuff as the medical authorities testify and it forms the chief foodstuff here because of sheer necessity. Therefore, it makes it obvious that malnutrition is rampant. Our women, who by custom are the planters of locally consumed foodstuff, have to climb to above mentioned heights… and on their return from the farms, they carry heavy loads. This causes our women to have early breakdown in health. The climbing of heights by mothers is also responsible for great infant mortality…"

To add insult to injury, natives who wanted to plant some economic crops had to rent land from missionary bodies thus paying for what, to all intents and purposes, belongs to them. Who would resist plunging into a state of confused lethargy when the means of subsistence is taken away and procreation become hazardous?

If the above do not constitute enough reason for the government to consider the peculiarities of the CDC in Southern Cameroons and that it ought to listen to the indigenous stake holders, through the well-established Bakweri Lands Claim Commission and the labour union and set aside a quota of the share holdings for the benefit of same, then it should be bluntly reminded that by privatizing the CDC, the regime merely wants to continue reaping where it did not sow.

After a decade of carting way benefits accruing from the original CDC for the wellbeing of French Cameroon, the Yaounde government has no qualms auctioning it. While time is still on their side, it could be said with no margin of error that, knowing full well that the days of the two decades- old kleptocracy that has presided over the fate of Cameroon are numbered, the regime has embarked on a looting exercise called privatization; an economy based on private enterprise, but which in reality is not an open-market system. John D. Sullivan refers to this type of behaviour as "rent-seeking".

If indeed the government is serious about a policy of state non-intervention in the economy, then it should give priority to indigenous private participation or else stand the challenge of taking

114

the policy to its logical end; namely a total abdication, not only from the economy, but also from power.

S-N F.

31

The Invalidity of Unitary State
Monday May 27, 2002

Now that the dusty and fluffy sentiments hanging over the 30th anniversary celebration of the unitary state have hopefully settled, it is time to recall and soberly reflect on a number of irrefutable historical facts in order to debunk and put to shame certain demagogues of annexation whose obsequious and stupid pronouncements in the media constitute a grave insult to our collective intellect.

The insipid, insincere and childish sentiments (not arguments) expressed by these quisling proxies and fifth columnists in defence of falsehood and the gigantic fraud of May 20, 1972, have disgraced and put a huge question mark on their intellectual qualification for the high offices they hold.

Illegality of 1961 Plebiscite

Every Cameroonian historian and intellectual worth the salt cannot deny that international law acknowledges the Southern Cameroons (Ambazonia) as a state with internationally recognized boundaries fixed by the League of Nations, inherited by the United Nations and which remains today.

In a scholarly write-up in West Africa magazine 20-26 March 1995, Chinedu Nwoko, historian and solicitor of the Supreme Court of England and Wales, reiterates some hard facts that are quite edifying and enlightening:

1) That according to Article 76b of the UN Charter, trusteeship over territory ends once the territory has achieved self-government or independence.

2) That Southern Cameroons (Ambazonia) achieved self-government in 1954 and in 1959, the UN passed a resolution

severing the territory from Nigeria and in October 1960, an independent constitution was promulgated for the territory. Therefore, the UN had no legal authority to conduct the 1961 plebiscite in which the Southern Cameroons voted to unite with La République du Cameroun in a confederacy instead of re-joining Nigeria.

In the magazine article referred to titled "No Win without Ambazonia" (in reference to the Bakassi border dispute), Barrister Nwoko questions the objective of the plebiscite. He recalls the terms of the UN manifesto, "The two Alternatives" stating that the plebiscite was to give the UN a mandate to either merge the Southern Cameroons with Nigeria or to unite it with La République du Cameroun in a confederacy. He questions further whether the UN implemented the plebiscite, recalling that the manifesto stated that if the people opted to unite with La République du Cameroun, then there would be a post-plebiscite UN conference to work out a draft constitution which the two parties would submit to their respective populations for approval. The draft constitution was never tabled before the Southern Cameroons House of Assembly.

The tragic failure of the UN to respect its own manifesto, albeit invalid, has had a devastating effect on the destiny of Southern Cameroons, which had "looked forward to its independence with quiet confidence."

May 20th Abomination

Many analysts have often puzzled over the total absence of both the UN and the administering authority Britain at the post-plebiscite Foumban Conference in June 1961, and Mr. Mwoko has already provided the answer. Both foster parents realized belatedly and shamefully that the February 11 plebiscite was illegal and instead of amending their irresponsible behaviour, they preferred pontiuspilating in a most dishonourable attempt to cover up their mess.

Britain had insisted on an illegal plebiscite as a ploy to achieve its ulterior objective of joining Southern Cameroons (Ambazonia) with Nigeria in a bid to expand its neo-colonial interest in the petroleum belt along the Bight of Biafra. It was confident a plebiscite vote would be in favour of joining Nigeria not only because of the long coexistence between the two territories but mainly because of the evident doom inherent in a choice of unity with lawless La République du Cameroun that was embroiled in a bloody civil war. Because of its hidden motives, Britain maliciously misled the UN to strike off a third option for the plebiscite, i.e. full independence for Southern Cameroons, under the pretext that the territory was not economically viable to stand on its own whereas there was evidence of petroleum resources in the territory.

Having failed to achieve its geo-economic objective, Britain turned tail with the satisfaction that if it did not get Ambazonia's oil belt, France may as well have it because unification was tantamount to delivering Ambazonia to France on a silver platter. Thereafter, President Ahidjo, France's chief comprador in La République du Cameroun, was free to proceed with its annexation agenda fraudulently achieved through the May 20, 1972 referendum that was a choice between YES and Oui, thereby destroying the 1961 federal state in favour of an aberration called unitary state.

On May 6, Ahidjo convened the federal parliament and announced the abrogation of the federal constitution dismissed the parliamentarians and ordered them to go out and campaign for a unitary government to be rubber stamped in a referendum in a matter of two weeks! They were to canvass for a unitary state they had not even the remotest idea about. Even a veteran politician like Ndeh Ntumazah, who is hostile to Ambazonian aspirations, has attested to Ahidjo's high-handed and autocratic coup d'état, which included the dismissal in 1970 of his Anglophone Vice-President, Foncha, with whom he shared the presidential ticket. When Foncha, Mukete, Jua and co. tried to resist, they and hundreds of supports were arrested, threatened with death and later released with a stern warning to join the bandwagon.

SCAPO Victory and Bakassi Imbroglio

Barrister Nwoko disclosed that La République du Cameroun was forced to drop its initial argument for its claim over the Bakassi Peninsula on the premise that Southern Cameroonian was part of a single Cameroonian nation, and is now claiming that it is suing Nigeria at the Hague in exercise of a mandate given to it by the Ambazonian people through the 1961 plebiscite – implying that the plebiscite gave it a mandate to annex the Southern Cameroons. God Forbid!

Having demonstrated that the plebiscite was invalid, Cameroon's fluid logic falls flat and one begins to see clearly the solidity of a judgment in favour of the Southern Cameroons passed in March, by the Abuja High Court, following a suit filed by the Southern Cameroons People's Organisation, SCAPO. The court asked the Nigerian government to take the case of the Southern Cameroons to the International Court of Justice and the UN. The implication as to which internationally recognized entities share a border at Bakassi is obvious.

Between 1884 and 1914, the Southern Cameroons was part of a German colony called Kamerun and that is just what it was – a part of a colony, but was never part of any legally recognized entity called La République du Cameroun. Unification sentimentalists who claim a common German colonial ancestry for what passes for Cameroon today should come forth and explain why, ever since the pre-independence era, not a single political current has raised a battle cry for the restitution of other parts of the defunct German colony which were ceded to Central Africa, Congo and Gabon. They should pursue their irredentist quixotism to its logical end.

Barrister Gorji Dinka Q.C., Cameroon's pioneer Bar Council president in exile, once raised the question that if the Kamerun idea carried so much magical attraction why is it that La République's foremost nationalist movement, UPC, which championed unification, did not style itself UPK? Let's stop the jiving and be serious.

S-N F.

121

32

Pros and Cons of Coalition Government
Friday, *August 23, 2002*

To talk of forming a coalition government after the June twin elections in Cameroon is politically inaccurate. Historically speaking, coalitions are formed when the leading party fails to win an absolute majority in parliament or presidential election, but in the present Cameroonian context in which the ruling CPDM party emerged with a crushing majority, questionable as it may be, coalition is uncalled for.

However, bearing in mind that the bulk of opposition militants throughout the country were deliberately disenfranchised, the ruling CPDM may be willing, in order to console its worried conscience, to form a broad-based government to include members of the opposition and for such a union government to have any semblance of credibility, the leading opposition party, the Social Democratic Front, SDF cannot be by-passed.

It is quite evident that no matter how well the opposition performs in the September re-run of the parliamentary elections, covering 17 seats, and given the highest level of transparency, its combined legislative force in the national assembly would hardly amount to 25 percent, confirming the fact that Cameroon has come back full circle to the one-party configuration.

Having excluded the majority of the electorate from the legislative process, is there a need now to seek ways of expanding the decision-making process to include the opposition, that is by inviting some its members to join a union government?

Political pragmatists have argued that the SDF, for example, stands to gain materially and experientially by joining the government. Materially speaking, they contend, its government members can give employment, influence appointments, award contracts and make timely interventions on behalf of their deprived constituents. Experience-wise, they would learn the art of governance and bring their style of administration to bear on a system widely regarded so far as inefficient, tribalistic and corrupt. Advocates of realpolitik also conjure the charms of political office such as immunity (not impunity, hopefully), red-carpet receptions and other trappings of protocol.

SDF purists have equally strong, if not stronger, arguments against joining a union government. They say joining the government would be lending credibility to an illegitimate regime, citing the theory of political contagion as a risky prospect and sure recipe for corruption by induction. Referring to the experience of Bouba Bello's UNDP party, they raise the insecurity of tenure of office and exposure to shabby treatment as the price to pay for such a political joint venture.

To be fair to the SDF, its leadership has never completely ruled out the possibility of joining the government but has consistently made it clear that it would not join for the mere sake of joining and would do so on condition of a joint political framework aimed at advancing the democratic process. This framework includes the setting up of an acceptable and transparent electoral machinery and constitutional reforms reflecting a republican presidential system as opposed to the quasi-monarchical polity now in place. In the minds of constitutional experts, such a union government would have a semi-transitional status aimed at levelling the political landscape and preparing Cameroon for political alternation -the hallmark of modern democracy- which the country has not experienced for two decades.

It is incumbent on the regime to demonstrate maturity by preparing for peaceful change. The June elections had the tragic effect of making nonsense of the ballot box, thereby inviting those excluded from power to resort to violence as the only way to achieve self-determination. The use of force to achieve democratic ideals is not desirable but could be made inevitable by the political entrenchment of a regime which has boldly inscribed its name in the universal hall of infamy by consecutively topping the world corruption index and dragging the country into the wretched club of Highly Indebted Poor Countries.

A union government based on globally acceptable democratic goals other than the desire to share the spoils of power is to be encouraged if the political time bomb must be defused.

S-N F.

33

Of Deprivation and Primitive Accumulation
Friday 30 August 2002

There is sufficient evidence to support the thesis that people born of deprivation and nurtured in the humiliating circumstances of deprivation-real or perceived-do become, again because of gratuitous circumstances, most contemptuous, arrogant, vain and vindictive toward those they perceived to have been better endowed (by dint of nobility or humility) and whom they regard as having been responsible for their deprivation.

Thus, child of ostensibly humble and parish upbringing, who by fortuitous circumstance, is elevated to the rank of a prince, instead of exhibiting the virtues of his lowly cradle, magically transforms overnight into a demo-god who must teach a lesson to all those who thought he was a NOBODY. Vengeance is mine!

If he ever wore a pair of slippers to school, he must now acquire a thousand pairs of designer court shoes of crocodile skin. If his humble parents never as much owned a bicycle, he now must acquire two private jets and the sheer magnitude of his vanity is arithmetically proportionate to his compulsive greed; a lust for vengeance born of deprivation. It is as if the world owed him something and he must have not only his pound of flesh, but also a gallon of blood. And that is the deal.

When power passes on to the hands of those who have a lesson to teach the world and who invariably recruit only those of their psychic persuasion, the rest of humanity is confronted with a senseless legion of Satanic power bent on teaching ordinary mortals a lesson in obeisance. "You think I am the carpenter's son? Sorry, I am now the king of…and I will out-Herod Herod." So be it.

The primitive instinct of over accumulation to compensate deprivation borders on madness,- a madness that reigns unchecked.

Framers of advanced republican constitutions were quite aware of the dangers of believing in the benevolence and decency of people of modest birth who may accede to power so they put checks and balances to curb excessive l power and political perpetuity. Human beings have an infinite capacity to inflict pain and suffering on fellow human beings, thus society must organize and protect itself against this tendency.

Primitive accumulation does not limit itself to those who aspire or are catapulted to power by circumstance, but also to those who unexpectedly and undeservedly find themselves in position of authority or influence. In their state of relative advantage over others, they tend to over compensate for an earlier stage of deprivation by hoarding ill-gotten property and to show contempt for virtue and nobility. This state of affairs is very glaring in societies where mediocrity has replaced excellence and roguery elevated to a pedestal of glory.

In such societies where embezzlers and hatchet men have become heroes, it is quite common to find those who have acquired wealth and authority by intrigue making a mockery of those they regarded yesterday as their superiors, the yesterday society of moral integrity, probity, respect for excellence and exemplary talent.

Academics have averred that when society plummets to such a grotesque state of debasement, the time is ripe for change. Yet social scientists have still to explain the delay in the eruption of revolution long after the dissection and exposure of the anatomy of corrupt polities and their henchmen.

Perpetuity breeds complacency and unless it is bled of its phlegm, the rest of ordinary humanity may just as well contemplate a return to the jungle and play by its predatory rules of primitive domination.

S-N F.

128

34

The Omenology of St. Cloud
Friday, October 4, 2002

Whoever took the snapshots of President Paul Biya and his Nigerian counterpart, Olusegun Obasanjo in the Parisian outskirts of St. Cloud on September 5 ought to be awarded the top prize for photojournalism.

The photograph captured the essence of a despondent yet arrogant Paul Biya and a beaming and triumphant Obasanjo who were being psychologically prepared for the forthcoming verdict of the International Court of Justice at The Hague with regard to the dispute over the Bakassi Peninsula.

It could be said that the summit meeting, brokered by the UN Secretary- General, Kofi Annan under the good offices of French President Jacques Chirac, incidentally the Senior Prefect of the French Overseas School of Democracy, was held in a location called St. Cloud. It was quite significant and ominous because as the saying goes, after the cloud, comes rain, and after the rain comes...

The nebulous background of the summit spells an augury yet to be deciphered. It is quite significant that the protocol of understanding reached as St. Cloud, i.e. the principle of abiding by The Hague's verdict, the withdrawal of belligerent forces from the dispute territory; and the placing of observers to oversee an eventual withdrawal – underlines the fact that Bakassi neither belongs to *La République du Cameroun* nor to Nigeria. It is also significant to recall that the Bakassi imbroglio cannot be disentangled without resolving the Southern Cameroons Question. The Hague and the corpus of international law recognize the international personality of the Southern Cameroons. Any attempt by *La République* to claim neighbourliness with Nigeria under the pretext that *La République* and Southern Cameroons are one and the same, has fallen flat on its face because the 1961 plebiscite (albeit illegal), in which the Southern Cameroons state decided to join *La République* du Cameroun did not give La République a mandate to annex the Southern Cameroons.

The federal arrangement under which the 1961 unification was operated was abrogated by systematic and consecutive constitutional aberrations and the final pull out from the federal arrangement by *La République* in 1984 when it reverted to its original name at the time of independence in 1960.In law and in any human arrangement, a partnership is automatically considered dissolved when one member dies or withdraws. *La République's* act of secession should go the whole hog and culminate in the withdrawal of its forces of occupation and quisling proxies.

Last year, CRTV dispatched journalists to cover Southern Cameroons Independence Day on October 1. We hope it does same this year on condition that the ethics of truthful and fair reporting are respected and the exponents of the Southern Cameroons cause allowed to air their views instead of confronting them with the dogs of war and showers of mayhem. Intimidation, wanton killing of unarmed citizens and blackmail cannot divert the God-ordained cause of a people in bondage. After the cloud comes…

S-N F.

35

Mamfe This Time Yesterday
Circa December 2002

Mamfe into the early 60s was a hotbed of political activism, trade and social interaction with people flowing endlessly from up-country in Bamenda, Kumbo, and beyond to distant Enugu, Calabar and Lagos in Nigeria. Sam-Nuvala Fonkem remembers some of the motley crew of strange fellows like "afaneekong" the mad man, hungry mallam the legendary beggar, and "doctor adiboloja" the conman… who, although on the fringes of mainstream society, nevertheless added the colour and zest that gave Mamfe its distinctive metropolitan character, and made the good old place tick…

Afaneekong chop die dog, cheiafaneekong! Can't remember if he was a violent type, but, virtually naked, dreaded Afaneekong scavenged from one rubbish heap to the other, and cleared the streets of cadavers of domestic animals. There was also "'ungry Mallam", the legendary panhandler who, it was alleged, had built storey buildings in his native Nigeria just from begging. It was said that he controlled a very long chain of beggars that had transformed a very charitable exercise of alms receiving into an enviable capitalist enterprise.

I remember these two as if it was yesterday- the butt of children's taunts and jokes. This was 1961 and for an eight year old attending Lala school, Mamfe conjured a wonderful world of possibilities and promise.

At school we took turns to water and sweep the earthen floor and fill the inevitable enamel bucket with drinking water fetched from the nearby brook in the palm grove. In standard one, you moved from chalk and slate to penholder, bottle of QuinckInk, exercise book and blotter. The acquisition of my first learners 'Oxford dictionary" and bible completed my initiation from infant school into the exploratory world of boyhood.

We did explore the neighbouring forest of Okoyong, learning to hunt squirrels and giant rats in gangs led by older boys. We plundered the bush mangoes, plums and exquisite Mamfe oranges that taste more like nectar than just juice.

At school the brunch-time fare was akpu and eru, ekpang, akara beans, agidi and akamu. A plateful worth a quarter penny (anini) was sufficient to still the worms until closing time when we all looked forward to a home variety of Calabar yams –grown in Mamfe of course! –greens, garri and ogbono soup or egusi soup, rice and beef or fish stew. There were treats of game meat when the old man returned from his occasional hunting sprees with deer, brown antelope and a variety of birds including the pheasant and hornbill.

Mamfe was the commercial nerve centre of the Southern Cameroons and was reputed to be one of the biggest in-land (entrepot) ports of West Africa-with vast warehouses stocking the bulks of goods and commodities coming from Nigeria through the Cross River that was navigable by boat and launch for most of the year and distributed throughout the interior.

'Motor go-up; Motor come- down'

The town roads were tarred but the trunk roads were of laterite and narrow, but regularly maintained. Because of this, the road to Bamenda was a one way route. Mondays, Wednesday and Fridays were 'motor come down; and the other days, 'motor go up.' Mammy wagons, usually of the Austin and Bedford make popularly known as kura or gbongboro, transported goods and persons. Passengers sat on fixed hard benches backing the driver's cabin and facing the driver's apprentice otherwise known as the lan boy (for learn boy), who usually hung precariously on the tail board swinging his hefty wooden block ready to wedge the tires every time the kura got stuck in mud.

No Telephone to Heaven

At moments, when the vehicle began to wobble dangerously from side to side, and one's heart was in one's mouth, one could not reflecting on some of the intriguing inscriptions boldly painted on the front and flanks of the wagon :SMOG{Satan must obey God}, NO TELEPHONE TO HEAVEN, GOD'S TIME IS THE BEST, GOD'S CASE NO APPEAL…

Inscriptions on the panelling were more forbidding and in smaller lettering: no talking to the driver! Don't put your head or hand outside when bus is in motion! No spitting!-a rather tall order considering the pungent fumes emitted by the petrol engines fabricated when motor engineering was still more or less in a primitive state.

Electricity was scarce then and ours was one of the few Government houses provided with diesel-power. So the promises of an ice block made our homestead an attractive playground for the boys on a scorching hot day. Bright Tilley and Aladdin lamps using delicate mantles were what kept Mamfe by night alive.

Downtown, my aunt ran what was known as a liquor license bar where revellers quenched their thirst with *mbu*(palm wine) from up country, the local *agbodari* served in thick glass mugs called *drumata*. It was always a thrilling and exciting opportunity when my elder brother and I could spend weekends and short holidays downtown to give a helping hand with her booming sales that soared every 'Motor-come-down.' Auntie Susanna had a gramophone that was battery-powered, and I was the DJ, with the task of oiling and sunning the pins and cleaning the breakable records. It was fun winding the machine and spinning the fashionable Ghana highlife music which have today become classic: Gyaesu, AmaBonsu, Ashiwo, Obekumi, All for You… The great stars included the Uhuru Dance Band, the Black Beats, Joe Atkins and the legendary ET Mensah.

From the promiscuous crowd of college boys, itinerant musicians, traders, to magicians like DD Mbah with his pointed alligator boots, hookers and con men, all was chic and exciting as they swung and shuffled to the upbeat rhythm of the hit songs of the day. Downtown held many attractions one of them being the performing art of outdoor advertising.

German X Mixture

I can't remember if they had any particular name, but there came a dancing couple, a driver and sales assistant, and packed their long-wheel-base land rover by the roadside equipped with a gramophone plugged to double loudspeakers fixed on the roof of the vehicle, selling some medicine they called German X mixture. The young man and girl, dressed in skin-tight jean trousers, performed a routine of high life dance and twist, which was catching on at the time. Their feisty dance style consisted of a combination of twist, jive and tap dance, swing and rock and roll. The Climax was marked by fast wobbling knees and horizontal leg strokes more like karate foot chops in the typical Ajasco style… just twisting, , kicking and well… twisting the night away to the tunes of Chubby Checker, Elvis Priestly and Chuck Berry.

Docta 'Diboloja, y don come!

Another itinerant medicine peddler was the inimitable Dr. Adiboloja who sold tooth powder and other panacea. He mounted his puppets on a mobile platform rigged with conic acoustic and percussive contraptions that danced and rattled to his original two-line lyric: "Docta Diboloja, y don comesah…Original kilinser y welcomesah." Dr. Adiboloja was not only an accomplished puppet master but also an advertising genius. He would peer into the crowd of onlookers, suddenly seize a boy by the collar and drag him to the centre of the ring. 'Make all man take eye look this one,' he would pronounce, pointing at the urchin as if he were a culprit. 'You see this boy here, something no di pass whey y no enter for him mouth. Cocoyam-oh, akara beans-oh, economic blockade y chop; garri y nyamaram, groundnut-oh, guru guru-oh, Congo bread-oh. Then after

134

when y no brush him mouth, james begin to rotten him teeth. And now ladies and gentlemen make I show wunaweti I mean by james. Boy, open your mouth!' Docta would then dab a toothbrush whose hairs I suspect were made of metal, not nylon, on a generous quantity of tooth powder – probably vim powder for scrubbing pots – and would vigorously brush the poor lad's gum to the point of torture. 'Spit the james, Nghia! Spit, Nghia! See the result! Nghia,' he would declare as if he had just made a scientific discovery, as the boy spat out nauseating blobs of bloody saliva.

That was Dr. Adiboloja, and did he sell! His range of products that sold like hot cakes were packaged in crudely fashioned paper sachets and could cure ailments ranging from snake bite, diarrhea, belly ache, rheumatism, and why not cholera, if he were alive today, no doubt he would he would also add AIDS!

How I would love to go on talking about Mamfe with its spectacular anthills that stood like monuments in honour of ancestral glory. And whenever I find myself somewhere with huge gmelina trees shedding their broad leaves on rain-soaked earth, whenever I get whiffs of that musty scent of casamango, sour sop, plums and oranges, I really can't help dreaming of Mamfe this time yesterday.

S-N F.

36

Will Fru Ndi short-circuit political career?

Monday May 17, 2004

As the opposition National Coalition for Reconciliation and Reconstruction NCRR, steps up its campaign to gain support for its platform, advocates of change are mainly preoccupied with the question of a single candidate to challenge the incumbent. Concern for a single candidate is based on the realization that the opposition does not stand a ghost of chance if it went to the October presidential election in dispersed ranks as it did in 1992.

The cliché about history repeating itself is a valid pointer to the way forward and it will be quite in order to revisit the circumstances surrounding the failure of the opposition to deliver the goods in 1992. At the time, there were five groupings to challenge the incumbent and the Fru Ndi-led coalition is widely believed to have won the election by a slim margin; a victory that was eventually hijacked by the ruling CPDM with the complicity of the Supreme Court. If claims of victory by the opposition were anything to go by, one must admit that Fru Ndi's margin of victory was slim (35.9% for Fru Ndi and 33.9% for the incumbent CPDM-led alliance. This ratio was reversed by the Supreme Court in favour of the incumbent).

If, for the sake of argument, we agree that Fru Ndi's coalition won by less than 40% of the votes, we must also admit that the score fell far short of advanced democratic standards that require a 50+1% majority. In effect, no contestant had a majority score, and to be fair to the opposition, a second round of voting was imperative to achieve that goal, but alas! The electoral code was deliberately tailored to prevent that possibility. The clause in the draft code providing for a second round of balloting was defeated on the floor of parliament, thanks to Bouba Bello of the UNDP who teamed up with the ruling CPDM to suppress that clause. An intense horse trading in which Mr.

Bello joined the vote against a second round in exchange for reducing the five-year residency requirement for presidential candidates to one year, was orchestrated to the detriment of healthy democratic practice. Mr. Bello had just returned from exile and would not have met the residency requirements when he put up his candidature for the presidential election.

Despite these flaws, it still came as a surprise that the Fru Ndi-led coalition failed to achieve a landslide score. His charisma and popularity were sufficient to guarantee such a score, but it would seem, paradoxically, that his coalition did not achieve the expected majority vote because of his charismatic profile. The opposition electoral platform today, as it was in 1992, seeks to flush out the incumbent, set up a transitional government that would level the playground for future elections by drawing up a genuine democratic constitution, an impartial electoral code and carrying out wide ranging institutional reforms. To ensure an unbiased transitional leadership, it is widely agreed that the leader of such a transition shall not be eligible for the subsequent presidential election.

The problem in 1992 was to find a candidate amongst the presidential hopefuls with a profile that cut across the various political divides, who was modest enough to set aside personal ambition for the common good and who was prepared to be guided by a broad-based collegial leadership of political heavy weights. The opposition was expected to find and present such a person to the electorate instead of going their individual ways. This was not done. Sceptics felt that Fru Ndi did not fill the bill because they could not imagine a man of mystified proportions would be modest enough to respect the terms of the transition. The Fru Ndi myth which was an asset for the forces of change became a liability and sceptics as well as the undecided segment of the electorate preferred, so to speak, to vote for the devil they knew rather than the angel they did not know. No doubt, the Fru Ndi myth has inevitably suffered the effect of political erosion with time and the image of intransigence painted by his critics has equally suffered some erosion. Does it mean he stands a better chance today to lead the proposed transition? It all depends on him and his cronies.

The implication of accepting transitional leadership is obvious. It means renouncing any ambition for long term leadership, and should Fru Ndi convince the electorate he is prepared to do so, then he would have scored an ace point. The suggestion that a transitional leader should be sought outside the political class may not be easily bought by some political gurus since there are hardly any precedents to go by and this is because elected civilian transitions have hardly been part of Africa's post-independence political culture. The only transition Africa has known have been perpetuated military dictatorships, not a short-lived civilian interim as is considered desirable in the present Cameroon context.

To prove their endorsement of the proposed civilian transition to be led, hopefully, by a member of the civil society, Cameroonians should fulfil their civic duty by massive registration and turn out at the polls. Failure to do this would endanger the credibility of the democratic process.

S-N F.

37

April Cabinet Shake-up: Biya's Royal Nod or Jolt from Slumber?

Monday 17 May 2004

The dust has yet to settle over President Biya's April 23 mini cabinet reshuffle primarily instigated by FIFA's disciplinary sanction of the national soccer squad-The Indomitable Lions- for violating sports regulation despite several warnings.

The prime target of the reshuffle was no doubt the ousted Minister of Youth and Sport, Bidoung Mkpatt who is charged with condoning and being complicit to FECAFOOT's violation of FIFA's dress code in order to promote the commercial interests of PUMA, the world renowned manufacturer of sporting apparels.

Grapevine sources have it that the financial incentives offered by PUMA to the nation's football authorities were so juicy and irresistible that they preferred to ignore FIFA's warning rather than lose the mouth-watering disbursements made by PUMA. Sources close to the team dispatched on April 24 to Geneva to plead with the world football governing body to review the sanctions against Cameroon indicate that an initial instalment of CFA 300 million francs might have been paid to obtain the ousted Minster's endorsement of the use of the controversial PUMA jerseys used by the Indomitable Lions during the recent African Nations Cup tournament in which Cameroon was ousted in the quarter finals.

Apart from the endorsement premium-"prime de signature"-a regular bonus in the thousands of dollars was disbursed to other football authorities while each player, we are told, earned as much as $1600 per match for sporting the irregular one piece (instead of two) jersey.

It cannot be said, a priori, that PUMA's package deal was illicit given that sporting events, which three decades ago were primarily funded by public patronage-spectators- have increasingly been hijacked by big business pumping in mega-billions for commercial and promotional purposes. Sportswear manufacturers like ADIDAS,NIKE,ROEBOK and other multinationals like VODAPHONE,MTN,FRANCE TELECOM pump in so much money in sport that the mere pleasure of fooling around an inflated leather ball has become such a glamorous pursuit among the youths and thus, they tend to shun more serious occupational and vocational endeavours.

What is however criminal in the PUMA scam is the non-transparency and lack of accountability surrounding the deal and it treasonable and unpatriotic consequence. The use of such funds for self-aggrandisement without the slightest regard for the collective national interest has become rampant and while sport officials are lining their pockets, infrastructures suffer from criminal neglect. At one time the nation's main stadium in Yaounde was banned from hosting international sporting events because it lacked toilets, running water, and the turf had degraded beyond minimum standards.

Somehow all these shortcomings may not have caught the attention of the Head of state until the FIFA hammer fell and jolted the "man of rigour" out of slumber. After castigating government officials for indulging in inertia, the LION, shortly after his invigorating New Year message, slumped into the legendary indolence of his catlike kith and kin.

It is possible that any report of the Bidoung scam might not have pricked the President's royal ears until he saw the possibility of his political mascots, the Indomitable Lions, being prevented from meaningful participation in the forthcoming African Nations and World Cup tournaments following FIFA's decision to slam a pre-tournament loss of 6 points on the LION as punishment for violating regulations.

Looking beyond FIFA's sanctions to explain the Aril cabinet reshuffle would be a frivolous exercise in political palmistry because when it comes to action, President Biya is simply unreadable. A popular columnist describes him as the imperturbable president.

142

The three other ministers who were removed along with Bidoung Mpkatt could be seen as victims of stray bullets. They were not the target. Post- reshuffle justifications for their dismissal may be valid but were not bilious enough to give the Lion Man a constipated nightmare.

For example, the scandal of the Postal Savings Bank and the loss without guarantee of recovery of depositors' hard-earned savings is a sheer re-enactment of the long standing misery and agony inflicted on the citizenry by the banking sector in the past two decades. The former boss of its titular ministry has been made a sacrificial lamb but would that solve the problem of the plunder of private and public funds by state-appointed officials whose greed the leadership has failed to put in check? If, as it is alleged, the Minister failed to scrupulously supervise the GM of the Postal Savings Bank, did the President have to wait to be jerked out of sleep by FIFA before taking action when it is common knowledge that depositors have been unable to make withdrawals since December?

Take another casualty of the President's royal nod-the Mines and Power Minister. What the hell had he to do with the privatization of the electricity corporation and the inability of the privatized utility to meet consumer demands; an inability attributed to inadequate rainfall to power the hydroelectric plants and infrastructural deficiencies? The man might have been an incompetent truant who had been sacked as Provincial Delegate a forth night to his cabinet appointment, but who takes the blame for the clumsy appointment in the first place?

The ouster of John B. Ndeh from the Transport Ministry has yet to elicit any convincing justification even from his detractors. The issue of road accidents and his attempts to put order in the ports sector have been half-heartedly cited but, for heaven's sake, what miracle was he expected to perform?

The bottom line is that the reshuffle was spurred by the spectre of Cameroon's potential relegation from international soccer events and anything that jeopardises the Lion Man's throne and the prospects of his political mascots must surely countered by the nod of his royal head.

In the meantime, ass FECAFOOT activities come under the scrutiny of a presidential commission of enquiry, we should expect more casualties of this deplorable yet revealing scandal.

S-N F.

38

G.W. Bush Jnr's Betrayal of Democracy
Monday 17 May 2004

(1)Bush's Unsettling Precedents

Of all American presidents in recent times, G.W. Bush Jnr can be singled out as one who has failed to symbolize the democratic ideals that the United States represents.

When papa's boy was declared winner of the 1999 presidential election after a controversial vote count and re-count coupled with allegations that his brother, Governor of Florida had rigged the election in that state in his favour, the forces of change in Africa took it as an ill omen for the nascent democratic revolution in the continent. The mere suggestion of vote rigging in the U.S. was viewed by democratic activists as an unfortunate encouragement for many an African dictator or autocrat to justify electoral malpractices by simply pointing a finger at Uncle Sam and declaring: "we have no democratic lessons to learn from abroad, least of all from the United States."

The tragic events of September 11 2001 became a turning point as American foreign policy went haywire. Mr. Bush lustily embarked on a " war against terror" that was widely interpreted as a war against Islam. He waged war on Iraq against the sound advice of the United Nations and even though he won the war, he failed to win the peace. The miserable trophy of the Iraq war was a half-dazed, dishevelled ex-dictator Saddam Hussein who was smoked out of hiding like a rat mole.

The consequences of the ill-advised war have exposed Mr. Bush as a reckless cowboy who is capable of tossing democratic principles to the wind if only to prove his sado-masochism. His international raids on suspected terrorists have resulted in the incarceration off hundreds of innocent people including children at Gwantanamo Bay without the least regard for human rights and due process. To justify his violations, he mischievously labels the suspects ass "enemy combatants" and has put them in indefinite detention without recourse to legal assistance.

Mr. Bush's awkward attempts to restore peace and stability in Iraq are likely to end in a fiasco. The brutal treatment of alleged Iraqi offenders in detention by American soldiers has tuned the image of liberators into oppressors. Recent incidents of sadism in which American soldiers force detainees into collective orgies of sodomy and other despicable acts are the ugly climax of a bellicose foreign policy equally reflected in his handling of the Palestinian question.

We learn from a certain biographer that GW Bush Jnr while in college was a member of an occultist club called "Skulls and Bones" which indulged in satanic rites and rituals involving the use of coffins and pirate symbols. Mr. Was shown on TV the other day turning hot steaks (or was it pancakes?) without the courtesy of donning a chef's cap; a campaign gimmick that may endear him to gourmets, culinary and con artists but not to a serious minded electorate that is likely to send him packing from the White House to the back house.

(2) The Albatross

Decidedly the Lion Man has been jolted from inertia following the creation of two commissions of enquiry in less than a month, giving the impression that a heavier axe is about to fall and much bigger heads are going to roll.

This time around, the matter in question is beyond the offence of lese majeste and misdemeanour in high office. It has to do with the sleazy purchase of a presidential jet that has proven to be a potential death trap for the Prince. And the sheer indication of regicide is not only treasonable but is by implication, beyond pardon.

The grapevine has it that the presidential Boeing which was not even on the "Okrika" (second hand) market had been fished out of a junkyard, having run for more than two decades for the Malagasy

146

Airways. We are told it was procured for a tidy package of CFA 100 billion.

American business moguls and Hollywood stars pick up custom made jets for anything between CFA1.5 billion to CFA 2.5-quote me!

Irrespective of Biya's unimpressive leadership and in respect for human life-the only ABSOLUTE right ordained by the Almighty-the scandal surrounding the purchase of the ill-fated jet christened THE ALBATROSS, purchased with tax payers money by managers of a Highly Indebted Poor Country and again for a royal president who ought to have been peacefully enjoying his retirement after 22 years of a disastrous management of the nation, is unpardonable. THOU SHALT NOT KILL!!!

No one wants an additional CFA 100 billion liquidation fee posted on Mr. Biya especially at the unaffordable expense of the impoverished tax payer.

The contenders of power, most of whom are of doubtful credentials, should hijack Prince Biya for a peaceful exit and it would not even matter to Cameroonians if his successor came from the so-called ruling party which has rather been reigning than ruling.

S-N F.

39

2004 Presidential Campaign: Time for people's verdict is now!

September 29, 2004

Campaigns for the October 11 presidential election are expected to gather momentum today after kicking off on a lame footing over the weekend.

Political activities including preparatory meetings, press conferences and public rallies have been less than hectic as the electorate is more preoccupied with verifying their names on the voter's registers and collecting their voter's cards. The issuing of cards has been marred by confusion in some opposition strongholds as some registered voters still find it difficult to locate their polling stations and to obtain their cards.

Campaigns themes

While the ruling CPDM party has hinged its campaign messages on the apparent peace and stability that reign in Cameroon and making a sing song of the shop worn slogan of Cameroon as an island of peace in the world beleaguered by strife and turbulence, the opposition in general have being capitalizing on the socio economic decline and moral decadence the country has experienced under 22 years of president Paul Biya rule.

CPDM

The ruling CPDM party campaign managers –the majority of whom are either cabinet or ex cabinet members-are wrapping their messages in a language of deification and a mood of over confidence, especially in the South, Centre and East provinces considered to be the fiefs of their natural candidate Paul Biya.

Launching campaigns in Yaoundé, Foubam and Mbouda, canvassing was centred on Biya as a winning president as speaker after speaker expressed confidence in a 100% victory for their candidate. They said a vote for Biya was a vote for democracy, economic growth and the fight against poverty. A Presbyterian pastor in a prayer session at Ambam called on God to ensure success for Paul Biya whom Education Minister, Joseph Owona, described as a veritable gift from God.

SDF

The nation's biggest opposition party has introduced a gimmick in its campaign by cashing in on the Anglophone problem. In a public rally in Bamenda, SDF chairman Ni John Fru Ndi cited statistics on the marginalization of the Anglophones, noting for example that only 20 Anglophones have being admitted into the school of engineering (polytechnique) ever since its creation three decades ago.

The SDF deputy for Momo, Hon. Peter Fonso, reiterated the same issues while launching campaigns in Njikwa, declaring that a vote for Fru Ndi would put a halt to the marginalization of Anglophones. In a more practical note, the SDF campaign spokesman, Martin Nkemngu, on Monday CRTV campaign forum, outlined his party's immediate plan of action including the abolition of tuition fees in state universities and the poll tax that goes under the name of "impot liberatoire" as well as pay compensation to victims of past political violence.

CNRR

The candidate of the Coalition for National Reconciliation and Reconstruction, Dr Adamou Njoya launched a crowd pulling rally at the Bepanda Omnisports stadium in Douala on Monday evening with a promise to restore social justice and reconcile the nation with its culture and history. He pledged to reform state institutions, brings the economy back to its feet, establish good governance and lead the fight against poverty. In the Coalition's TV campaign spot,

150

introduced by a rather impressive jingle with images portraying Ndam Njoya as a man of the people and a devoted Muslim, campaign manager, Sanda Ouarou, decried President Biya's rule as 22 years of betrayal and reiterated that the Coalition was committed to reconciling Cameroonians with politics. The Coalition, he said, proposes to reconcile and reconstruct a dislocated country, revive a moribund economy, and restore the tarnished international image of the country.

He concluded by remarking that Paul Biya cannot do in 7 years what he had failed to do in 22 years.

SLC

The candidate of the Social Liberal Congress, Dr George Nyamndi, performed eloquently on his TV campaign spot, passing on his message in impeccable French and English. He paid polite homage to outgoing president Paul Biya whose achievements, he said, would only be judged by history and invited the incumbent to avail himself of a well-earned retirement. He called the electorate to break with the past and cut out a new path to progress and prosperity.

UFDC

Hamenei Bieleu of the Union of Democratic Forces proposes in his TV message to tackle the issues of embezzlement of public funds and unemployment which he believed can be solved by industrialization. He extolled the virtue of procreation and promised to pursue a pro-natalist policy.

UPA

Hubert Kamgang of the Union of African Peoples outlined what he calls his miracle recipe (les recettes du miracle) which includes the creation of enterprises and the financing of small and medium size industries. He told TV viewers that he proposes to reduce interest rates on loans –up to 22%, create a national currency and pull out the country from the Bank of Central African States, BEAC.

MP

Jean-Jacque Ekindi of the Progressive Movement, a CPDM splinter party, also talked of Biya's betrayal and charged the head of state with failing to respect the constitution, citing the fact that he holds two executive offices as chief executive and as CPDM chairman.

MEC

Fritz Pierre NGO of the Ecological Movement, in a less eloquent performance, proposed to tackle the issue of environmental conservation, fight deforestation, pollution and industrial waste.

MANIDEM

The leader of the Africa Movement for New Democracy, Anicet Ekane, launched his TV campaign by a socio psychological posters, which he said portray President Biya as a leader who is alienated from his people and a neo-colonialist prototype who has never experienced the stressful daily life of Cameroonians and has never been encumbered with the responsibility of paying for utilities such as water, electricity and telephone ever since he was born. Anicet Ekane suggested that President Biya does not even know the price of bread or that of a kilogram of meat.

DC

The president for Cameroon Integral Democracy, Gustave Essaka, in his usual lachrymal tone, declared that the country is being ruled by liars and that in politics, lies can kill. He castigated those clamouring for the return of the remains of the first president, Ahmadou Ahidjo, who died in exile in Dakar, describing him as a puppet of France who ordered the massacre of thousands of nationalists fighting for independence. He declared his modest assets and those of his wife, saying he earns a monthly salary of 208.000 franc as a worker of the Douala urban council.

JDP

The candidate for Justice and Development party, veteran journalist and publisher of the Herald newspaper, Bob Forbin, we are told, adhered to the adage that charity begins at home by inviting residents of his Bastos neighbourhood to launch his campaign through the media. Most candidates do not have the means to embark on elaborate an campaign as state subventions promised political parties to facilitate their campaign are yet to be disbursed.

S-N F.

40

Coalition Split Revisited
Wednesday 29 September 2004

The decision a fortnight ago by the Social Democratic Front (SDF) to pull out of the coalition of a dozen opposition parties following the disagreement over the choice of a single candidate for the October 11 presidential election dealt a severe blow to popular aspirations for political change.

Dr. Adamu Ndam Njoya of the Cameroon Democratic Union (CDU) who emerged as the coalition's choice attributed the split to the SDF's refusal to play by the laid down rules of the game while the SDF Secretary-General, Professor Tazoacha Asonganyi has blamed the other coalition members for violating the principle of consensus. SDF spokesman Martin Nkemngu charges that the candidature of SDF Chairman Ni John Fru Ndi was side-lined by a conspiracy. In the midst of these accusations and counter accusations, one is bound to wonder who is right and who is wrong. Where does the truth lie?

One keen observer DROSHOT put this question to responded diplomatically that each side was half right. So under the circumstances, how does a less philosophically-minded citizen establish what was half-truth?

Any attempt to unravel the ramified circumstances of the split must necessarily revisit the origins of the coalition formed a year ago to work out a common political platform and most importantly to choose a single candidate for the presidential election. In fact it would even be instructive to review a similar exercise in the 1992 presidential election, the first since the restoration of multipartism a year earlier. In 1992, the opposition umbrella group, the Union for Change, recorded failure when Adamou Ndam Njoya pulled out of the union with an opposition coalition he led known as the Patriotic Opposition Parties while Fri Ndi led the SDF to the election. At that time the split was attributed to a personality clash between the two opposition leaders, none of whom was prepared to step down in favour of the other.

Twelve years later, the opposition devised a more systematic approach to achieve what they failed to attain in1992. What became known as the Coalition for National Reconstruction and Reconciliation (CNRR) put emphasis on the need to fashion a common platform, promote solidarity among its members and embark on a nation-wide political sensitization campaign, leaving the very sensitive issue of a single candidate to the last minute.

With regard to the procedure for selecting a single candidate, it was agreed that the principle of consensus was overriding. Members shall proceed to apply a 15-point list of criteria outlining the profile of the most suitable candidate. Should the coalition reach an impasse, then an independent broker would be called upon to mediate.

The first flaw to be observed in the coalition's terms of reference was the deliberate avoidance of the criterion of party numerical strength and popularity. With 22 seats in the 180-seat parliament and 34 local councils to its name, the SDF's strongest point was ignored a priori. From a pragmatic point of view, numerical strength should not only have been among the 15-point criteria but should have been weighted bearing in mind that we are dealing here not with ideological politics but with electoral politics.

Another flaw in the application of the 15 point criteria is that each criterion should have been allocated a maximum mark and candidates awarded grades per criterion as opposed to the "yes" or "no" method of assessment. And so when it turned out that the selection committee of the Coalition led by Issa Tchiroma and with a membership of personalities like Professor Hogbe Nlend who did not conceal their intellectual contempt for Fru Ndi's candidature published the result of their selection exercise, Fru Ndi's score was 11, Sanda Oumarou - 12 and Adamou Ndam Njoya - 15.

The winning camp held that there was no longer need to resort to an independent broker after the selection while the SDF insisted that the consensus exercise should be pursued.

It can be said with the benefit of hindsight that the SDF candidate might have taken too many things for granted. Ni John might have considered the endorsement of his candidature a forgone conclusion to the extent that in one coalition rally in Douala, he said to have improvised a swearing ritual in which he held up the hand of a young girl and swore that whosoever shall pull out of the coalition should be considered as having drunk the blood of the kid. Fru Ndi assumed that the 1992 scenario in which Ndam Nyoya pulled out of the Union for Change would likely repeat itself and the makeshift ritual was intended as a move to pre-empt such a split. Now that he is the one who has pulled out of the coalition, could it be said that the hunter became the hunted?

It would appear that the two protagonists of the coalition, Ndam Njoya and Fru Ndi were engaged a in ploy to trap the other. Fru Ndi's bait was his popularity while Ndam Njoya's decoy was the 15 point criteria. It is still unclear how the 115 points were arrived at and how they were implemented. One point of contention raised by Fru Ndi when he spoke to THE WITNESS shortly after the coalition candidate was made public was the criterion concerning transparency. He suggested that the public service record of a certain nominee was not as lily white as the tiles used in renovating a public building in downtown Yaoundé when he was Minister for a tidy sum of CFA 3 billion francs.

At his inaugural election campaign in Bafoussam last Sunday, Fru Ndi attributed his withdrawal from the coalition to what he described as an incomplete selection process and a lack of democratic spirit.

It is only fair to say that the coalition doggedly adhered to the letter of the selection procedure that was obviously tailored to achieve a hidden agenda interpreted by Southern Cameroonians (Anglophones) as a ploy to exclude them from the presidency of the country.

While the letter of the coalition exercise was said to have been respected, could the same be said of the spirit of the coalition mission?

Given the intrusion of the personal ambitions of coalition members, it might have been more practical, as one political scientist has suggested, for coalition leaders to act as king makers and select a common presidential candidate from without their circle. To be graded by one's own peers who share the same ambitions or have deep-seated preferences for one candidate or the other was an exercise loaded with danger and discord.

S-N F.

41

45th Anniversary of Southern Cameroons Independence: Southern Cameroons Struggle at Crossroads

Monday, October 2, 2006

Two years ago, President Biya of La République du Cameroon in his traditional New Year message broadcast on CRTV reminded his audience that the first of January marks the date in which one part of the country (French Cameroon) gained independence (January 1960).

It was indeed a very thoughtful reminder that what passes for La République du Cameroon is in effect a fractious entity made up of two states of equal status which came together on 1st October 1961 to form a federal republic that was subsequently abrogated in 1972 by political fraud and subsequent presidential fiats.

Biya's motive for that reminder can only be perceived as a cynical exercise in downplaying the significance of the Southern Cameroons struggle to restore its sovereignty and nationhood that has been trampled upon by the assimilationists and annexationists forces of the Francophone led regime in Yaounde. I do not recall any instance in which Mr. Biya mentions the October 1st 1961 unification in all his 24 years in power. The man would go down in history as the President who, with a reckless stroke of the pen, buried the last relics of unification by simply changing the name United Republic of Cameroon (1972) to La République du Cameroon (1984) the name of French Cameroon when it attained independence in 1960.

Despite all political acrobatics to undermine and obliterate the political identity of the Southern Cameroons, the vanguard for the restoration of the territory's sovereignty and self-determination for its people has made significant diplomatic breakthrough to win international recognition and support at the African Union Human and People Rights Commission the Unrepresented People's Organisation, the UN Human Rights Committee etc.

The vanguard movement for the restoration of Southern Cameroons, the Southern Cameroons National Council, SCNC has experienced the rise of faction leaders like Justice Ebong and Mr. Henry Fossung but this has had little or no effect on the validity of the restoration struggle. When leaders of the Free West Cameroon Movement, the Cameroon Anglophone Movement which later became the Southern Cameroon Restoration Movement and many others converged at the Mount Mary Maternity in Buea in April 1993 to give birth to the SCNC, all Southern Cameroonians spoke with one voice and one sentiment and expressed the unshakable desire to take their destiny into their hands.

All political processes based on the right to self-determination must overcome the first and most difficult hurdle i.e. that of creating a political consciousness. In this light, the Southern Cameroons struggle has scored very high marks. Gone are the days when the demagogues in Yaounde tried to falsify the Southern Cameroons predicament as a mere minority question to be equated with that of minority tribes like the pygmy and the Baka of the Equatorial rainforest and the cattle rearing Bororos of the grass field who are clamouring for equal rights and opportunity

True enough, Southern Cameroonians have been treated like second class citizens and relegated to the background in the management of public affairs. A recent and shameless manifestation of this attitude was the appointment last week of six assistant government delegates each in the urban councils of Yaounde and Douala. I don't recall any of them being of Southern Cameroons origin, yet Southern Cameroonians form a significant part of the population of these cities.

True enough Southern Cameroonians form at last one quarter of the Cameroon population but that does not make them an ethnic minority. The former British-administered Trust Territory of Southern Cameroons is basically English-speaking with regard to the two official languages (French and English) but that does not simplify its aspirations to those of a linguistic minority.

The restoration movement has succeeded in dispelling the false notion that the Southern Cameroons question is an ethnic or linguistic minority issue. Attempts to dissemble the issue by the Yaounde regime has resulted in exposing the regime as a bunch of congenital liars with an incurable penchant for dishonesty and corruption. There is absolutely no doubt that the regime shall never relent in its reductionist agenda, yet no amount of political chicanery can halt the momentum for self-determination. Examples abound. Take the Ethiopian province of Eritrea which began its struggle in the early 1970's. Take the Soviet satellites of Latvia, Estonia and Byelorussia. Take East Timor and very recently Montenegro in former Yugoslavia. Sovereignty has nothing to do with numbers.

At the time of unification in 1961, the Southern Cameroons population was officially estimated at 800.000, much larger than Equatorial Guinea, Burma and dozens of other smaller entities that are today enjoying full independence. The Southern Cameroons was already operating a parliamentary system in 1954, three years before French Cameroon had a French-teleguided territorial assembly. Multiparty politics was the order of the day in Southern Cameroons. The political and socio-economic institutions in the autonomous Trust Territory of Southern Cameroons before unification were indicative of a greater political maturity. Economic prosperity was guaranteed by the Cameroon Development Corporation with its vast plantations of cash crops like oil palm rubber and banana; the West Cameroon Marketing Board and the West Cameroon Development Agency, a well-grounded cooperative system and a promising public works Department, PWD.

The actual and potential wealth of the Southern Cameroons coupled with the discovery of petroleum along the west coast in the 1960's fuelled the piratical instincts of the francophone-led regime in Yaounde to embark on the annexation of Southern Cameroons.

The story of the marginalization of the Southern Cameroons is a tragic tale of greed, dishonesty and plunder. The restoration

161

movement under the auspices of the SCNC has succeeded to a large extent in exposing the predatory nature of the annexationists and while it is at present intensifying representation in international bodies, it must be reminded that Yaounde will not willingly withdraw its forces of occupation and its colonial appointees just for the asking. It would be naïve to think that as long as the regime continues to tap the resources of the territory while occasionally dropping one or two crumbs for a few Anglophone lackeys, the gold-digging marauders of Southern Cameroons will suddenly realize their thieving injustice and voluntarily pack out of the territory, with or without apologies, sorry!

Thirteen years after Mount Mary, the Southern Cameroons nationalist struggle has succeeded in establishing machinery for the reaffirmation of its people's identity and a psychological tool for asserting self-pride. A Southern Cameroonian today more than ever before, can now say with confidence that "I am not a second class citizen. I know I have a homeland, a mentality and a world view." But what he cannot assert in truth is "I am in control of my homeland." Thirteen is the age of puberty and a critical age at that. The direction of the restoration movement henceforth would determine the kind of support it gets. Failure to match aspiration with appropriate action could usher in a more radical and revolutionary force to the centre- stage that would not be bothered with intellectual niceties; a force that would not be too eager to caress western diplomatic circles with anti-terrorist lullabies and the virtues of no-violence.

Southern Cameroons consciousness did not reawaken only 13 years ago. The late Dr. Bernard Fonlon made timid noises about Anglophone marginalization in highly private memos to President Ahidjo as far back as 1964. Twenty years later the late S.T. Muna former Vice President and Prime Minister of West Cameroon at the time President of the National Assembly also made a rather sheepish memo to Paul Biya about some problems facing Anglophones. None of these highly restricted memos touched the crux of the matter i.e.

the Southern Cameroons truncated march towards total independence.

The non-negotiable position for sovereignty was sounded by the Free West Cameroon Movement at the All Anglophone Conference at Mount Mary Maternity in Buea (AAC-1) in 1993 and was only adopted at AAC-II in Bamenda in April 1994. It had dawned on participants that the accommodative federalist approach of AAC-1 had become irrelevant and that the path to self-determination called for a more drastic appraisal of the plight of the Southern Cameroons. Only drastic measures can move the struggle to its logical conclusion.

In as much as people pretend that secession is not the answer to the question, a dispassionate diagnosis of the malady dictates that there can be no relief unless the boil is excised. It is rather paradoxical that the advocates of accommodation with La République du Cameroon at the expense of Southern Cameroons God-given right to self-determination are the very surrogates licking the crumbs from the francophone table. They are usually rewarded with cabinet and another lucrative positions forgetting that they owe their appointments to the nationalist struggle, the bearing in mind that Southern Cameroonians and deceive international public opinion that national integration is a reality in Cameroon.

Integration is a voluntary process not imposed by high-handed political manipulation. Integration is not synonymous to annexation and unless the forces of occupation peacefully withdraw (which is not likely), they would have to be evicted – one way or another.

S-N F.

42

Economic Sabotage
Friday, May 9 2008

Snapshot has received reliable information that there is some sharp black marketing of imported rice going on the creek port of Ekondo Titi, while Cameroonians are languishing and paying exorbitant retail prices for that essential foodstuff and other basic commodities.

Eyewitness accounts speak of dozens of 20-tons trucks and converted Dyana buses on a daily mad rush to deliver huge consignments of rice destined for Nigeria by engine boats docked at the creek port under the watchful eyes of a few uniformed men of the Customs department and the armed forces. From the look of things, it would not be an exaggeration to put the daily smuggling of rice at 1000 tons of the foodstuff, which, presumably, has just been cleared from the Douala port by importers who are now taking undue advantage of recent duty-free measures taken by government to alleviate the crucial shortage of basic commodities and the attendant galloping inflation.

These importers and wholesalers are taking undue advantage to do brisk business and make windfall profits at the expense for the Cameroonian consumer. The entire business cannot be described merely as economic crime. The penal code ought to be amended to consider such activities as a treasonable offence deserving capital punishment.

It would seem that what is happening to rice is the same as what is happening to cement and other commodities. It is the same hide-and-seek game whereby unscrupulous businessmen are bent on a serious campaign of economic sabotage, not only for profit, but to undermine the regime of president Paul Biya, who should have known before long that he had it coming to him. As they say, what goes around comes around.

When Mr. Biya was alerted 20 years ago about embezzlement of state monies by government officials, he waived the matter aside, saying there were no proofs. When he began his selective anti-corruption campaign by piercing a few sharks, he should have known that the fish begins to rot from the head, not the body. He should have known that the every cleansing act or ablution begins with the head down to the toes.

The regime's spin doctors are quick to explain Cameroon's economic woes as a consequence of globalization but that cannot convincingly justify the fact that a bread basket like Cameroon cannot now boast of feeding itself. It cannot feed itself because of ill-timed policies, bad faith, egocentric interests and a shameful lack of patriotism on the part of the ruling class.

Instead of deploying its uniformed men to do meaningful work, hundreds of thousands of troops are deployed along the highways to harass peaceful travellers under the pretext of checking identity cards and the imaginary transportation of arms by the public transport network, for the purpose of overthrowing the regime. Uniformed men are idling about, intimidating impoverished citizens in the towns and cities, while a crippling economic sabotage is taking place in remote places like Ekondo Titi.

Eyewitness reports emphasize the mad rush with which the smuggling of rice is being conducted, probably because the saboteurs want to hit the jackpot before anyone takes notice and probably because the muddy roads to Ekondo Titi may soon become intractable with the coming of heavy rainfall. The quagmire Mr. Biya has dug for himself is rougher than the road to Ekondo Titi and if he cares to read the handwriting on the wall, he should be able to see the monstrous hydra head of the G11; the Frankenstein monster he gave birth to and which, willy-nilly, is out to get him despite his ambition to rule Cameroon for life.

What is happening in Ekondo Titi is a mere tip of the iceberg and when the avalanche finally sweeps down the May 20th avenue, right in his backyard, then shall the story be told. I have always pondered why the Ondo Ndongs and the Abah Abahs did not border to flee the

166

country even when it had become clear that they had been earmarked as sacrificial lambs. They had all the opportunity to escape, passport or no passport. But they did not. They are out to defy Ali Baba and if they must go, Ali Baba too, must go.

It is a nasty power game in which the poor unsuspecting and docile citizens of Cameroon, who, having been anaesthetized by the false political doctrines (the absence of war) for so long, have been caught up in. And they too had it coming. The obsequiousness of our de facto one- party parliament that has been blessed with a dubious political opposition has finally brought Cameroon to its knees and the perpetrators of our collective misery shall pay with their bones.

The demise of the Abah Abahs and co has provided solid dramatic material for our TVs, an unwholesome distraction for a poverty stricken population; a childish play that smacks of naiveté and intended to cover up the greater crime. But when the hour of doom strikes, the political jesters will have to pay the ultimate price.

S-N F.

43

Morning Safari Takes Us for a Ride
Friday 1ˢᵗ June 2007

For quite a very long time now, the English-language interactive early morning talk show broadcast live over the national station of Radio Cameroon has actually been taking its audience for a ride; and a rough ride indeed.

This programme which occupies a rather demanding prime slot, we believe, is targeted at an audience that expects to be treated to thought-provoking issues of crucial interest to a nation that, from all indications, has lost its sense of direction. Unfortunately, that has not been the case. Serious-minded listeners are mindlessly served a tasteless porridge of blabber for breakfast. What comes across on 'Morning Safari' is an incoherent babble from an improvised mutual admiration club of a randomly selected crop of broadcasters who give the impression of having been jolted, half-asleep, from their beds to the studio, with a drowsy notion of what their duty to inform and educate is all about. Topics for discussion are haphazardly chosen by proponents and propagators of issues they themselves do not master or have bothered to master. Issues are broached and discussed, not only amateurishly, but in an annoyingly tentative manner that leaves much to be desired by a highly demanding and critical audience which expects journalists to do their homework; that is to be informed in order to inform.

One critic remarked: "These Safari boys, perhaps, should first of all be informed before they can inform." The blatantly ad-hoc manner in which the programme is conceived and operated only confirms the aphorism that "talk is cheap." And the talk on Morning Safari is cheap. Every member of the mutual admiration club chimes in with half-baked ideas, inconsequential observations, uninformed opinions, disjointed and illogical statements, childish argumentation, a flimsy and approximate mastery of facts foisted down the throats of helpless listeners. The majority of listeners who have the means and bother to phone in are those with a personal agenda, which usually does not have any bearing on the whimsical topic of discussion.

The rather capricious choice of topics, the deliberate attempt to avoid a soul-searching examination of any given issue, the disorganised and confusing debate that has become a hallmark of the programme constitute one more gimmick that Cameroon's poverty-stricken taxpayers cannot afford. CRTV is financed by citizens who demand their money's worth.

Granted that a talk show is basically conversational and allows for a certain degree of colloquialism, this should not be an excuse for laxity in language. The media ought to set language standards that can be emulated by society, especially pupils and students. Morning Safari has not only failed to set proper language standards but has also been promoting sloppy diction. We do not expect our broadcasters to speak through their nostrils like white men, but for heaven's sake, there is something known as Received Pronunciation (R.P) which has been widely accepted as the universal standard for the English language. One does not have to go to London to find R.P because it is right there in the dictionary.

Morning Safari, of course, has its positive side in that it provides an opportunity for those who can afford it to express their opinion and that it occasionally raises important issues which have provoked spirited debate.

The programme, despite it defects, can be improved upon if the panellists would take the trouble to do some minimal research on the topic of discussion so as to make the programme more informative and less speculative. Some homework and a little dose of intellectual humility would ensure a more comfortable ride on Morning Safari.

S-N F.

44

Bridge over Troubled Waters
Monday June 25, 2007

Once again a new bridge has been erected over the River Mungo after the old one collapsed in July 2004. Thank God.

According to the Prime Minister who presided over the inaugural ceremony recently, the new bridge symbolised the recovery of national unity. No one is oblivious of the fact that when the old bridge collapsed after an accident caused by a reckless truck driver, detractors saw it as part of Southern Cameroons National Council's (SCNC) secessionist agenda. Far from it.

The SCNC preaches secession but not violence. Its motto is "the force of argument and not the argument of force". It cannot serve the SCNC's purpose to go about blowing up bridges because it has not, a priori, ruled out the prospect of diplomatic and trade relations with La République du Cameroun once it recovers and establishes its sovereignty. That notwithstanding, the collapse of the old bridge, albeit accidental, was viewed by Southern Cameroonians as an ominous pointer to the collapse of the fake union in 1961 between the Southern Cameroon's (Anglophone) and La République du Cameroun (Francophone). For one thing, the highway on which the Mungo Bridge stands is the very symbol of the vicious exploitation of the natural and human resources of the Southern Cameroons for the sole benefit of La République du Cameroun. It is through that road that products of the SONARA oil refinery in Victoria are transported to the rest of the country as well as products of two agro-industrial giants east of the Mungo: the Cameroon Development Corporation, CDC, and PAMOL plantations. The carting away of all this wealth and the concomitant impoverishment and degradation of the standard of living in the Southern Cameroons is a constant and painful reminder of its colonial status. The colonisation of blacks by blacks is as bad, if not worse than the colonisation of blacks by whites.

The Prime Minister, a Southern Cameroonian stool pigeon of the coloniser, has a right to believe the new bridge symbolises the recovery of national unity, implying, perhaps unwittingly, that unity had ceased to be a reality. If that which was lost, according to him, has been found, so be it. All one can say for now is that peddling illusions is not a realistic approach to the Southern Cameroons Question.

So much water has gone under the Mungo Bridge, old and new and not a single drop can be recovered. Perhaps the new Mungo Bridge could be said to be an auspicious landmark on the road to the recovery of Southern Cameroon's' sovereignty.

CPDM Wins Bali Council by Forfeiture

When the Bali-Bawock crisis erupted in March, keen observers were quick to see the hands of some barons of the ruling party behind the manipulation of the Bawocks for political ends.

They were not wrong. The rejection of the list of prospective councillors of the opposition Social Democratic Front, SDF, in Bali Subdivision in view of the July municipal and parliamentary elections might not have been the original intention of the manipulators, but is a clear consequence of that manipulation.

The Santa mafia did not succeed in getting Bawock carved out of Bali and added up to Santa Subdivision to form a new division, but they, at least, succeeded not only in obtaining a special electoral constituency, but also in fuelling hatred against Bali-Nyongha.

The Santa CPDM mafia would use any means fair or foul to please its paymasters in Yaounde. Thus, it did not come as a surprise that the Chief of Bawock instructed his subjects not to join the SDF Council list in Bali, knowing fully well in advance that a list without adequate Bawock representation would be rejected. Only one Bawock candidate was bold enough to agree to join the list.

And so the council election in Bali-Nyongha will be a no-contest show; a football match with one goal post; nothing to write home about. When victory is cheap, it loses its taste. The CPDM following in Bali-Nyongha certainly has people of sterling qualities and leadership potential but to win by forfeiture is to dampen the excitement and fulfilment of victory.

Child Labour and the Hierarchy of Capitalist Exploitation

The United Nation's Day of the Child has come and gone with its usual noises about child labour. The sing-song about child labour or the evils associated with it is, at times, unbalanced and ill-defined. The campaign against abusive child labour occasionally verges on a blanket condemnation of child labour as if manual labour which was part and parcel of our primary and secondary school educational system had no virtue whatsoever.

Parents or guardians cannot be blamed for encouraging children to take an active part in household chores, fetching water or firewood for home use and doing some gardening and handicraft during their spare time. In fact, it is a salutary policy to encourage children to engage in purposeful and gainful chores as an exercise in productivity and such productive activity is even more imperative in low-income earning households as a means of making ends meet. What society condemns is the inhuman treatment and abusive exploitation of children for personal gain without taking their education and welfare into consideration.

The fight against the inhuman exploitation of children did not begin today. The famous English writer, Charles Dickens, in the wake of the Industrial Revolution in the 19th century, had taken up the crusade against abusive child labour which he so graphically depicted in his novel "Oliver Twist". The novel is the pathetic tale of a ten-year-old boy who was taken out of an orphanage to join a gang of his peers in a public workhouse where they were compelled to drudge the whole day to produce industrial inputs, were fed a miserable bowl of oat porridge and not allowed to take a bath. In a

173

bid to revolt against their starvation rations, the children drew lots which fell on Oliver Twist who, after gobbling down his porridge, moved up to the master of the workhouse and pleaded, "I want some more". The authorities cried scandal and were on the verge of pronouncing the death sentence, when it dawned on them that more gain could be made if Oliver were sold to whoever cared to buy an impertinent brat for three pounds.

As Western capitalist countries made giant advances in technology, child slave labour gradually diminished and began gaining grounds in the Third World. The more the West or First World grew richer, the Third World became poorer as the phenomenon of child slave labour gained more grounds. The world economic order of exploitation is glaringly explicit. The industrial cum imperialist nations exploit the politically vulnerable nations of the Third World by agencies of Third World dictators and their compradors who, in turn, exploit the more vulnerable strata of society including children.

The prevalent slave wages in Cameroon's public and private sectors are a vexing testimony of this deplorable hierarchy of exploitation. The exorbitant price indices of vital commodities such as water and petrol are pegged at par with the so-called capitalist free market standards even though Cameroon is hydrologically and petrologically well endowed. And this policy of impoverishment has been piously sanctified under the nebulous doctrine of globalisation; a doctrine whose most vulnerable victim is the African child, the Cameroonian child.

Two types of child exploitation, in my opinion, do not fit into the abusive child labour category. These involve juveniles forced to take up arms as child soldiers and those being "trafficked" through the black market for the sexual gratification of Western paedophiles. These dreadful types of exploitation constitute a raving madness and perpetrators ought to be perpetually confined in mental asylums.

While we are all called upon to wage a relentless war against child exploitation, and all forms of exploitation for that matter, crusaders, especially the media, should take the pains to *distinguish between wholesome child labour and abusive child labour*. The one operates for the benefit of the child while the other operates to the detriment of the child.

S-N F.

45

Dan Kisob Goes Marching In
6th July, 2007

With the obvious exception of the so-called state funerals of venerable politicians like John Ngu Foncha and Solomon Tandeng Muna, hardly any other funeral in Bamenda has in recent times mobilised and galvanised the populace like that of my bosom friend and soul brother, Justice Dan Akum Kisob.

Dan should have made it to the rank of chief justice were it not for his most untimely and painful death on the road to Ebolowa, of all places. And why was he on the road to Ebolowa, the land of rotten chimpanzees? Dan and two of his colleagues had been jettisoned into internal exile purportedly for disciplinary reasons in connection with the infamous murder trial of Fon Doh, the traditional ruler of Bali Kumbat and a mignon of the ruling CPDM regime, who last year was sentenced to prison for murder even though he is today moving about freely following a legally dubious and immoral grant of bail on health grounds.

If I were to write an epitaph for you, Bobs, I would simply say, "Dan died on the Altar of Vindictiveness." Enemies labour in vain. Your life, Bobs, was glorious, but your very hot exit has brought immeasurable sorrow and consternation. If I should write a book about you, that book would be like my heart and me. When you checked out unceremoniously, you took away a part of my soul and all those you came across during your hectic time on earth. I recall the decision we took (you, Chinanga Suh Boma (RIP) and myself); the decision, after completing CCAST Bambili, to go to Yaounde instead of overburdening our parents about the UK, USA or à la rigueur Nigeria, Ghana, or Liberia, all of which were the cherished and conventional destinations for Southern Cameroon and later West

Cameroon's high school leavers. We strapped our boots and journeyed to Yaounde in a spirit of adventure and defiance. Who was excited about Yaounde University where bright Anglophone students found themselves repeating classes or whose chances of gaining admission into the school of engineering (Ecole Polytechnique) where narrowed by Government policy?

Yet we took the challenge to defy the Yaounde myth with a self-designated mission to imprint the Anglo-Saxon way of life on the other side of the Mungo. We were going to turn the other cheek, but not at every bend of the road. Our watchword was HONESTY. We were subdued in comportment, but not intimidated; respected authority but licked no asses (or is it arses?).

Throughout your life, as anyone can testify, you lived by noble principles. You had a heart of gold, a sense of humour, and a generous soul, which left no one you came across indifferent. The 70-seater omnibus that conveyed your colleagues from Ebolowa (where you had hardly stayed for six months) to your funeral in Bamenda (22-23 June) was eloquent testimony of your outgoing nature and outstanding human relations. For most of your 55 odds years on earth, you left a legacy of refinement in taste and deeds.

You never settled for less than the best in dress, drinks and victuals. And you have also left behind three promising boys, a lovely daughter, a tearful and devastated wife, Jackie, the entire Kisob family, the magistracy, friends and acquaintances (from the highest to the lowest) to grieve for you.

Water Rationing In Buea

While in Bamenda recently, I stumbled on a number of friends who sought to know how we were faring in Buea. Well, I said, apart from the hectic political electioneering, we are suffering from shortage of potable water, even in the rainy season.

"What?" exclaimed one of them, "you mean to say that after having supplied two prime ministers in quick succession that is all they can bargain for? That is rubbish!"

178

"Easy my man," I countered, "at least we have the new Mutengene-Muea macadamised road." The bearded one, dubbed Sam Nujoma on account of his grey beard, dismissed my observation." A one-centimetre density road. Can you compare that with the Dschang-Melong road? A masterpiece in civil engineering? "

Of Intellectuals and Politics

The issue of intellectuals getting involved in politics and what attitude is expected of them was brilliantly handled recently in the national radio programme, Cameroon Calling. Professor Ndiva Kale's contribution was so edifying and clarifying that intellectuals need not be embarrassed by taking active part in politics, as long as they do not fall prey to sycophancy and obsequiousness.

For quite a long time, a simmering tension had been building up within the rank and file of the opposition SDF party between those who held brief for intellectuals and those who contemptuously dismissed the role of intellectuals, pointing, as evidence, to the CPDM government as one made up of good-for-nothing professors and technocrats, who have failed to deliver the goods. You cannot blame them for such irrefutable evidence. However, the intellectual versus the hoi-polloi debate, if not kept in reasonable check, could constitute a debilitating and expensive distraction to the detriment of political dynamism.

In one of the episodes of Charles Dickens' *Oliver Twist*, Oliver encounters, in rather misadventurous circumstances, a would-be benefactor, Mr. Brownlow, who most charitably adopted him. When Mr. Brownlow, a respectable book dealer, later suggested to the boy that he could groom him to become a writer, the young Oliver, in all his blissful innocence, replied that he thought it was more profitable to be a bookseller.

The reality is that in the enterprise of intellectualism, both the bookman and the bookseller need each other to succeed.

179

The Ondo Ndong Verdict

When the Ondo Ndong verdict was passed last Thursday, the population and the media worked overtime, expressing all kinds of opinion and feelings. Some said he should have been slammed a 100-year prison term for his part in embezzling State funds to the tune of FCFA 53 billion. Others also suggested that those who benefited from his largesse such as the First Lady, the church, eminent and not-so-eminent personalities, should have to appear in court to answer as accomplices. I sought to have a legal opinion as to whether all those who received financial gifts from the ex-General Manager of the Special Council Support Fund was answerable before the courts except may be as prosecution witnesses. The answer was in the negative.

I am inclined to think that were it not for my own sheer ignorance, I would not have hesitated to solicit Mr. Ondo Ndong's financial assistance. Perhaps Mr. Ondo Ndong was a very generous man, just that he was too generous with State money while our municipal councils were financially crippled and unable to provide basic services.

Although people have expressed fears that the ex-General Manager may eventually end up being freed on bail like another CPDM baron, the one and only Fon Doh of Balikumbat, one must acknowledge the fact that the judiciary in Cameroon is struggling hard to establish its authority as the Third Estate of government. We only hope that whatever assets are recovered from Ondo Ndong and his accomplices, such assets should find their way to the national treasury and should be accounted for.

Advance Salary Propaganda

Hundreds of civil servants are already lining up at the Ministry of Finance with application files for advance salary. It is about two decades since the Government suppressed this facility because of liquidity problems. Reinstating the advance salary facility would no doubt come in handy for most civil servants even if it is going to deepen their indebtedness.

Our Highly Indebted Poor Civil Servants who were expecting to see a salary increase after the recent cancellation of the national debt by international creditors are instead being offered the possibility of three-months salary interest-free loans payable over ten months. And the government is now making political mileage out of it.

What is even irritating is their attempt to palm it off as a humanitarian gesture as civil servants go a borrowing and a sorrowing.

S-N F.

46

Looking Beyond July 22
Friday 13 July, 2007

If president Biya intended his nation-wide address last Friday to pep up the electorate, I am afraid he did not impress his audience. Besides, his usual platitudes about guarantees of free and fair elections, the act of voting as a fundamental and civic right, the pursuit of the anti-corruption drive, and the sanctioning of reprehensible conduct, the thrust of his message was his appeal for a massive turn out at the polls as evidence of vitality in order to determine "clear and incontestable majorities in the National Assembly and the municipal councils".

Of course, a massive turn out would be evidence of political vitality, but the question of determining clear majorities is moot. There can be no doubt in anyone's mind that when President Biya, who doubles as chairman of the ruling CPDM party, spoke of clear and incontestable majorities he meant the consolidating of the state-contrived majority of the CPDM which occupied two-thirds of the out- going legislature of 180 seats. The fact that Mr. Biya made an unprecedented nation-wide address on the eve of campaigns for the July 22 general elections is a clear indication that he is anxious, indeed, very anxious about the outcome of those elections.

Biya's current seven year term of office, the second since 1997, ends in 2011, making a total of 29 years as Chief Executive. In 1996, he manipulated parliament to endorse constitutional reforms extending the presidential term of office from five to seven years while his French political mentors were reducing their own presidential term of office from seven to five years. The man was not about to play by the rules and this self-proclaimed best pupil of the French Overseas school of democracy was set on outdoing his masters. Why then should "the best pupil", who had secured by constitutional manipulation, two 7- year terms of office, be so anxious about the forthcoming general elections? For the obvious reasons that he is constitutionally barred from running for presidential office come 2011, the seven-year term being renewable only once. Mr. Biya more than ever before must, by hook or crook, ensure a "clear and incontestable" two-thirds majority in order to stage-manage further constitutional reforms that would guarantee him the legal status of president-for-life.

If less intelligent pupils of democracy a la francophonie like Omar Bongo next door have clocked four decades in power, he, Mr. Biya was not going to settle for less. Notwithstanding his total grip on power and his mastery of personal rule (which is worse than dictatorship), Mr. Biya is visibly uncertain about the CPDM emerging with the two-thirds parliamentary majority he so desperately requires to foster his egoistic grand ambitions for very obvious reasons.

The wear and tear, bruises and broken limbs sustained by the CPDM in recent weeks of intra-party competitions, that is, the renewal of local party executive bureaus and primaries for the forthcoming parliamentary elections, have inflicted a heavy toll on the party and exposed a not-so-pretty backside of the political machinery that has ground this nation to a halt for more than two decades. The sheer amount of backstabbing, cloak and dagger tactics, greed, corruption, and the unbridled quest for power for the sake of it, shocked the bulk of unsuspecting CPDM militants who had all along been made to believe that their party was holier than the opposition.

Paradoxically, the timid anti-corruption drive, which has been put on hold for electoral reasons, and which has been highly commended, though with reservations, has had the effect of alienating the tribal clans of Mssrs Ondo Ndong and Siyam Siewe, two CPDM sharks-turned-scapegoats, now languishing in jail for devouring huge chunks of the commonwealth. Everything being equal, Mr. Biya knows that he has lost beforehand at least one-sixth of the two-third majority he enjoyed in the last legislature because of the awkward political acrobatics of his circus clowns and the greed of

184

his fellow diners who preferred to eat with cooking spoons instead of table spoons.

The litmus test for Cameroon's opposition parties would be to ensure that Biya does not obtain a majority (simple, absolute or two-thirds) by the end of the July 22 exercise. Failure to do so would provide an excuse for a return to a de facto one-party state and divine rule. Perhaps divine monarchical rule would be a blessing if only it were embedded with a spirit of benevolence, a benevolence which is woefully lacking in our not-so-royal presidency.

I am always slightly amused when I hear some people declare that Biya will not seek another term of office come 2011. The political emasculation of the citizenry has rendered it so helpless that it can only find solace in wishful thinking. The wishful thinkers have conveniently forgotten that barely three years ago when it was rumoured that the President had died in a European hospital after a brief illness, the man organised a triumphal return to Yaounde during which he buoyantly declared to those who wanted him dead that they would have to wait for another 20 years. Of course, Mr. Biya is not stupid enough to let himself be caught in his own constitutional trap. He has the agility of not only being one step ahead of the pack, but also the unusual ability of running with the hares and hunting with the foxes. He is certainly not going to wait for 2011 when his eligibility would have run its course.

Political pundits envisage a game plan whereby, Mr. Biya, armed with a parliamentary majority, would obtain constitutional reforms in 2008 that would shorten the presidential term of office from seven to five years, run and rig elections in 2009 when his eligibility will not be contested and go in for yet another five-year term of office, renewable once. And the beat goes on... until he drops dead... in keeping with his own prophetic calendar.

Numerologists believe Mr. Biya's game is being played under auspicious weather conditions. July 2007 is the seventh month of the seventh year of the new millennium; so the man has got a double seven going for him. There is usually one joker in a pack of cards. But Biya has seven jokers and seven trump cards and he is playing

185

them so close to his chest that any attempt to second guess him may prove futile.

Centralisation, Personality Cult and Impunity

Shortly after Mr Ondo Ndong was appointed to take over the management of the Special Council Support Fund (FEICOM), news of his profligacy reached the supervisory body, that is, the Ministry of Territorial Administration, headed at the time by Koungou Edima who immediately dispatched two of his inspectors to investigate. Ondo Ndong flew into a rage and chased the inspectors away. He fumed and complained to that rather elusive centre of power in Cameroon usually referred to as the hierarchy. He argued that his predecessor, Gilbert Biwole, a man of integrity whose death in office paved the way for Ondo Ndong's rise to power, had never been subjected to an investigation and that Koungou Edima was setting a bad precedent. The matter died a natural death. And Ondo Ndong was left to his own devices by bullying his supervisory authority into inaction. The new FEICOM boss had gained admission into the exclusive club of sacred cows and the cult of impunity.

Perhaps Koungou Edima might have subsequently resumed his battle for supremacy had he not been prematurely given the sack in the wake of the 2002 general elections which were postponed on polling day for one week when word got to President Biya that the Ministry of Territorial Administration had failed to ensure the dispatch of sufficient voting materials to certain stronghold of the ruling CPDM party. Poor Edima got the sack for negligence of duty while the Ondo Ndongs and the Siyam Siewes went on a wild looting spree. They kept fleets of expensive SUV'S, bought lavishly furnished villas for their mistresses and imported exquisite household items. Siyam is even said to have ordered a dining table for fifty million francs ($100,000 US).

What else could have been responsible for this state of affairs if not the over centralisation of incredible financial resources in the hands of these sacred cows and would you blame them for behaving like demi-gods? Were it not for the conditionalities imposed by the international community for Cameroon's attainment of the HIPC completion point and debt cancellation, it is doubtful if Biya would have bothered about sacrificing a few scapegoats in his make-believe campaign against corruption in high places

S-N F.

47

Violence Begets Violence
20th July, 2007

Vanity of vanities, says the preacher, all is vanity. Humbug of humbug, says the radical, all is humbug. You all know, ladies and gentlemen, that when we say in pidgin that "Massa no hambog me; you di hambog plenty" we understand it to mean: don't pester me, don't disturb me, don't be a boor, you are such a nuisance! Words have a plastic quality and fluidity, which intrinsically permit them to assume multiple semantic faces.

And so, brothers and sisters, my sermon this evening is about violence and to remind you that violence of violence, says the revolutionary, all is violence. The choice of the theme of violence has been triggered by an overflow of adrenaline that has been poisoning and contaminating the blood veins of the fictitious body politic called 'La République du Cameroun' that, in recent weeks, has been caught in a frenzied atmosphere of election fever. The attitude, actions and pronouncements of political actors, confused militants and sycophants of partisan political associations have become such a great cause for concern that if someone does not sound the alarm, we, both gangsters and bystanders, will find ourselves engulfed in a senseless mayhem of actual, not virtual, backstabbing, butchery and savagery.

Revenons à notre mouton. Now, when we talk of violence, what are we talking about? It is the use of force to cause harm, pain and suffering. The impression we all have is that violence, of necessity, is physical. Violence is physical. It is also moral, spiritual, and psychological. The operational phrase here is: to cause harm. And for what purpose? Egoism, self-aggrandisement, envy and greed. When Cain murdered his brother over an issue of offerings to God, that was a sheer case of envy, jealousy. And when King David dispatched his top army general to the war front so he could get killed and so he could get the general's wife to bed, that was a sheer case of covetousness. Thou shall not covet thy neighbour's wife!

These may be deadly sins, but the deadliest sin is greed! Seneca, the venerable ancient Greek philosopher, it was, who observed that "gluttony (the love of money) is the root of all evil." Geoffrey Chaucer, in the 14th century, re-echoed this aphorism in the Canterbury Tales, the Pardoner's Tale, to be more specific. Very few philosophers, ancient or modern, have ever been against money (material well-being). Certainly not. They crusaded and shall always crusade, against the 'LOVE of money'. The sheer love of it! The sheer love of money, wealth and accumulation of wealth, power, just for the sake it. And this business of greed (langa throat) has increasingly become so rampant during the past two decades that even a pope cannot fold his arms, genuflect in piety, without violently sounding the alarm. Of course, His Eminence, Cardinal Tumi, has done so. So, after that, what next?

Those who engage in violence or have been tagged and stigmatised as violent just because they have dared to demonstrate, in public, their bitter discontent with a political arrangement that has reduced them to sub-humans, zombies, in a land well-endowed by God, are for all intents and purposes NOT VIOLENT. Those who have engaged in acts of violence (and they are well-known) are the upstarts and brigands who have made a duty to inflict on a society (of which they lay no claim to have built or nurtured) almost irreparable damage; a damage that could easily result in carnage.

When a Prime Minister, Head of Government, makes a punctual electoral home-coming visit to his so-called area of origin and declares that "everybody is free to militate in any party, but here in Buea and Fako in general, we (whoever we is supposed to be) shall not accept the opposition. Militants of the opposition parties should go to their area of origin for militancy." The PM reportedly vomited this unfortunate statement in Buea a few days ago and for this kind of declaration to come from a prime minister-cum stool pigeon; from someone you would expect a certain modicum of decency, smacks of mischief and desperation. And when he talks of areas of origin, what, in God's name, is his own area of origin? Someone could be referred to as 'Lagos boy', on account of the fact that he was born in Lagos. But when the Prime Minister is referred to as 'Calabar boy', was he born in Calabar, or is he a congenital Calabarian? In which case, he should aspire to become Prime Minister in Calabar, not to perpetuate his status as a comprador Prime Minister of la République du Cameroun.

What the Prime Minister and Head of Government succeeded in doing was to unleash violence on our normal sense of decency and dignity. When those who are posturing as the advocates of national integration propound and exercise of the principle of divide-and-rule, primitive tribalism and exclusion, we all have reason to wonder and be perplexed.

Cameroon is an ISLAND OF PEACE. Yes! But it is the peace of the graveyard because when a system that is run by brigands hijacks the laws of the land, grabs power for the sake of greed and the populace stand by as helpless onlookers, that is violence. The silence and helplessness of a people forever condemned to swallow the bitter spittle of anger cannot be construed as total and unconditional submission to the forces of evil, of Satan. So, no one is surprised when conscientious activists ripped political campaign banners off the streets of Douala because the ruling CPDM party had arrogantly placed them in locations expressly forbidden by law. And those conscientious activists have been branded as lawless troublemakers even though they had petitioned the Minister of Communication and the Senior Divisional Officers about the irregularity.

When you have a legislative body that owes its legality to a two-thirds ruling majority by broad daylight fraud and that even the laws passed and enacted by that same ruling majority are openly flouted by those expected to uphold the law, you don't have to ask who is promoting violence. And when the violence of the oppressor can no longer be borne by the oppressed and the oppressed by natural law begin to agitate, the agitator cannot be held responsible for violence. The international community of philosophers has defined the

191

agitation of the oppressed as legitimate self-defence against which no amount of fraudulent legality can prevail. Legality cannot be equated to legitimacy. So be it.

The Duel That Never Was

Apart from violence, the current fever of electioneering has been spiced by a healthy dose of sensationalism. The much-trumpeted radio debate between mayoral-aspirant Mbella Moki of the ruling CPDM party and former SDF Buea Mayor, Mokake Endeley, ran into an anti-climax last weekend when Endeley failed to show up at Radio Buea whose premises were jammed full of political enthusiasts, who had turned out like ancient Romans in an arena to be thrilled by gladiators who were out to draw blood. We are told Mbella landed much earlier at the studio, literally jogging vigorously in 'track suit', warming up and spoiling for a fight. Mbella, the prize fighter and challenger with red gloves intact was already bouncing and sparring when news came that his opponent had thrown in the towel without the courtesy of even making a show of presence. The challenger and the huge crowd of fans piled out of the radio, crestfallen and disappointed. Who would not have been? In Pidgin English we say: 'man no run.'

Political actors, like stage and movie actors, just like athletes and sportsmen, even the most intelligent and talented, need coaches, managers and consultants. And until these categories of professionals in Cameroon realise this, the likes of Mokake Endeley would continue to whet our appetites, trigger our adrenaline and our morbid penchant for bloody entertainment only to end up in a rather kill-joy frigidity by chickening out. Poor show. Why Mokake Endeley had picked up the gauntlet in the first place and against good sense is his business. Everyone knows that Mbella Moki was not only going to give him a bloody nose and roll him in cow dung but Mokake was likely going to quit the ring with a fracture that could severely compromise his political career.

Mbella Moki, as incumbent Mayor, had an obvious edge over Endeley. Both gentlemen are intelligent except that Endeley had failed to realise that intelligence is not cleverness because to be clever is to be cunning. To be cunning is to be street wise and Mbella seems to know something about street mentality.

S-N F.

48

Lion Man, Lion's Share
Friday 27th July, 2007

If anyone says he is surprised at the results of last Sunday's general elections, just know he is deceiving himself. Apart from the rigging carried out by the ruling CPDM machinery, what is even most disturbing was the very low voter turn-out estimated at 30 percent; a figure which is far below the credibility benchmark. Now that the CPDM has bagged in 153 out 180 seats in Parliament, President Biya, the Lion Man, should be as pleased as Punch. He wanted a comfortable majority and he got it.

Perhaps it would not be a bad idea, after all, to replace the lone star on the national flag with the picture of the lion; a predatory beast that symbolises greed and indolence. It may not also be a bad idea if all the opposition parties resolved to dissolve and fuse into the ruling CPDM. Such a move might ensure that every citizen gets a share of the national cake; that is after the Lion Man would have sliced off two-thirds of the pastry.

Someone has suggested that civil servants may go without pay this month owing to the fabulous expenditure incurred by the ruling CPDM at the expense of State coffers to fuel its election campaigns. This is not likely to be the case because we can take advantage of debt relief to borrow from European financial clubs. The elections are over and we can at least heave a sigh of relief and return to business as usual.

What one gathers from the low voter turn-out is that Cameroonians are so preoccupied with poverty and misery that politics no longer holds any attraction for them. The business of survival has taken up the little energy in them with nothing left for politicking

Stop These Quack Medicine Men

Traditional doctors play a major role in the country's health delivery system given their proximity to the masses and the comparatively low cost of treatment. However, the proliferation of certain unethical practices by a good number of them is a great cause for concern.

I was taken aback the other day by a commercial announcement over radio Buea about a certain traditional doctor residing in Bomaka claiming to cure blindness, river blindness and cataracts in fifteen minutes!

Media managers and journalists ought to be a bit more circumspect in handling these kinds of information. Medical doctors are ethically barred from making commercial advertisement and one should expect same to apply to traditional doctors especially those who make fabulous claims; some of them even claim to have discovered a cure-all drug, a panacea for 200 kinds of ailments.

The Ministry of Health and National Council of Medical Doctors ought to take vigorous action to stamp out this dishonest tendency and why not punish the offenders.

Another variety of offending traditional doctors could be described as itinerant charlatans who usually commute in express buses of travel agencies. One cannot help the feeling of being part of a captive audience when traveling in these buses. They do not only violate one's sense of decency with their uncouth language and vulgar references to sex in general. You don't have to be prudish to feel a great amount of discomfort when these charlatans harangue passengers for hours on end about their merchandise. Some idle-minded passengers are thrilled by these charlatans, some of whom, it should be said, are quite adroit in salesmanship. They are good at hoodwinking a generally gullible set of unsuspecting passengers and so passengers who would prefer to journey in tranquillity, read a magazine or book, or chat among themselves, are virtually held hostage by those rascals. Nobody can have peace of mind when these charlatans board the bus. Their lewd and explicit description of sex,

196

even in the presence of children is simply unacceptable and the Ministry of Transport ought to issue an order banning these mind corrupters from violating peoples' right to peaceful enjoyment of their bus ride.

God alone knows the content of the concoctions and decoctions they offer for sale. So, apart from the moral harm they cause, the graver danger is the hazardous game they play with the health of citizens.

Continental Government for Africa

The recent African Union Summit came and went with little attention paid to it by the national press even though the meeting was attended, very uncharacteristically, by President Biya. Cameroonians were so engulfed in electioneering that the importance of the AU Summit agenda, that is the creation of a continental government for Africa, did not quite get the attention it deserved.

Kwame Nkrumah's vision of a continental government is as relevant today as it was yesterday but rather than leave the matter entirely in the hands of heads of state, who might view the project as a means of eroding their power and glory, the ordinary people, political parties, trade unions and civil society in general ought to be involved in expressing their opinions and ideas as to how to go about achieving this dream.

I share the opinion that African regional groupings such as ECOWAS, CEMAC, ought to take concrete steps to ensure the free flow of persons and goods within their region as a first major step towards concretising the vision of continental government. Regional groupings have so far been pussy-footing on a number of objectives aimed at establishing economic integration which, in my opinion, should precede political integration. The Osagiefo Kwame Nkrumah would not agree entirely with me even in his grave. He had posited that one should "seek first the political kingdom and everything else shall be added onto it."

Once the freedom of movement and goods, and the breaking down of intra-regional barriers have been achieved, each country should then proceed to organise a referendum for the people to decide whether or not to join continental government. Even the United States of America and the European Union went through a process of gradual expansion.

S-N F.

49

Stop The Pretence! Boycott Parliament!!

Friday 10th August, 2007

There has been quite a lot of useless talk about the way forward following the July 22 general elections that were dogged by massive fraud and irregularities that gave the ruling CPDM party an overwhelming majority in the National Assembly and the municipal councils. CPDM spin doctors and incorrigible apologists argue that their Pyrrhic victory is the result of their party's political programme and the inability of the opposition parties to put a united front, strong enough to wrest power from the entrenched oligarchy.

Cameroonians are a strange lot; a confused set of people, so confused that one cannot help believing that they truly deserve the kind of government they have got. The question as to which way forward after the unparalleled electoral fraud of July 22 has elicited varying responses such as the need for the opposition to form alliances, the need for an independent electoral commission and the need to overcome voter apathy. How all these constitute a way forward beats my imagination. How these selling-after-the market suggestions constitute a pointer to a way forward remains a mystery to those who have not been initiated into the convoluted pathways of Cameroon politics.

Some self-appointed defenders of the status quo have attributed the CPDM stolen victory to that party's political programme and the opposition's lack of an attractive political platform. If this is not a case of either selective exposure or selective perception, I wonder what else it could be. The CPDM has offered a high sounding programme called Grand Ambitions, which has left the populace in a famine of great expectations. They have shifted from fighting poverty to the slogan of poverty reduction. Their much-trumpeted fight against corruption has not only lost steam but has fizzled down to shadow boxing. Their understanding of political decentralisation has been translated into administrative decongestion; hence the illegal and haphazard creation by Presidential fiat of numerous sub-divisions and special electoral constituencies soon after the electorate was convened for the July 22 merry-go-round. Decentralisation means the devolution of power from the centre to the periphery of the political centre and not the crude carvings of non-viable administrative units. Gerrymandering is not a synonym for decentralisation.

The frontline opposition parties have, ever since the restoration of multi-party politics in the early 1990s, come up with solid and desirable programmes adapted to the aspirations of their followership. These programmes include a truly independent electoral commission, the reform of the constitution to put in place a two-round presidential election, the endorsement of independent candidatures for general and presidential elections, the vigorous pursuit of embezzlers of public funds and the repatriation and restitution of same and the upgrading of the standard of living by ensuring a more equitable distribution of the commonwealth. The opposition has never, and may never, have the chance to concretise these objectives because the electoral fraud machinery of the ruling junta has always short-changed them at every electoral jamboree since 1992.

Perhaps the deepest pitfall of the opposition is their naïve persistency in believing that any meaningful change can be achieved through the ballot box. This naivety of the opposition, which has failed over the last decade and a half to achieve a level political playground, has reinforced the widely held opinion that their continued participation in electoral exercises is motivated by personal pecuniary gains. Why would they want to continue lending credence to a diabolical circus show when it is clear that every step the electorate has taken to the ballot box has resulted in two steps away from the democratic culture?

Cancelling the July 22 elections would have been a logical way forward. But, alas, that option is a dead letter. Petitioning the

Supreme Court as the opposition has done to seek redress can only amount to a cosmetic surgical operation that provides work for idle spin doctors who can only be too happy to fulfil their role of eye servants. Imploring the international community to stand witness to the electoral sham of July 22 is tantamount to begging a stranger to mourn for your dead. The international community, the majority of whose electoral monitoring institutions had refrained from observing the elections, the outcome of which were predictable, are tired of midwifing the political miscarriages that have become the trademark of Cameroon.

The responsibility to cause change lies squarely on the doorsteps of national political actors, not the international community. The international community can only act or react in consequence of internal action and so long as the opposition are contented with giving credibility to the regime by dancing to the tune of the pipers and their paymaster, then we may just as well go on shuffling and smiling and stop grumbling.

If the opposition truly wants to erase the image of their role as self-seeking clowns of Biya's circus, clowns who are merely interested in lining their pockets with the spoils of aborted democracy, they must put an end to all the pretence and relinquish the demeaning number of seats that the oligarchy has grudgingly accorded them. Let the National Assembly be seen for what it truly is - a one-party affair. The moral, trade and investment sanctions that would inevitably result from such a move remains the only hope for bringing the regime back to its senses. Philanthropists have argued that international trade and investment sanctions resulting from a total withdrawal of legitimacy from the ruling junta can only be harmful to the ordinary citizen. That is sheer propaganda because international aid and foreign investments have hardly been of any benefit to the people of Cameroon, who, for the past two decades, have been called upon to roll up their sleeves and face up to hard times till they drop dead, while gangsters are feeding fat on the sweat of slave labour.

If opposition leaders think they can also ride on the backs of their gullible followers, then it is up to that followership to take their destiny into their hands, swing the club of people's power and ensure that none of their parliamentary aspirants take up a seat at the National Assembly under the pretext that they would create a storm in Parliament. A storm by 16 members out of 180 is a storm in a teacup.

S-N F.

50

To Go or Not To Go
Friday 17 August, 2007

Even if the opposition, especially the Social Democratic Front, SDF, were to decide not to go to parliament following the severely flawed general elections of July 22, it would require MPs with a flawless attachment to principles and a high sense of sacrifice to resist the lucrative possibilities and the seductive charms of office that come along with a parliamentary seat.

It is obvious that candidates incur considerable financial debts to run for political office and those who make it consider their success as an opportunity for recuperation. This is where personal motivation seems to have the upper hand over collective principle and the rules governing the National Assembly make it impossible for any political formation to legally restrain any elected member from taking his or her seat in the House. The flip side of the coin reveals a different scenario wherein those who genuinely or fraudulently lost the election will have to accept their financial losses in a spirit of true sportsmanship. And if we expect losers to demonstrate a sense of sportsmanship, why should proponents of boycott not demand that same spirit of sacrifice from the winners? If the SDF were to decide on a boycott that may not be respected by successful parliamentary candidates and proceeded to expel defaulters from the party, it would, at least, go on the record that the party had resolved not to be part of a legislature in which it never could have been possible for it to play any role at all. With only 14 seats going for it until the yet-to be scheduled rerun in five constituencies, the SDF will not be in a position to form a parliamentary group, which by regulation requires control over at least 15 seats.

Some critics have expressed the opinion that should the SDF eventually be in a position to form a group, it should refrain from accepting positions in the parliamentary bureau. They argue that SDF membership of the bureau with all the perks that come with the territory, exposes office holders to corruption and makes them accomplices of the ruling CPDM party and its anti-people policies. In my opinion, the presence of the opposition whose combined strength as at now is a mere 21 seats in a 180-seat parliament, automatically makes them accomplices of the CPDM. Even if they were to occasionally stage a walk-out to demonstrate disagreement over certain draft laws and resolutions, they would still be morally responsible for every decision taken by parliament.

Another major question on the minds of many Cameroonians is whether or not the SDF should eventually join the new government that President Biya is widely expected to appoint in the days ahead. The SDF has persistently dismissed the idea of joining the executive. It may have very good reasons to hold firm on that position.

It is not my intention to provide its leadership with any justification for not joining the government, but it would be recalled that the late Professor Emeritus Bernard Fonlon had examined the implication of a coalition government as far back as 1964 when the Federal Republic of Cameroon was hardly three years old. Dr. Fonlon, in a memo to President Ahidjo in which he deplored the marginalisation of the ruling West Cameroon (Anglophone) party, the Kamerun National Democratic Party, KNDP, in the conduct of national affairs, which had been completely monopolised by the ruling Francophone party, the Union Camerounaise (majority), reminded the Francophone hegemony, that "when you share a government, you share full responsibility for its action: you share the credit for its achievements, the blame for its blunders. Thus, it cannot be a matter of indifference to you how this government is constituted or what policy it espouses."

Biya, in his nationwide address on Tuesday, was explicitly dangling the carrot when he spoke of the possibilities of a broad-based government; a union government, which he said, would include parties whose election results may have fallen below expectation. What he was telling the opposition, in effect, was that

204

they should not feel excluded and that a coalition government would be in the higher interest of the state. Dr. Fonlon had remarked in his memo that "any chief of government or state picks his team as he judges best, but this surely does not exclude consultation with his partners in coalition to hear their views about his choice." Biya is not the consultative type and could get up one morning full of mischief enough to include a sprinkling or two of SDF militants in the new government and the party can go to hell with its policy of non-participation in-government.

Successful candidates of the legislative election have up till Monday to validate their parliamentary membership and by the time you read these lines, the SDF should have made its stand clear on whether or not to join the National Assembly.

Whichever way the die is cast, the question remains: is it more useful for the SDF to join a parliament in which it cannot even create minimum impact or to join a government in which its members can, at least, imprint its own style of governance and avail themselves of the opportunity for apprenticeship?

S-N F.

51

Where Is The Oil Money?
Friday 5th October, 2007

It was with a bit of surprise that I learnt the caucus of Southwest traditional rulers presented a motion to Prime Minister Ephraim Inoni last month demanding a fair share of revenues from the National Oil Refinery, SONARA, to be ploughed back in development projects in the province.

Their demand for a fair share of oil royalties and not all revenues is quite in order and in keeping with the broad principles of economic deprivation, but one would have expected the chiefs to target the National Hydrocarbons Corporation SNH, which collects oil royalties from multinational consortiums such as ELF and Mobil, not SONARA which buys and refines crude oil from SNH and elsewhere under free market conditions and is constrained, like all other enterprises, to pay Value Added Taxes and a host of other fictitious taxes, imposed by a rent-collecting regime whose taxation policy has ruined productivity, scared away venture capital and impoverished the citizenry.

The principle of derivation dictates that a people have a God-given right to derive benefits from commercially exploited natural resources within their geographical area. It is a natural endowment which no government, legitimate or otherwise, should mess around with. Government has demonstrated a certain amount of transparency with regard to derivation in the timber exploitation sector even though the timber exploitation policy in itself leaves much to be desired in terms of sustainability and environmental conservation. Perhaps the regular disbursement of timber royalty in recent years is motivated by the fact that 90 percent of beneficiaries are in the Francophone part of the country while petroleum exploitation is entirely in the Anglophone section which must be impoverished to maintain its second class status.

The Southwest chiefs would be well advised to monitor the activities of SNH, which is collecting juicy windfalls from oil royalties as a result of the skyrocketing price of oil in the world market in the past two years. Huge sums of unexpected royalties have swollen the national treasury and should not be allowed to lie fallow to tempt the ever-increasing bundle of long fingers that dabble with the commonwealth of the nation.

Official figures indicate a windfall of FCFA 14.25 billion for the first quarter of the current fiscal year, bringing the figure to FCFA 119.94 billion. This impressive figure was attained despite a drop in crude oil production, which stood at 83.604 barrels a day as at May 31, 2007, compared to 87,357 barrels a day as at December 31 2006. Apart from royalties, SNH company tax for the current fiscal year is expected to reach FCFA 75 billion while royalties for this year is estimated at FCFA 613 billion.

All these statistics are fine on paper but how they do translate into concrete and sustainable development projects such as manufacturing industries, small and medium size agricultural and construction enterprises is what remains to be seen. About two decades ago, we were made to dream about moonshine projects such as a cement factory, a motor tyre industry, a fish canning factory and the building of the Natural Sea Port in Victoria (Limbe) - all these in the Fako Division.

At present, even the prospects of fish canning has been dealt a severe blow by the government's rent-seeking policy that has preferred to give concessions to unscrupulous Chinese fishermen who are wreaking havoc along the coastline with monstrous trawlers that spell doom for our entire marine life. You can't find a single shrimp at the Victoria dockyard these days and the availability of tuna fish may soon become a thing of the past even though the name Cameroon is derived from Rio Dos Cameroes (River of Prawns), the name given to the Cameroon estuary by Portuguese sea-faring explorers in the 15th century.

The persistent squandering of our natural resources with little or no thought given to the reinvestment of some of the fruits of exploitation, reminds us of the nagging questions: what legacy are we going to bequeath to the next generation?

Structural Terrorism in Schools

Structural terrorism is an expression I only came across very recently during a group discussion on the rights of the child which I was consulted to moderate over Radio Hot Cocoa in Bamenda and it was pronounced by the no-nonsense human rights lawyer, Barrister Harmony Bobga, who is reputed for calling a spade a spade. The learned gentleman observed that school children in some select private schools were more likely to assimilate the teachings on the rights of the child than those in our public school system because of the structural terrorism that has been instituted in those schools.

No one can deny the fact that overcrowding in our schools, especially the government schools has been a persistent cause for concern for a long time and that in the academic year that has just begun, the magnitude of the problem has attained the threshold of psychological violence. Classrooms designed for 30 pupils are now crammed to the brim with 100 pupils and you don't need to stretch your imagination to visualise the perpetual atmosphere of terror in which pupils are condemned to receive formal education. You don't need to be very observant to notice the dilapidated state of the infrastructure of state-run primary and secondary schools, especially in the countryside. The eyesore that passes in the name of schools is a sheer indication of our underdevelopment. We have moved from a developing country to an underdeveloped country.

Every time I travel to Bamenda and pass by the Government School Up-Station, my heart bleeds. My late father graduated from there in 1939. The late Rt. Honourable S.T. Muna left there a decade earlier and I did in 1965. We are now in 2007, the 21st Century and yet there is not a single infrastructural innovation to boast of. And yet our politicians keep on telling lies about their concern for a better future for the younger generation.

The leadership of this country, if leadership it is, stands accused of squandering the nation's resources for their egoistic interests. The demagogues in power who shamelessly want to be seen as benefactors of society do not need to engage in the shop-worn rhetoric of what legacy to pass to the youth because they damn well know the answer to that one. The leadership of this country stands accused of an incurable tendency to regard the youths as being in a perpetual state of infancy which probably explains why it has done little or nothing to reverse the alarming trend of school leavers and graduates hovering around their mothers' kitchens at the age of 35 or more because they never had a chance to earn a living. A good number of these managers of state affairs have conveniently forgotten that they were already holding top positions of responsibility when they were still in their early 20's. They are still in business as usual because they believe they were divinely ordained to lord it over the rest of the miserable lot of mankind, who must forever moil and toil for them to live in exaggerated luxury.

The structural terrorism instituted by the leadership is not only in schools, hospitals, streets, markets and so on; it is everywhere. Those of them who are found guilty of making life miserable for others shall answer for their deeds on earth, not in heaven.

S-N F.

What Good Is University?
October 2007

The university academic year has officially kicked off with Francophone authorities making so much euphoric noise about "le systeme LMD" - Licence, Master's, Doctorat.

For many weeks, Yaounde University campuses have been flying banners proclaiming the Bachelor's, Master's and PhD university degree system as if it were some accidental discovery that would make Archimedes jealous in his grave.

The recent adoption of the Anglo-Saxon BMP system by the Latin-oriented university systems worldwide has come as a blessing to Cameroon, which, despite its colonially derived bicultural educational system with Francophonie having the upper hand, had stubbornly resisted embracing the more rational Anglo-Saxon academic formula because, according to Francophone thinking, it would have been an act of submission to a numerical minority and by extension, a clear admission of inferiority.

In an attempt to mollify Anglophones and temper their agitation for secession, the government created the University of Buea, alongside five others, in 1993, stating, for public relations purposes, that it had been conceived in the Anglo-Saxon tradition.

Now that the BMP format has been dictated nationwide by global circumstances, what distinguishes the University of Buea from the rest at the moment is ceremonial: the rituals of matriculation and convocation during which graduates in rented academic robes are awarded degrees.

Besides the fact that lectures at UB are delivered in English, the institution's destiny and possibilities for distinction lie in its recently published Strategic Plan for 2007-2015, a rationally conceived blueprint spelling out an action programme aimed at moving UB "from a mainly teaching institution to a teaching, research and service university."

According to the document, the programme of reform has been designed within the context of the new university governance policy that advocates professionalism, relevance and quality.

With regard to the University's primary objective of teaching, the master plan envisages the quantitative and qualitative improvement of the teaching staff, noting that junior staff predominate in some faculties thus, some faculties have a very high number of lecturers who are MSc holders.

According to the draftsmen of the blueprint, junior staff means lecturers with qualifications below PhD. It is quite doubtful if this definition reflects the true Anglo-Saxon notion of junior staff in academics.

In my relatively limited academic experience, I have had the privilege of being tutored by the likes of Bud Wilde (BA), Professor and Dean of the School of Journalism of the University of Western Ontario, London Ontario, Canada.

He was an unassuming scholar who in 1976 was nearing his retirement after two decades of university teaching. He was not only the mentor of dozens of PhD holders, but had attained the rank of professor and dean by dint of his academic experience and his immense contribution to knowledge through renowned publications and inspiring lectures. I am sure if a Bud Wilde were to be recruited in UB today, we would gladly forget our academic manners by classifying him as a junior staff.

Cameroon's preference for terminal degrees has had the unfortunate effect of demotivating a good number of academics who seem to attain intellectual menopause soon after obtaining the so-called terminal degrees. Degrees may be terminal, but the quest for knowledge is not.

With regard to research, the UB master plan pledges to conduct research for sustainable development and to enhance the quality of life of Cameroonians. Both fundamental and applied research, it

212

states, will be done to address issues of local, national and global concern as well as those of relevance to industry.

The draftsmen have identified principal themes on which to focus research activities. These include health, food security, the environment, gender and governance. It is, however, the opinion of many observers that next to political atrophy, Cameroon's most aching problems are economic and managerial.

Economic development, trade and commerce, banking and other services, industrial processing, packaging and marketing seem to constitute areas with problems begging for urgent solutions. Perhaps the Social Management Sciences Faculty ought to be accorded greater space in the area of applied research for it to become relevant to industry.

Cameroon is awash with a multiplicity of development agencies such as MIDENO and SOWEDA that seem to have long forfeited their raison d'etre. We have utility providers like the defunct SNEC for water and AES Sonel for electricity which had long become moribund even before the arrival and spread of the privatisation epidemic.

The banking and housing sectors are suffering from a pestilential virus that may soon render them terminally paralysed. UB ought to identify such ailing institutions and contract with them to finance research and find practical scientific solutions to their problems.

For one thing, the master plan does honestly acknowledge that even though there is increasing collaboration with national institutions and enterprises, enterprises for now only provide facilities for practical training of students. It is time to go beyond that horizon.

UB must embark on a wooing spree to charm the private sector out of slumber. This requires a serious marketing effort to be especially initiated by the Social and Management Sciences Faculty with a select committee of journalists, economists, management gurus, public relations whiz kids and people with drive and gumption.

S-N F

213

53

Motions of Commotion

October 2007

All hell has broken lose again as the demons of "advanced democracy" are bent on not letting sleeping dogs lie with their petitions of support for their party Chairman Paul Biya to become life president.

The orchestrated flow of motions of support for Mr. Biya on the occasion of his quarter century in office is a sickening reminder of the authoritarian dispensation of the one-party days and a clear indication that Cameroon's multipartism is mere window dressing.

When you listen to the wording of their motions, you cannot help asking the Almighty what Cameroonians have done, or not done, to deserve this unholy and unwholesome invasion of their consciences by political adventurers whose prime motivation is the preservation of their undeserved privileges, booty looted from state coffers and the perpetuation in power of the man who made it possible for them to have access to the public treasury.

The demagogues of the ruling CPDM party have advanced a number of unconvincing reasons why they want Mr. Biya to remain in power after November 2011 when his current seven-year term comes to an end.

They argue that the constitutional limitation of the presidential terms of office is undemocratic. They say there is no limitation on other elective offices and that to do so for the president would be unfair. They also claim that the constitution should not constitute a stumbling block to the exercise of sovereignty by the people if they express the wish to have President Biya to rule for life.

They also believe Mr. Biya still has a heavy load of unfinished business and ought to be given a chance to accomplish his design for the nation. Where were these demagogues in 1996 when the constitution was amended to prolong the term of office from five to seven years with a mandate renewable once?

Perhaps it did not occur to them that the man would live up to 2011. Who does not know that there has never been any constitutional amendment or violation that was not drafted and sponsored by the president ever since the Ahidjo days? By calling for the abrogation of constitutional provisions limiting the mandate of the president, CPDM cheerleaders should be reminded that the public cannot be deceived to think it is a spontaneous and sincere expression of the wish of party militants.

They talk of fairness and the free expression of the sovereign will. Who does not know that Cameroonians in what is today referred to as La République have never had a chance to experience free and fair elections?

At a time when Cameroonians are struggling to keep the past behind them, pick up the pieces and carry on with their broken dreams and aspirations; at a time when people are trying to figure out a way to deal with the problems of survival on a daily basis, the spoilers of peace should spare us the nightmares of yesteryears when the sing-song of motions of support was the order of the day.

People are tired of sycophants whose songs of adulation can only be a source of irritation and provocation. Biya himself has said 2011 is still far ahead and it would be a good idea to cross that bridge only when we get to it.

In the midst of this entire hullabaloo, the opposition, which has regrettably narrowed their political vision to electioneering, has become a helpless and silent observer. They have always failed to seize the opportunity to ignite and galvanise their militants for a common cause after the operation go-slow of the early 1990's.

I don't want to believe, like the deist, that God created Cameroon but has abandoned control of it. Clerics of every religious persuasion have tried to bring sanity and to instill the fear of the Lord in Cameroon but it would appear that they too, are weary. Has God forsaken Cameroon?

Coup Plots and Border Clashes

One is tempted to believe that reports of a military plot to overthrow the government and the attack on Cameroonian soldiers in the Bakassi Peninsula may not have been a mere coincidence, especially as they occurred against the background of President Biya's silver jubilee in office.

It may appear to be wild speculation to link the three events, but leaders have very unorthodox ways of gaining public sympathy. While the theory that the border attack could have been carried out by Nigerian rebels may sound plausible, the alleged coup plot does not augur well for Cameroon since both matters are currently under investigation.

It would be prudent to withhold premature comment. It suffices for the moment to remark that the two incidents are omens of terrible things to come. No one has to be a doomsday prophet to sense that.

Democracy and National Sovereignty

I was impressed the other day listening to Morning Safari as a certain Mr. Hilaire Kamga, twice presidential candidate, elaborated his theory that there cannot be democracy without sovereignty. He posited that a country, which does not exercise control of its sovereignty thus, a neo-colony cannot pretend to establish a democratic dispensation.

He was referring to Cameroon and other French-speaking African countries that are inextricably tied to the apron strings of mother France through fictitious cooperation accords that leave crucial matters such as national currency in the hands of their neo-colonial master.

If anyone had any doubts concerning Mr. Kamga's statements, he ought to have followed the current diplomatic row between Chad and France over the issue of a French so-called charitable organisation whose members were caught red handed as they

217

attempted to abduct hundreds of child refugees purported to be orphans from the Sudanese region of Darfur.

The intervention of French President, Nicolas Sarkozy, who personally flew to Chad to rescue some of the culprits from the hands of the Chadian judiciary, is a case study that lends credence to Mr. Kamga's theory.

Sarkozy did not only rescue journalists and the crew of the aircraft that was destined to fly out the refugees, some of whom were Chadian nationals, but he has also threatened to repatriate the member of the French NGO in total disrespect of Franco-Chadian cooperation agreements and contempt for Chadian sovereignty.

The racist undertones of Mr. Sarkozy's interference are unmistakable, especially when you compare them with previous statements he made in Senegal on the occasion of his first presidential visit to Africa.

Mr. Sarkozy believes Africans are inferior and he makes no apology for his beliefs. Chad, like Cameroon, is an oil producer whose citizens are wallowing in poverty, thanks to their umbilical relations with France whose President has the cheek to treat his neo-colonies and their rulers with contempt.

S-N F

54

How Far, 2011?
Friday 2 November 2007

Paul Biya's latest diplomatic offensive in France is quite remarkable for two reasons. He returned home punctually instead of globetrotting and gallivanting as he usually does whenever he has an official excuse to go abroad.

Secondly, the man mustered enough courage to face the media on thorny issues of national interest, even though he did not have much of a choice. The media coverage, especially his express interview on the esplanade of the Elysée Palace and the chat with a French TV channel were very instructive, even though I suspect the special reportage in the French rightist daily newspaper, Le Figaro, as usual, was a publicity stunt known in French journalism as "Publi-reportage".

Since November 1982, when Mr. Biya came to power by constitutional arrangement following the resignation of his predecessor. Ahmadou Ahidjo, most crucial pronouncements concerning the destiny of what has become known as "La République du Cameroun", today, have invariably been made from France.

Mr. Biya has never had the courage to confront or accost a pluralist national press. As a self-confessed pupil of French democratic institutions, he is inclined to feel more comfortable with France's establishment media when it comes to giving an account of his stewardship to his countrymen, than with the Cameroon media. So be it.

Biya's performance at "France 24" was quite remarkable in that the anchor man screened two televised questions from Cameroonians in the French Diaspora, a significant departure from the neo-colonial tradition whereby the voices of dissidents-in-exile were routinely stifled. One is inclined to attribute this media revolution to French President, Nicholas Sarkozy's personal discomfiture with contemporary Francophone African leadership that has been characterised by ineptitude, corruption and bad governance.

Biya didn't have much of choice with regard to his media encounters. In other words, his choices, besides facing the music, would have been considered inappropriate or ungentlemanly if he had walked out of the TV studio in anger (like his French counterpart in a CBS 60-minute programme), punched his interviewer or spat invectives at him.

He braved the media encounters under very tense and nervous conditions as you heard and felt his very deep and stressful breathing. He managed to circumvent the question of his hidden agenda to prolong his tenure of office when his current and second seven-year term comes to an end in 2011: after a quarter century in office!

Biya artfully dodged the question whether or not he intended to run for office in 2011. In fact, all he said was he was not thinking about it now, which is not to say he will not run in 2011. When he pointed out that 2011 was still far away, you begin to wonder how far it is. You ask yourself how deep the ocean is. How high is the sky? How far is far? Time is tricky, intangible, inelastic and immeasurable. Time is relative.

The length of time from now till 2011 could relatively be equated to the length of time from 1982 to 2007. In trying to give the impression that the crucial year 2011 was too far off to be of major concern to Cameroonians today, Mr. Biya was merely confirming that his leadership lacks, and has always lacked, vision and purpose other than a mindless, callous and cannibalistic perpetuation of personal rule.

He made some rather inaccurate statements since it is not polite to say he lied, in his French interviews with regard to his promise made on Radio Monte Carlo in the very early 1990's to meet the Cameroon opposition. He has never done so. He has yet to do so. He claimed, and for the first time in history, called Fru Ndi by name, that the latter boycotted a scheduled meeting with him. Not true. He claimed his latest government is broad-based. That is inaccurate. He claimed his urgent priorities are fighting corruption and upgrading the standard of living of Cameroonians. That again is not evident.

Interestingly, Mr. Biya also declared he had no reservations if the remains of his predecessor who died in exile and was buried in Dakar in 1989, were to be repatriated if the deceased family so wished.

One wonders how the repatriation of a deceased head of state could solely depend on the wish of his family. Biya knows better than anyone else that the day Ahmadou Ahidjo's remains touch the soil of Cameroon would spell doomsday for him and the ruling oligarchy.

If Cameroonians have anything significant to look forward to before 2011, it should be the return of Ahidjo's bones to Cameroon; a prospect that has haunted Mr. Biya and his henchmen for nearly two decades.

S-N F.

55

When Silver Begins To Rust

To make a balance sheet of President Paul Biya's stewardship is an exercise in futility. It is even more frustrating, uninspiring and debilitating when one attempts to make an assessment of his 25 years in power because the man's performance lacks latitude - a graph of longitudes without curves and character.

Historians, like mathematicians and geographers, need significant markers and pointers without which their story falls flat, their narrative becomes insipid and commentary is rendered tedious instead of illuminating.

The sheer monotony of the man's pronouncements can be so irritating that many are those who turn off their radios and TV sets every time he comes on to harangue the nation in his not-so-angelic voice.

For 25 years, we have heard him churn out his favourite stock phrases such as "rigour and moralisation", "appeased democracy", "advanced democracy", "grand ambitions", "fight against poverty", "peace and stability", "Cameroon is a state of law", "we have achieved so much but much still has to be done", "we must roll up our sleeves and work harder." Etc., etc., etc., etc.

Mr. Biya's speeches are so predictable that one can conclude his discourse even before he opens his mouth. He exhorts everyone else to roll up their sleeves but no one recalls when he ever sweated in his armpits except during the April 6, 1984 coup attempt when 'putchists' came knocking with bazookas. He does not sweat and does not like to sweat, but he expects everyone else to sweat so that he and his cronies can continue to live in style.

How many cabinet meetings does Biya hold in any given year? Ever since he promised to personally supervise the construction of the Bamenda Ring Road in 1985, one wonders if he can identify that region on the map.

Any historian or journalist who ever bothered to chronicle Mr. Biya's first 25 months in power would not need to strain to map out his 25 years in power. The nature and itinerary of his leadership were indelibly imprinted from the outset. The spokesman of the April 6 coup plotters had unbelievably diagnosed the cankerworm of the regime when he stated over the national radio that Biya's acolytes were recklessly siphoning the wealth of the nation as if there was no tomorrow.

They were looting the state coffers with impunity and even if that was not the ulterior motive for their coup attempt, it was, nevertheless, a tangible excuse to take up arms against Ali Baba and the forty thieves. Even though the tables turned against the coup plotters, the looting continued in higher gear and one of the kingpins of the white collar robbers, Roger Melingui, who depleted the produce farmers providence fund - the National Produce Marketing Board - shamelessly came on TV to justify his extravagant life style by stating that he hails from an ethnic group which believes in high living.

In the latter part of the 1980s, Cameroon became notorious for being among the top ten world consumers of champagne. The new boys were really living it up. They had arrived. It was their turn, the turn of Biya's tribesmen to rule and ruin the nation and they succeeded. They have not only succeeded but also believe they can get away with it.

For 25 years, the ship of state has been drifting with a highly distracted pilot and no navigator. In 25 years, the country has circumnavigated full circle to a de facto one-party state. The political balance sheet is not only in deficit, but indicates an irredeemable bankruptcy.

Economically, we twice won the world trophy for corruption and shamelessly carried the banner of Heavily Indebted Poor Country.

224

When Biya moved into state house in November 1982, the five-year development plans and other development blueprints fled through the window.

From a social point of view, the number of liquor off-licences began competing with the number of schools and health centres. Boozing became a full time occupation while work became an occasional distraction. Religious and ocultic sects flourished as Rosicrucians and Free Masons held the instruments of power hostage, demanding blood as ransom. What have we not seen? What have Cameroonians not gone through?

On many occasions, President Biya has assured his countrymen that there was light at the end of the tunnel, but what they discovered every time they came close to it was the flame of a one-eyed dragon poised to swallow up the innocent citizens of this God-forsaken nation.

The evildoers, kindred spirits of the flaming dragon have always gone scot-free, but for a handful of scapegoats that have been sacrificed on the altar of earthly powers and principalities, the manipulators of international finance whose greed cannot be appeased with anything short of human blood.

Mr. Biya celebrated his 25th anniversary in power exclusively with sycophants of the ruling CPDM party and was honest enough to admit the fact that when he addressed the crowd of his party vanguards who had come to jubilate with him on the esplanade of State House on Tuesday.

When a Head of State celebrates his silver jubilee and expresses gratitude exclusively to members of a party he created 24 months after he came to power in November 1982, you know it cannot be an error in political arithmetic. He was merely acknowledging, perhaps inadvertently, that the entire nation is not with him.

Mr. Biya's silver jubilee was indeed a non-event or at best a media event. What Cameroonians expect of Mr. Biya is action, fast action. Next time he bothers to come on the air, he should be able to make meaningful pronouncements such as so many hundreds of billion francs were embezzled by so and so, and the State has recovered or has begun recovering so and so amount, instead of dwelling on intentions and wishful thinking.

Anything short of concrete results carries no weight. In the meantime, that is until February 11 2008, the National Youth Day, we expect the President to show proof that he too, has rolled up his sleeves and is prepared to sweat it out like the rest of his compatriots so that when he comes on the air to address his docile countrymen for the umpteenth time, they would have good reasons to cheer him.

S-N F.

56

Street Power versus State Terrorism
Saturday 1 December 2007

Now that it has become abundantly clear that the Cameroon parliament is a toothless bulldog as it has always been since the country's flag independence, the citizens have been given no other choice but to take to the streets to express their profound disillusionment with the State and its institutions.

Jan Schreiber says "government is an organisation designed to protect those who subscribe to it and to assist them in acquiring basic needs. To do this, it must be at least minimally responsive to the expression of those needs."

When we are told that MPs of the ruling CPDM party accosted the Minister of Finance to persuade him to cause a raise in civil servants' salaries weeks after the 2008 budget had been tabled before the National Assembly, one wonders whether they were not merely playing to the gallery, in which case, it was a joke in bad taste.

It is merely stating the obvious to say the government has failed woefully to respond to the basic needs of the people and has admitted its failure to check inflation, ensure the smooth running of public utilities, provide jobs and guarantee the purchasing power of the masses.

In his budgetary speech in Parliament nearly a fortnight ago, the Prime Minister was honest enough to remark that despite efforts to protect consumers' purchasing power by intensifying dialogue with entrepreneurs and monitoring the distribution of essential commodities in a bid to check galloping inflation and speculative price hikes, the State, in the long run, was not in a position to adequately contain market forces.

The solution proposed by government is the enhancement of alternative supply channels for essential commodities, which in reality implies the encouragement of cheaper imports, as was the case this week with regard to cement. The long-term effect of such measures on local industry is anybody's guess.

The refusal of government to raise wages and salaries on grounds that such a decision would trigger inflation is frivolous when we know that while public sector salaries were not only curtailed by 70 percent 14 years ago and have witnessed no increase ever since, and that the annual inflation rate has been officially estimated at three percent, one wonders which came first: the egg or the chicken? Can we honestly attribute the current inflation rate of roughly 20 percent to salary increase?

Civil servants, like the sacrificial lamb, have been fleeced without mercy for too long. Their representatives in parliament have barked to no avail and are suffering from sheer fatigue and powerlessness and have hit back the ball squarely on the court of the people.

The threat by civil servants to take to the streets on Wednesday is the result of the realisation of their collective helplessness and despondency. The government is not ruffled by such a threat because it controls the sophisticated apparatus of violence and would not hesitate to unleash its dogs of war to quell any street demonstration.

When a policeman or soldier pulls a gun and fatally shoots at striking students or any unarmed civilian, he is comforted by the fact that he shall suffer no consequences. He even believes he has an official mandate to use human beings for target practice.

Civil disobedience is the least harmful form of violence employed by helpless and oppressed members of civil society whose only crime is that of publicly expressing their disgust with institutions and governments dedicated to the destitution of society to gratify their inflated egos, and ensure compliance and acquiescence of the very citizens from whom they pretend to derive legitimacy.

Natural law dictates that the exercise of violence in any context must be proportionate to the real or perceived threat. Even the law of the jungle forbids the killing of an enemy in retreat. When a trigger-happy policeman shoots an unarmed civilian on the occiput, it can no longer be a question of exercising state authority or self-defence. It is a sheer act of depravity and madness. And these depraved acts of State violence have been rather too rampant in recent times when one reviews the casualties recorded last year at the University of Buea, and a few weeks ago in Kumba, Bamenda and Abong Mbang and so on, involving students in some cases, motorcycle taxi-men protesting police harassment and civilians disgruntled about prolonged electrical power cuts.

Can it be said that the mayhem unleashed by government forces and the wanton molestation of citizens were merely acts to establish State authority? Can it be said in all honesty that the killing in Kumba was calculated to contain a mere students' strike? Certainly not. Who gave the order to shoot and kill students; unarmed students?

Social scientists have attributed the militarisation of the forces of law and order to what has been described as a repercussion of an exaggerated defence consciousness. The steady increases in Cameroon's defence budget over the years is inversely disproportionate for a country that prides itself as an island of peace in a continent plagued by armed conflicts. Whereas the reverse should hold true, it seems the State is purchasing much more arms and ammunition than rations with no real or perceived threat of war or armed conflict.

The result is that the devil must find work for idle bullets and blank bullets that should normally serve in extreme cases of civilian unrest have been substituted with live bullets. The State has substituted dialogue and conciliation with truncheons, tear gas and live ammunition even though the Minister of Labour declared on Tuesday that the planned civil servants' strike was illegal, announcing that his doors were open for discussions.

There comes a time when dialogue is meaningless and civil servants are saying that if parliament has admitted its inability to mediate and obtain solutions to their grievances and thus providing no other civilised channel to obtain solutions, then they have no other alternative than civil disobedience.

Jean Schreiber, the expert on State terrorism, is merely stating the obvious when he says "in order to retain its mandate, a government must continue to appear concerned with the condition of its people." And what happens when a government fails to show that concern beyond lip service? It means it has lost its mandate. It has simply abdicated.

Budget of Grand Ambitions

In Cameroon, one can only take budgets for what they are - statements and estimates of good intentions. You can't quarrel with good intentions. One can only be critical about the implementation of the 2007 budget, a job meant for MPs, who, sadly enough, have confessed that their opinion and critical examination of the budget, old or new, does not count. They are expected only to rubber-stamp their approval. Period.

However, from a layman's point of view and going by the Prime Minister's budgetary speech, one can make a cursory remark or two. Somehow the Cameroon government, it would seem, has always shied away from investing in mineral exploration and exploitation, preferring to leave that sector entirely in the domain of foreign investment.

Foreign investors, for their part, hardly express sufficient enthusiasm because government would not and does not make provisions to engage in joint ventures, especially with regard to exploration. As a result, one could only remark in passing that (foreign) investors have expressed the desire to embark on exploration and exploitation of nickel, cobalt and bauxite.

The bauxite deposits at Mini-Martap and their commercial value are well known, but because of some obscure arrangement with the French conglomerate Pechiney, Cameroon, has for the past several decades, preferred to import bauxite from Guinea for its aluminium industry.

The budgetary speech casually mentioned plans to rehabilitate some state-owned hotels, but no specific mention was made about

230

Buea Mountain Hotel, which has been allowed to rot into oblivion and the Atlantic Beach Hotel in Limbe, which is now a ghost of itself. One cannot help feeling that such criminal neglect is aimed at killing tourism on this side of the Mungo.

Another astonishing item of the budget is the privatisation of the drinking water provider SNEC, which will be taken over by l'Office National de L'Eau Potable du Maroc. If my knowledge of French is anything to go by, this Office National of Morocco is a state or para-public corporation, which has performed so well that it qualifies to take over Cameroon's water corporation.

Maybe tomorrow, one of Cameroon's corporations would perform so well that it can win a privatisation bid to take over a failing corporation in a foreign country. We have a long way to go indeed.

S-N F.

57

Red Carpet for Monkeys
Friday 7 December 2007

The red carpet reception given last week to four gorillas that had been rescued and repatriated and are now being rehabilitated at the Limbe Zoo looked like the final act of a comedy inspired by the theatre of the absurd.

A high-powered delegation led by the Minister of Forestry and Wildlife were on hand to receive the highly-priced endangered species in a solemn ceremony that would have won the admiration of great satirical playwrights like Ionesco and Samuel Beckett.

We were all brought up to show kindness to animals and most religions do prescribe civilised ways of slaying them for food. No one quarrels with that. However, the exaggerated concern and near reverential treatment of wildlife species especially in a society where government pays little attention to the general well-being of citizens, smacks of hypocrisy. The whole show smacked of hypocrisy.

Sometime ago we were treated to a less exaggerated show of hypocrisy when a certain lion died, I suppose from old age, at the Mvog-Betsi Zoo in Yaounde. It became such a veritable media event that I half expected the government to declare a national day of mourning with the national flag flying at half mast especially as the lion is the totem of the Lion Man.

With regard to the four primates which were accorded a hero's welcome from captivity, it may not be wrong to assume that huge financial and human resources by far greater than the black market value of the great apes were deployed to track their whereabouts and repatriate them from South Africa.

One can imagine the quality of detective networking that was put in place (and I won't be surprised if Interpol or even the CIA,

SPECTRE were put on red alert) to rescue our distinguished super primates, not your regular stuff for pepper soup.

Yes, we should be kind to animals even though I take exception to certain kinds of animals like snakes and rabid dogs. And talking about dogs, I recall lounging once upon a time on the terrace of one of these de Luxe hotels and waiting to catch up with an appointment. I was beginning to get bored when I saw this stooping old white lady walking this petite breed of dog they call Chihuahua on a leash.

When she passed by me, I decided to put on a menacing look, pointed mischievously at the dog and remarked that her companion would make a very nice and juicy dinner. She pretended not to have heard me, so I further explained that since it looked rather fragile and tender, it would taste better if it were barbecued, not boiled. The poor lady stopped abruptly on her tracks, dumbfounded and speechless.

Her cheeks flushed crimson and she did not know whether to flee, scream or just buckle under and weep. It would be unwise, I told her as a matter of fact, to stroll around with such a specimen of good meat in my part of the country. She glared at me in disbelief. Her hands began to tremble as she stammered in a quavering voice: You – a – not serious! She cursed and cursed and cursed and when I realised she was on the verge of a nervous breakdown, I burst out a belly laughter to let her know I was only joking.

She obviously didn't think I was joking, but I eventually managed to calm her anxiety by telling her the name of her breed. By the time I got around talking about St. Bernard's, German Shepherds, Alsatians, etc, she had regained her composure and was reassured no harm would come to her dog.

White people in general, excepting those from Latin - speaking countries, have carried their culture of individualism to such an extent that it is regarded as unbecoming to bodily express emotions towards their fellow humankind in the form of handshakes, hugging and holding hands.

They tend to recoil from such gestures and by the time they are past middle age, they resort to lavishing their pent up sentiments on pets and think nothing of sharing their comfortable beds with cats, dogs and even horses. Hence they have special supermarkets for pet food, clinics and even day care centres for pets. That's their cup of tea.

However, while I think it is salutary to respect international norms governing the conservation of nature's fauna and flora, I suggest that the over eagerness we have demonstrated in certain instances to please our foreign donors is at times disproportionate to the concern we should show for human well-being.

We went to the four corners of the world to bring back four gorillas, but would we have done same if four times forty Cameroonians had been abducted by human traffickers who are now plying their trade in Cameroon and elsewhere un-apprehended?

It is good to be kind to animals but much better be kind to fellow humankind.

Bear Named Mohammed

The recent controversy over the sentencing to 15 day imprisonment of a British lady teacher in what has been described as an elitist school in Khartoum, Sudan is just another instance of Western European insensitivity to other people's culture. The way I see it, there was nothing innocent about the naming of a classroom teddy bear after Prophet Mohammed, Founder of the Islam religion.

I think her act was deliberately provocative and was done to spite the predominantly Moslem regime of Sudan where the famous terrorist and the world's most wanted man Osama Bin Laden is said to have operated networks of his Al Qaeda, anti-capitalist terrorist organisation.

That woman had no business in stirring the generally volatile anger of the Islamic regime, even if that regime operates a Sharia-based legal system. What is even more irritating were attempts to rationalise her behaviour by two Moslem members of the British parliament who were dispatched to Sudan to negotiate her release.

One of them said over BBC that it was not a bad idea to inculcate the respect for religion in young people when they are still at a tender age. He suggested that by naming the teddy bear Mohammed, the pupils were being taught to show respect for the Prophet at a young age. Balderdash!

If I understand the qualification of the school as being elitist, I would suppose that it is referring to one of these international schools to be found in most capitals of Third World countries for the privileged children of foreign diplomats, senior executives of international organisations and non-governmental organisations.

Such schools would normally have a sprinkling of children of the local ruling class and the nouveau riche. I can safely assume also that the school in question is not an Islamic institution in which case, the teacher had no business promoting the lineage of Mohammed. Islam expressly forbids the making of or the representation in any form of the image of Allah and his Prophet Mohammed or any holy man of the Koran for that matter.

That teacher should have known that and all Westerners ought to know that one of the main reasons for the failure of the United States and its allies to pacify Iraq stems from this stark insensitivity to the cultural and religious values of non-Westerners.

S-N F

58

S.O.S Santa Isabelle

Thursday, 13 December 2007

The violent pogrom unleashed on Cameroonians by soldiers in neighbouring Equatorial Guinea last week was just one in a series of xenophobic outbursts demonstrated by that former Spanish colony in recent times.

Victims of this latest incident also included Nigerians, who like Cameroonians, are looked upon as "Jews" who have invaded Equatorial Guinea to make a fortune out of their new-found oil El Dorado.

The pretext for last week's military brutality against Cameroon nationals was a spate of bank robberies allegedly involving some suspects in possession of Cameroon passports and identity cards.

Every Cameroonian in Equatorial Guinea automatically became suspect and transformed into an endangered species, 5000 of whom were forced to take refuge in their diplomatic mission in Malabo (formerly Santa Isabelle) and Bata.

The Yaounde government should be commended for its timely humanitarian response to the crisis as it organised an airlift of emergency supplies to the distressed Cameroonians whose lives were molested, property looted and their dignity rubbed in mud.

The humiliation and constant indignities Cameroonians are made to suffer could be attributed to a number of factors ranging from xenophobia, poor diplomacy and the regional perception of Cameroon as a giant with clay feet.

As children in the late 1950's and early 60's, we referred to Equatorial Guinea (Spanish Guinea in pre-colonial times) as Panya - a Pidgin appellation of Espana. In the colonial era, Panya was known as Fernando Po, the Portuguese (?) explorer who "discovered" the Gulf of Guinea and is credited with having made the earliest cartographic record of the Western tropical coastline of Africa in the late 15th century.

At some point in time, the British took advantage of Spain's tentative and negligent control of Fernando Po and baptised it Clarence Island as the strategic location for monitoring and policing the anti-slavery campaign and a potential resettlement haven for freed slaves.

Fernando Po, and later, Clarence Island, became a staging post for Protestant evangelists including Joseph Merrick of the American Baptist Society who used to paddle his canoe to Douala and Ambas Bay (Victoria, now Limbe) in the early 1940's to propagate the Holy Scriptures.

He was later joined by eminent evangelists like Alfred Saker and co., all of whom were erratically expelled from the Spanish enclave in 1844 when the pro-Catholic monarchy in Spain imposed a ban on the activities, religious or humanitarian, of all non-Catholic religious bodies in the island.

In fact, it is a result of this expulsion that Alfred Saker relocated to Ambas Bay and negotiated the sale of a four square-mile parcel of land from the chiefs of Bimbia and named it Victoria in 1858.

It would be recalled that in 1979, Nigerian military ruler, Murtala Mohammed, who had just overthrown civilian President Shehu Shagari, had to send a task force to Equatorial Guinea to rescue thousands of Nigerians who had gone there to make a living by trading and tilling the cocoa farms because Panya people had been brought up by their 'Spanish ancestors' to refrain from soiling their hands.

There seems to be a certain amount of evidence to indicate that Equatorial Guinea, because of its new-found oil wealth within the past two decades, has been demonstrating undue violence against nationals of neighbouring countries it has resented for their big boy status in the region.

Panya was inevitably regarded in Cameroon as a "petit frère." It had even been jokingly suggested at one time that former President Ahidjo and his French masters should pursue their annexationist

238

venture, as they had done with the Southern Cameroons, by declaring Equatorial Guinea the eleventh province.

I recall that on several occasions, Ahidjo used to put an aircraft at the disposal of Panya's head of state to attend summit conferences of the Organisation of African Unity, now African Union.

Panya's presidential automobile fleet, if it can be so called, was occasionally replenished with hand-outs from what used to be known as the Administrative Garage. Today, the boys have become men and if the big boys don't want to reckon with that then Panyas are going to teach them a lesson.

Panya may feel resentful against its petty status of the past, but the policy of brutality against innocent foreign nationals is certainly not the acceptable manner of asserting its sovereign personality. Panya has no doubt qualified to enter the Gulf Club in a big way, but it sorely needs to be circumcised in order to be fully initiated into the club of producers whose prominent badge of honour is the abject poverty of their citizens.

Panya has grown horns with oil wealth and can therefore challenge Cameroon to a fight and with good reason. While Panya's coffers are swelling, Cameroon's oil reserves, if any, are said to be dwindling with little or nothing to show in terms of socio-economic development since it struck black gold more than three decades ago.

As a result of its deplorable economic performance, Cameroon nationals have become economic refugees and have invaded other neighbouring oil producers to eke out a living doing menial jobs, petty trading and why not conmanship (feymania) and armed robbery which have become a regular way of life in Cameroon.

This is thanks to a degenerate socio-political system which visits its own citizens with infernal holocausts, ethnocentric doctrines like "cam no go," high-handed repression of peaceful demonstrations by students, impoverished civil servants and the civil society. We should not be surprised tomorrow if Equatorial Guinea, because of Cameroon's irredeemable fragility, contemplates annexing the territory.

59

The Soft Underbelly of the African Union
Friday, 04 July 2008

Since all lizards crawl on their stomach, it is difficult to know which one of them has a belly-ache (Achebe).

The summit conference of the African Union which took place in Egypt early this week did not only expose the naked underbellies of African heads of State, but equally demonstrated that they have no stomach for upholding their own laid down principles.

With the few exceptions of Botswana and Liberia, who made it clear they would no longer stomach the presence of Robert Mugabe of Zimbabwe in their midst, the majority of African leaders at the summit welcomed Mr. Mugabe who arrived the summit barely a few hours after declaring himself winner of a highly controversial election he alone contested. He even received accolades from his compeer, Omar Bongo of Gabon who described Mugabe as a hero, declaring that the man had just won the presidential election and had been sworn-in and was therefore qualified to be one of them.

The rather perfunctory manner in which African leaders regard their accession to and maintenance of power, irrespective of legality and legitimacy, without respect for fair play and consideration for the feelings of their fellow citizens and the opinion of the international community, all add up to constitute the mentality on which politics of the stomach (bellytics) in predicated.

As long as one can get himself declared the winner and is sworn-in by a handpicked acolyte, that does the trick! The sheer self-centredness of African leaders whose one and only preoccupation is to remain in power "till death do us part" has now become an entrenched political tradition which makes a mockery of democratic values.

Mr. Mugabe is so very conscious of this mentality that despite the overwhelming evidence that he deployed his arsenal of violence and brutality to scare all his opponents from contesting last weekend's presidential election, he felt no qualms about going to the AU summit where he was sure to be embraced by birds of the same feather.

The man arrived the Egyptian city of Sham-El-Sheikh just in time to clink champagne glasses with the likes of his host Hosni Mubarak (in power since 1981) who is reputed for keeping 15,000 political detainees in a dungeon without hope of a fair trial; Museveni of Uganda (in power for 24 years) who is bent on going in for a 4th term of office; Obiang Nguema of Equatorial Guinea, who would be clocking 30 years in power next year; the Zenawis, Dos Santos, the Campaores as well as freshmen like Musa Yar'Adua of Nigeria who emerged last year after flawed elections.

Mugabe must have felt very much at home and certainly did not miss the company of our own right royal president Paul Biya who from all indications is bent on beating all the others at their game as he braces himself for yet another term of office in 2011 after he would have clocked 29 years on the throne with his special brand of 'advanced democracy'.

When I occasionally catch a glimpse of Mugabe on TV, gesticulating vigorously with his fist like a student protester of the late 1960's, I wonder why someone cannot politely remind him to carry his 84 years of age with grace and dignity and leave revolutionary rhetoric where it belongs.

Those who are wont to ascribing Africa's developmental failures to Western interference take so much delight in Mugabe's rabble rousing to the extent that they fail to see where the man himself went wrong. He is very articulate when it comes to denouncing the "dictates" of Western nations, British imperialism, the "colonial stoogery" of his rival Morgan Tsvangirai, but ever since he came to power in 1980, Mr. Mugabe has been unable to conceive and implement a clear and viable programme for the appropriation and

242

redistribution of 80 percent of Zimbabwe's arable lands that were confiscated by white settler farmers since the late 19th century.

He has vacillated between a policy of appropriation with financial compensation and outright nationalisation of white-owned commercial farms without compensation. You can't tell where the man stands but every now and then, especially when elections are around the corner, he raises the spectre of nationalisation, authorises war veterans (ex-nationalist guerrilla fighters) to invade white-owned farms, sack the proprietors, and assume occupation without the slightest managerial know-how and no financial backing to run commercial farms.

There is no doubt that the restitution of the land was the legitimate raison d'être for the war of independence and no one can deny Zimbabweans their God-given inheritance. But then, what has Mugabe made of the land issue? He has merely used it as a subterfuge to perpetrate his grip on power regardless of the collective plight of his countrymen.

Every time the realities of Zimbabwe are discussed in the international media, it is not uncommon to hear a sycophant dismissing them as the work of western media propaganda aimed at painting Mugabe, the nationalist hero, in Satanic colours. No one is dismissing the existence of western propaganda, neither can we be blind to the massive exodus of Zimbabweans to neighbouring countries especially South Africa and the resultant spate of xenophobia that recently raised its ugly head in that former bastion of apartheid.

No one can remain indifferent to TV footages of acts of physical violence against opposition sympathisers in Zimbabwe, the 1600 percent fabulous rate of inflation; the general insecurity of life and property; the battered face of opposition leader Morgan Tsvangirai which was self-evident of brutalisation and the mass hunger and famine that have struck the peasantry.

By undermining and making a mockery of the democratic process, African leaders are deliberately sowing the seeds of mass rebellion in the belief that they shall be protected from its attendant hardship when it breaks out. They comfort themselves by the fact that they have the army and police at their beck and call and to hell with everyone who is envious of their divine right to reign.

Their roguish manipulation of power and their rascally abuse of the commonwealth of their nations to gratify their selfish pursuit of aggrandisement, luxury and debauchery are not enviable. It is pitiful.

S-N F.

60

The Travails of Southern Cameroons
Thursday, 17 July 2008

At a gathering of friends in Buea last weekend, one member of the group broached the idea about the need to convene another All Anglophone Conference, AAC, along the lines of AAC I in Buea in 1993 and AAC II in Bamenda in 1994.

While we brainstormed about the opportunity of such a conference, another member expressed a contrary opinion, stating that the problem of Cameroon today goes beyond the Anglophone/Francophone divide, adding that the real problem is a generational one i.e. the generation born in the 1950's is a lost one that has been deprived of the opportunity to take up a leadership role by the older generation which has monopolised power since independence. He suggested that the 1950's Anglophone generation should rather explore the possibilities of finding a common ground with their Francophone peer group to chart a way forward for Cameroon in its present configuration.

Proponents of the idea of reaching out to the Francophone, just as the pro-unification Anglophone politicians of the latter part of the 1950s, can be classified as sentimental irredentists who believe in the One Kamerun myth based on the defunct German protectorate that was split into French Cameroon and British Cameroons in the wake of the First World War.

The two entities evolved separately as mandated territories under the League of Nations (1919-1945) and later as Trust territories under the United Nations system until October 1961 when the two came together in a federated state following a U.N.-organised plebiscite on 11 February 1961 in which the British Southern Cameroons expressed the wish to form a union with French Cameroon as equal partners.

The travails of Southern Cameroons consists of an unending list of dishonesty, treachery and falsehood exhibited by the more populated partners, French Cameroon, whose authoritarian leader Ahmadou Ahidjo failed to respect the terms of the union, systematically turned the union into a one-party state, dismantled the federal nature of the union and proceeded to annex the Southern Cameroons whose gullible citizens have ever since been tacitly classified and unabashedly treated as second class citizens.

In last Monday's issue of this newspaper and in an article titled "The Travails of West and East Cameroon", Nfamewir Aseh made some fallacious statements which must be promptly rectified before it creates confusion in the minds of many who have not bothered to acquaint themselves with the historical facts regarding the Southern Cameroons.

Aseh states that "between 1958 and 1961, Southern Cameroons became the State of West Cameroon". False! The federated state of West Cameroon came into being on October 1, 1961, while French Cameroon became the federated state of East Cameroon.

He also claims that "while East Cameroon did produce a cream of nationalists who rallied under the freedom cry of the UPC national liberation movement, West Cameroon did not produce even a single nationalist and are still to catch up with political arguments that seek to counter the intrigues of neo-colonialism..."

The above assertion smacks of a selective interpretation of historical facts. If Aseh understands nationalist to mean a guerrilla war fighter such as the UPC could boast of, then he may be right. Guerrilla warfare was the only language of political struggle in French Cameroon which seriously lacked a culture of open dialogue, freedom of speech and political discourse-all of which were entrenched in the political culture of the Southern Cameroons.

No one was obliged to take bush cover and resort to arms to express his political opinion or pursue his legitimate political aspirations. I understand nationalist to mean someone who is

246

committed to the ideals of his nation and is prepared to sacrifice his personal interest for the common good of the nation.

When Aseh declares that West Cameroon did not produce even a single nationalist, you start wondering which nation he is referring to. How would Aseh classify personalities like PM. Kale, S.A. George and Fon Achirimbi of Bafut? Where would he place the nine out of thirteen Southern Cameroonians who declared neutrality and walked out of the Eastern Nigeria House of Assembly in Enugu in 1953, swearing never to engage in Nigerian politics unless the British who were administering the Southern Cameroons on behalf of the U.N. gave the green light for the establishment of an autonomous Southern Cameroons endowed with a separate executive, legislative and judiciary?

These gentlemen decided to forego the prestige and material benefits they enjoyed as MPs for the sake of the nationalistic vision they held for their country. And they succeeded in achieving their demands. Ask any of the Anglophone hand clappers in the Yaounde National Assembly today if he is prepared to make a similar sacrifice, the answer would be in the negative.

Aseh talks about "this point in time when there is a need for a rereading of our history in a way that can lead to a new synthesis possibly emerging in what Hubert Kamgang calls a neo-pan Africanism which must counter neo-colonialism in Africa in the 21st century". In as much as I share the idea of Pan-Africanism, I would refrain from being romantic about it.

The neo-colonialism the Southern Cameroons is experiencing is one perpetrated by an African state against another state of 'equal status'. Pan-Africanism is the desirable goal of all the free nations of Africa and does not countenance the subjugation of one state by another.

Pan-Africanism, like pan-Europeanism, can only be concretised through a voluntary and transparent process, not by falsehood and political chicanery. It may be a good idea to reread our history as Aseh recommends, but it is grossly sacrilegious to rewrite that history

247

for the sheer purpose of distorting the facts and confusing the present generation and generations yet unborn.

Even the two leading Southern Cameroons politicians, John Ngu Foncha and S.T Muna who initially championed the idea of unification, made a full circle turn around when they attended AAC I in Buea in 1993, made their mea culpa and proceeded to the U.N. headquarters in New York in 1995 to deliver a petition for the rectification of the self-determination process of the Southern Cameroons. They died like true Southern Cameroons nationalists.

S-N F.

61

El-Bashir's Problematic Intransigence
Thursday, 31 July 2008

The application by the prosecutor of the International Criminal Court, ICC, for a warrant of arrest of Sudanese President Omar el-Bashir on grounds of crimes against humanity, ethnic cleansing and genocide, has cast a long shadow of doubt over an internationally acceptable definition of genocide and the procedure for tackling the phenomenon.

Whereas human rights organisations the world over have welcomed the prosecutor's initiative, the UN and the African Union are not quite comfortable with the dare-devil courage and timeliness of the prosecutor's move.

While the European Union has obviously not objected to any attempts to bring El-Bashir to book, the Arab League, on the contrary, and for obvious reasons, has condemned the application for a warrant of arrest of the Sudanese leader.

The ICC prosecutor's application has sparked such a terrible controversy and discord among world political groupings that one begins to wonder whether the world can ever come to a full agreement on how to deal with political rascality and leadership impunity.

Even though the ICC is operating under a UN mandate which grants it independence of action, the UN Secretary-General, Ban ki-Moon, is nonetheless sceptical about the possible repercussions of any indictment proceedings against the Sudanese president that might jeopardise the lives of members of the UN peace mission in Sudan, and compromise a fragile peace process that is making no head way as a result of El-Bashir's recalcitrant attitude.

And it is precisely because of this uncompromising attitude to the peace process that the prosecutor is seeking his arrest. In as much as the arrest of an incumbent president on charges of crimes against humanity is unprecedented, one must admit that the perpetual atrocities perpetrated by the Sudanese regime against the people of the Darfur region considered as second class citizens, had reached untenable proportions that warranted drastic measures.

The notion of racial superiority of the Sudanese ruling class was fabricated and established by British colonialists long before Sudan attained independence in 1956. The Nilotic ethnic groups which found favour with the British have lorded it over the darker-skinned tribes of the South and Western regions, and have monopolised power and the wealth of the nation to the detriment of the peripheral groups who have been forced since independence to put up resistance against marginalisation.

The 20-year civil war between the Arab-led regime in Khartoum and Southern Sudan ended with a fragile peace settlement in 2005, but the regime's continued attempts to exterminate inhabitants of the Western region of Darfur has led to a heavy toll in human lives.

International bodies put the casualties at 300,000, while the number of displaced persons is estimated at close to two million in the past five years of unrelenting turmoil. Come to think of it, Sudan, by all standards, is not a poor country with annual oil revenue estimated at US $ 7 billion.

Yet, the bulk of this wealth is used mostly for the benefit of the regime and its cronies. The vast disparity and inequality between the "chosen tribes" and the rest of the country is largely responsible for the emergence of armed rebellion of the marginalised people of Darfur, who see no solution to their plight other than autonomy or outright secession.

Despite efforts by the UN to put a stop to prevalent violence as a pre-condition for working out a peaceful settlement to the conflict, the Sudanese leader, with the tacit connivance of China, his main supplier of arms and importer of Sudanese oil, coupled with the nonchalance of the Arab nations, has defied all civilised attempts to call him to order.

Robert Mugabe of Zimbabwe has obviously defied the norms of civilised governance, but his threshold of violence falls far below the Sudanese bench mark. And if Mugabe can attract so much international vehemence, then El-Bashir ought to be physically restrained before all hell breaks loose.

Extremism must be matched by extremism when it comes to violence, the only exception being that, in the case of Sudan, measures taken on the ground so far to contain the situation have been grossly inadequate. Initially, the Sudanese government had been unequivocally opposed to the deployment of UN peace keeping troops, leaving the few thousands of AU troops at the mercy of government-sponsored militia or killer squads known as Janjaweeds.

Even with the present joint UN and AU forces of 10,000 troops and policemen, far short of the required minimum of 26,000, it is not likely that the violence in Darfur can be brought under control very soon.

In the meantime, the international community must realise that speedy measures to beef up the peace-keeping in Sudan despite El-Bashir's stubbornness should not be taken lightly because there is danger in delay. The vulnerability of the present dissuasive international force and the threat they now face from the belligerent Janjaweeds, despite, or perhaps, because of the move to arrest El-Bashir, calls for a more decisive action irrespective of self-serving insinuations of foreign interference.

While the ICC prosecutor's move should be regarded as salutary, we are equally compelled to admit that diplomacy should be given yet another chance to prevail on the cantankerous regime in Sudan to conduct itself according to the norms of civilised behaviour.

The call by the heads of the UN and the AU to put a hold on penal procedures should be heeded to even if it is only a ghost of chance that President El-Bashir, who has rightly been branded a pariah by the ICC prosecutor, might amend his ways.

The ICC prosecutor has done his job as is expected of him and nothing, but his job. The path of diplomacy might be tortuous, long and weary, but then it should be allowed to trudge to the end of the road before the mighty arm of justice descends on those who have vowed not to give peace a chance.

S-N F.

62

1st October Frenzy
Sunday, 30 September 2007

October 1, the day Southern Cameroons theoretically gained independence in 1961 by joining East Cameroon to form a federation, is round the corner.

Once again, as it has been the case since the birth of Southern Cameroon's National Council, SCNC, security operatives and the dogs of war of the Francophone-led regime in Yaounde are warming up to brutalise unarmed, harmless Southern Cameroonians who dare to commemorate the event.

The sadistic delight with which the forces of repression have often anticipated the October 1 event since 1993 – the year of the Buea All Anglophone Conference – is a clear indication that the regime desperately wants to suppress the truth.

Adventurers and warmongers have used the occasion to line their pockets with state funds under the pretext of mounting counter insurgency operations. One wonders how many billions would be deployed the day a real liberation war is launched by a more radical movement that would not share the SCNC slogan of 'The force of argument'.

Somehow, the government's belligerent attitude towards Southern Cameroons' aspirations has been aggravated by some local tabloids, which for sensational reasons conjure the image of bloody confrontations in advance of the anniversary. President Biya is on record for having reminded Cameroonians in one of his New Year messages that January 1 marks the date in which a part of the nation (French East Cameroon) gained independence in 1960. No one raised an eyebrow when he made the declaration. So, why then should there be a frenzy of belligerent activities when Southern Cameroonians plan to commemorate a historical event?

October 1, 2007 comes against a background of renewed vigour within the ranks of the Diaspora to mobilise international support for Southern Cameroons' struggle for secession. The indispensable role of the Diaspora cannot be overemphasised, but the prime movers of the movement abroad must guard against exploiting the situation as an enterprise for self-enrichment.

Even the most noble of human endeavours have invariably been plagued by self-seeking adventurers who have no scruples feeding fat on the collective misery of a people with a genuine cause. They should be reminded that wherever they find themselves today was only made possible because of the sacrifices made by nationals of their host countries, and it is their duty to, in turn, make sacrifices to make their own fatherland a safe and prosperous haven for Southern Cameroonians and humanity at large.

Biya's Latest Observatory

One wonders why President Biya had to airlift an entire village to New York just to announce to the UN General Assembly his latest fancy to set up an observatory for global climate change. He even went further to shamelessly beg for international assistance to make his dream come true.

Perhaps, the man should be reminded that in my primary school days, weather observation equipment such as wind vanes, rain gauges, barometers and thermometers were set up and operated even in the remotest primary school without foreign aid.

The habit of perpetual begging for foreign aid has eaten so deep into the national psyche that the achievement of the HIPC (World Bank categorization of heavily indebted poor countries) completion point has merely signalled another round of begging and borrowing.

Does Mr. Biya need an observatory to realise the main cause of global warming in Cameroon? If he claims not to know the answer then he ought to set up an observatory to monitor the number of logs of raw timber that is carted abroad on a daily basis from our forests. There is supposed to be a law banning the export of raw timber, but that law has been circumvented by a loophole in the legislation that exempts so-called species that are not well known.

The wanton rape of our forests by compradors of the regime constitutes a legacy for which Mr. Biya shall never be able to atone even if he were to live a hundred life spans. Who needs another observatory for climate change to realise that the reckless exploitation of natural resources including marine life by unscrupulous Chinese operators of fishing trawlers, and the unchecked dumping of toxic chemical and industrial waste in our waterways and streams are causing irreparable damage on the environment and the health of the citizens?

At what price has this regime auctioned the national patrimony for immediate personal gains, and what purpose does it serve to mount the international forum to deceive world opinion that the Cameroon government is a respecter of environmental norms?

As I write these lines, the BBC has just broadcast a live report of mass demonstration by Cameroonians and other Africans booing at the Cameroon delegation to the UN General Assembly and clearly chanting 'Biya is a dictator!' The anti-Biya lobby is a clear signal that the New York diplomatic stunt has backfired and that the hypocritical posturing of the regime can no longer hoodwink the international community, which is so well informed about Cameroon that no amount of chicanery can paper over the cracks.

Biya has pitifully run out of ideas to the extent that nearly every institution he creates simply emerges as a mere observatory. He fabricated a National Elections Observatory, NEO, which now belongs to the museum of political history. The other observatories for good governance, the fight against corruption and hopefully, there is going to be another one to alleviate poverty and why not another one to fight inflation, to create employment and so on will all end up in the waste paper basket of history.

The only meaningful favour Mr. Biya should do for his countrymen is to go on CRTV and declare that he shall step down from power by 2011, and why not before so that people can pick up the broken pieces of their lives and reconstruct a more coherent and sober society that would cease to witness its citizens desperately seeking ways to escape abroad because living in Cameroon has become untenable.

The pathetic obsession with observatories is a childish gimmick that has failed to impress even the most naïve and gullible segment of the Cameroon society.

S-N F.

63

Soft-Selling Biya's Ambition
Friday 25 January 2008

In public relations parlance, the word spin is used to refer to the art of intentionally manipulating public opinion to buy a product or service and to rally support for an idea or issue without regard for truth or reality.

After unveiling his ambition to rule Cameroon for life, President Biya seems to have instructed his spin doctors to adopt a soft-selling approach which now consists in diversionary tactics.

The idea is to steer public opinion from the heated and controversial debate over the proposal instigated by Mr. Biya, and his CPDM party cronies to cause parliament to amend article 6.2 of the Constitution, which bars the President from seeking another term of office when the current mandate expires in 2011.

A brief recap of events will demonstrate that Mr. Biya, contrary to the wishful thinking of political green horns, has never entertained the idea of quitting office and has skilfully exploited the naiveté and gullibility of the masses to entrench his personal rule.

It would be recalled that a few months after the October 2004 presidential election, a mischievous group of Mr. Biya's kinsmen, self-styled G8 began floating the idea of lifting constitutional limitations on the presidential term of office.

Whereas the masses quickly brushed aside the proposal as a joke in bad taste, arguing that it was too early for anyone in his right senses to be suggesting the renewal of Mr. Biya's mandate when he had barely begun a fresh seven-year term and that at any rate, the Lion Man would certainly not be interested in staying in power come 2011 when he would have clocked 29 years in power at the age of 78, keen political observers did not fail to recognise the G8 move as a deliberate test balloon aimed at gauging the political atmosphere.

What the G8 did in 2005 was unfortunately perceived as a premature move on the political chessboard, but can now be identified as the early stages of political salesmanship. They were at the stage of soft-selling the idea of a life Presidency for Mr. Biya, but promptly withdrew into their shells when they discovered that the idea had failed to capture the imagination of the public.

Political strategists with a long term agenda are hardly in a hurry. The results of the July 22, 2007 twin elections had hardly been proclaimed and litigations resolved by the Supreme Court when the G8 syndrome raised its ugly head once more in a hard-selling extravaganza as the state-owned media were inundated with an avalanche of motions of support orchestrated by CPDM stalwarts calling for a constitutional amendment to allow their Messiah - President to run for election in 2011.

Many are those who wanted to believe the whole exercise was a hoax by Mr. Biya's acolytes to lure the Lion Man into buying the idea of perpetuity in order to guarantee immunity for their misdeeds, and ensure their access to the corridors of power and ill-gotten wealth. They all swore that Mr. Biya was not going to fall for such a cheap ploy.

They got it all wrong. Even though Mr. Biya in an interview with a French television last October failed to declare categorically whether he was for or against the amendment of article 6.2 of the Constitution, preferring to dribble with the fact that 2011 was still a long way from now and that he had other priorities on his agenda, the wishful thinkers, like the Biblical Thomas, were bent on seeing before believing.

They did not have to wait for long as Biya in his New Year message let the cat out of the bag, confirming, even to sceptics, that he had all along been the originator, band leader and puppet master of the constitutional amendment circus.

Now that there is clearly a very hostile public reaction to the unpalatable notion of monarchical rule in this new-found age of 'advanced' democracy à la Camerounaise, Mr. Biya's spin doctors have embarked on a desperate attempt to focus public attention on

258

what they have suddenly discovered as "other salient aspects of the constitution, which require urgent attention such as the senate, regional councils and decentralisation."

What is it that has made the above institutions, consecrated in the revised Constitution of 1996, a matter of urgency after 12 years of non-implementation? And if Mr. Biya has suddenly realised that the time was ripe for implementation, how do they constitute a matter for public debate?

It was clearly inscribed in the 1996 Constitution that institutions such as the senate constitutional court, regional assemblies etc., would be put in place 'progressively', a term which can be equated to stagnation.

The President had made it clear that even the idea of decentralisation was too delicate to be implemented and he confirmed his attitude to that aspect of governance last week when he issued a decree establishing a National Decentralisation Board whose terms of reference are as vacuous as they are misleading.

The mission of the Board is "to follow up and evaluate the putting in place of the decentralisation process. The Board submits annual reports to the President of the Republic on the state of decentralisation and the functioning of local services. The Board gives an opinion and makes recommendations on the annual programme of the transfer of competences and resources to decentralised structures as well as modalities of the transfer."

The vagueness of the Board's mission is a clear indication that decentralisation is the least concern of a leader who is not only used to the exercise of centralised authority, but one who is looking forward to legalising an existing despotism.

In their attempt to divert public focus from the crucial issue at stake, the regime's political salesmen are now peddling a new vocabulary that ascribes a new meaning to old words such as 'undemocratic'.

After Mr. Biya's description of the constitutional limitation of the presidential term of office as "undemocratic", the Coordinator of the Islamic Union in Cameroon, a certain Ibrahim Moubarak Mbomobo, is reported to have criticised recent public demonstrations in Douala against the proposed constitutional amendment, qualifying the demonstrations as "undemocratic!"

He said those who are against the modification "should put their worries to the parliamentarians who make and unmake laws." In effect, Mr. Moubarak is expecting Cameroonians to surrender their collective destiny to an unrepresentative parliament that emerged after a heavily rigged general election in favour of the ruling CPDM.

If that is what he and the likes of him who believe that civil society should be deprived of the right to peaceful demonstration think about the democratic process, then they will have to think harder.

By advocating a confrontational response to the hostile public reception of the constitutional amendment idea, the regime is about to squander whatever gains it might have made in trying to soft-sell their obnoxious political package. In opting for a brutal police and army response to the public outcry, the regime would only be confirming its desperation to remain in power at all cost.

Perhaps a violent confrontation might after all turn out to be the only option left for a regime which has failed to sell a political idea to its people, especially after its tactics of persuasion and deception have failed to convince even its own sycophants.

S-N F.

64

Bilingualism: A Badge of Honour or Shame?

Friday, 08 February 2008

Shortly after his installation as General Manager of a major State Corporation in Douala last week, the newly installed General Manager held a press conference during which he categorically refused to make any pronouncement in English.

He had been pressed by a reporter to make a statement in English for the benefit of the English-speaking audience, but he bluntly replied; "Je vais parler en français!" Not long ago, another top official, a Minister of State again at a press conference, made it clear that he was not going to take any questions in English. Period.

It cannot be said that these gentlemen, like many other Anglophobes who hold high office in Cameroon, were in breach of any law. The constitution provides for the use of two official languages i.e. French and English, but does not make it compulsory for any official to use the two languages interchangeably. That would be a tall order indeed.

It could, however, be said that while the constitution allows the use of any of the two languages in the conduct of public affairs, the hostile attitude of the Francophone hegemony towards the English language, which up till the 1996 revision of the constitution was considered subordinate to French, is tantamount to a breach of the spirit of the constitution.

What realistically obtains in Cameroon is what linguists define as diaglosia wherein two different language groups operate in their language of origin with the hope of achieving a reasonable measure of intelligibility. The one speaks in English and the other in French and the experiment goes on.

The use of language is a cognitive, not intuitive, process and to think that we have had bilingualism as a cardinal policy of national unity since 1961, one cannot help questioning why the present generation of Francophone public officials and managers should prefer to exhibit a negative and unfriendly attitude towards the English language.

If one bothers to find out, he would discover that the negativity of those who publicly display this phobia do actually understand and speak English. These are usually the very hypocrites who have overcrowded Anglophone colleges with their offspring and wards to the extent that Anglophone children do not have it easy gaining admission because, unlike Francophones who have unlimited access to the state coffers, not many Anglophone parents can promptly fulfil the requirements for their children's admission into these schools.

It is an open secret that while Anglophone parents can barely manage to installmentally settle the exorbitant tuition and boarding fees in especially the Anglophone mission colleges, which have no doubt, established high academic and moral standards over the years, the affluent Francophone parents are not only prepared to pay the annual fee at a go, but are in the dubious habit of making fabulous and unsolicited 'donations' to the school authorities presumably as an inducement or compensation for 'taking good care' of their offspring.

The corruptive nature of this practice could readily lead to discriminatory treatment of students and compromise the ethics of equal opportunity and merit. When Francophones hasten to enrol their wards in Anglo-Saxon educational establishments, one is bound to suspect a hidden agenda behind their motives.

Cameroon has been operating an unwritten principle of regional and linguistic balance, even though, in reality, attempts to achieve that balance have been severely flawed by bias, dishonesty and majority complex in favour of Francophones. Attempts to achieve regional balance have been plagued by the inequitable sharing of the national wealth and the excessive exploitation of the Anglophone

262

minority's natural resources, notably oil for the benefit of the Francophone hegemony.

Apart from natural resources, the distribution of power and authority has put the Anglophones at the beggarly end of the equation and even the little they hold in terms of public office would eventually be taken away from them and given to the new generation of Francophones who would quickly brandish their Anglo-Saxon qualifications as a justification for monopolising power and authority.

Language is a cultural and scientific asset, which has yet to be valorised in Cameroon. One would expect that by now the government should have devised a formula for rewarding public officials who practice bilingualism rather than condone those who merely pay lip service to that policy.

Granted that the inability to demonstrate mastery of the two official languages does not constitute a breach of the law, would it not be desirable to draw up a code of conduct that should call to order or sanction public officials who exhibit outright contempt for any of these languages?

Last week was celebrated as the Week of Bilingualism under the theme: "Bilingualism for Progress and Unity." These yearly celebrations should be backed by rules and regulations to guide the effective application of the language policy. Official decrees, decisions and announcements generally conceived and published in French are hardly translated into English and when that is done, the quality of such translations has always left much to be desired.

The failure to publish all official literature in English is a discriminatory practice calculated to put Anglophones in a disadvantageous position when it comes to matters of employment, tenders for public contracts, in short, all socio-economic opportunities. You only need to flip through every single copy of the state-owned daily newspaper, Cameroon Tribune, to understand how this unwritten policy of discrimination is being implemented.

Despite its reluctance to implement a genuine policy of bilingualism, the government is fond of making cosmetic applications of it for public relations purposes especially when it comes to the naming of state-owned enterprises such as Cameroon Tribune, Cameroon Shipping Lines and Cameroon Airlines. We only realise the ugly side of bilingualism when the lipstick wears off leaving the public with ghost enterprises that are merely a tragic reflection of a degenerate system.

The government has misused its bilingual status to canvass for positions in international organisations yet when it comes to filling such positions, the Anglophones are treated like Cinderella.

It is high time the government re-examine its bilingual policy and ensure that enough money is invested in it. It cannot continue to rely only on an unstable asset like football to project its image at home and abroad. The persistent failure to promote bilingualism only reinforces and justifies the political stand of Anglophone nationalist groups that are clamouring for secession.

S-N F.

65

Pharaoh, Let My People Go!

Saturday, 16 February 2008

It is never a good thing to rejoice over the misfortune of others, that is if one considers the failure of the Indomitable Lions to bring home the African Cup of Nations a misfortune, especially to those who were counting on making political capital out of an eventual victory.

Last Sunday's defeat of the Lions at the continental soccer competition in Ghana, does not diminish the heroic image the team has built for more than two decades, and only those who take delight in basking in the glory of others who have had the opportunity to excel would feel disappointed.

The tendency to equate the successes of the Indomitable Lions with the deplorable socio-economic and political performance of Cameroon has been very misleading, deceitful and illogical. The tendency to misconstrue the image of an ad hoc football team as a symbol of national cohesion, unity and stability distorts the true sentiments on which genuine patriotism is founded.

Selfless attachment to the fatherland is the real stuff of which patriotism is made and not the ephemeral excitement and pleasure derived from kicking or watching a team kick an inflated leather ball on a pitch. Patriotism is made of sterner stuff; sterner than the fluffy sentimentalism, fanfarism and fanaticism that have impacted on the Cameroonian psyche and elevated football on a religious pedestal.

It is sheer coincidence that the defeat of the Indomitable Lions by the Pharaohs of Egypt came on the eve of celebrations to mark an event which is generally referred to as National Youth Day and whose true significance has been distorted and eroded since 1965.What passes for Youth Day today is the day on February 11, 1961, when the UN, in total disregard of its cardinal policy of decolonisation, organised a plebiscite for (Anglophone) Southern Cameroons to decide whether to achieve independence by joining Nigeria or French Cameroun, both of whom had attained independence in1960. The UN has yet to explain and clarify the international community about its definition and understanding of the concept of an autonomous territory having to achieve independence by becoming an appendage of another entity, which itself had just been conferred the status of independence.

It is very disheartening to note that even some educated middle-aged Southern Cameroonians erroneously refer to February 11 as the day the territory decided to break away from Nigeria and join French Cameroon. That is inaccurate!

The Southern Cameroons broke away from Nigeria and set up its House of Assembly in Buea in 1954 when it established its autonomy and looked forward with quiet confidence to attaining full independence. Its leaders had realised that Britain, which was administering the territory as a Trust on behalf of the UN, had no business managing the territory as an extension of its Nigeria colony. When they saw themselves becoming increasingly embroiled in Nigeria's internal political wrangling, Southern Cameroonian MPs staged a definitive walkout from the Eastern Nigeria House of Representatives in Enugu and prevailed on Nigeria and the UN to sever the umbilical cord with Nigeria.

That was a bold act of patriotism and attachment to the Southern Cameroons fatherland. Some have wondered aloud why February 11 was re-baptised Youth Day instead of maintaining its original significance. The answer is simple. When you subjugate and enslave a people, it is in your interest to distort and destroy their identity, history and personality.

The process of obliterating the identity of the Southern Cameroons was skilfully implemented by President Ahmadou Ahidjo of La République du Cameroun who later became the President of the *Federal Republic of Cameroon*, the artificial political entity that emerged after the plebiscite.

He began by coercing Southern Cameroons political parties to join him in forming a single party in 1966. In May 1972, he coerced Southern Cameroons politicians to campaign for the dismantling of the federal system in favour of a unitary state styled the **United Republic of Cameroon**. According to Ndeh Ntumazah who led the One Kamerun Party in the early 1960s, the late Right Honourable J.N Foncha, Chief V.E Mukete and other top Southern Cameroonian political leaders were briefly arrested and bullied to comply or resist at their own peril.

President Ahidjo's successor, President Paul Biya, merely consummated the process of de-personalisation when he issued a decree in 1984 changing the name of the artificial state *from the United Republic of Cameroon to simply La République du Cameroun*, the name adopted by French Cameroon when it attained independence.

In between these political gravestones, misconstrued as milestones on the path to national salvation, every single institution of Southern Cameroons political and socio-economic personality was brutishly dismantled, cannibalised, coveted or destroyed.

The Mobile Wing, its paramilitary force, was dismantled; the Produce Marketing Board was transferred from Victoria to Douala along with more than FCFA 80 billion of farmers' savings. The rape of the Southern Cameroons (later West Cameroon) economy has been well documented and needs no elaboration in this column.

It would be recalled that Ahidjo pursued the process of distortion to ridiculous heights. On the eve of his official visit to the UK in 1982, he issued a decree changing the name of Victoria to Limbe under the pretext of cultural authenticity.

In effect, Ahidjo was cynically jabbing the British monarchy below the belt, a disguised message to Queen Elizabeth II that her grandmother's name and the British legacy had no place in a new found Cameroon where he was the one and only overlord.

The sheer arrogance of that act can be appraised only when it is realised that Ahidjo's idea of cultural authenticity excluded other colonial emblems such as Avenue De Gaulle, Rue Foch, Lycée General Le Clerc, etc.

Any attempt to brainwash a people by distorting and misinterpreting their history may enable the oppressor to play for time. It simply cannot work especially in this age of literacy and information.

All oppressed peoples should take comfort in the fact that history is on their side and should remember the words of the Mighty Lord who, after realising the indignities suffered by the Hebrews in the hands of their Egyptian overlords, commanded Prophet Moses to go down to Egypt and tell Pharaoh "to let my people go!!!" This was more than 3,000 years ago.

The other day, the white rulers of Australia, the descendants of convicts and miscreants who were banished from England two centuries ago, plucked up the courage to ask for forgiveness from the Aborigines, the dark-skinned indigenes of the land, for the injustices and inhuman treatment meted against them.

Maybe when Mr. Biya is crowned King after his proposed constitutional amendment would have been passed into law, he may want to borrow a leaf from the Australian government and withdraw his regime of predators from Southern Cameroons.

S-N F.

66

Technocracy, Technology and Technopoly
Friday, 22 February 2008

The plethora of cabinets formed by President Paul Biya ever since he came to office in 1982 have invariably been tagged as technocratic in order to distinguish them from those of his predecessor, Ahmadou Ahidjo, whose governmental team mates were usually composed of politicians and administrators.

How technocratic Mr. Biya's endless string of governments have been and what goods they have been able to deliver is quite a different matter altogether. What remains indisputable is the fact that his governments have had a significant dosage, perhaps an overdose of members of the intelligentsia including economists, sociologists, jurists, engineers, medical scientists and what have you.

It was believed during the early years of his regime that his apparent fondness for modernism as opposed to Ahidjo's traditionalist style of governance was going to enable Cameroon to leapfrog into the 21st century and become a pacesetter in political and socio-economic advancement.

Cameroonians were sold dreams of a country linked by magnificent bridges and glittering super highways, a country where every rural community and urban neighbourhood would be provided with a health centre and a general practitioner; a country where a universal primary educational system equipped with decent classrooms filled with beaming pupils and enthusiastic teachers; a country where people go to bed with the certainty of waking up to a healthy breakfast and three square meals; where people can go to sleep without keeping one eye open for fear of night marauders.

It would be quite simplistic to conclude that the failure of the regime to concretise these dreams after a quarter century of leadership has been entirely the fault of the intelligentsia or the collective responsibility of the educated class. The problem lies in the fact that when members of the educated class accede to leadership, they tend to discard their toga of scientific knowledge and prefer to don the mask of sycophancy.

So, instead of using their expert knowledge to move forward the country to prosperity, the majority of these technocrats have preferred to play the role of court jesters in order to grab a chunk of the national cake. And would you blame the man on the street who expresses scorn for intellectuals in government?

The label of technocracy might have been a misnomer after all. A good number of these so-called technocrats, especially in the early years of his regime, were Mr. Biya's schoolmates who were selected on the basis of cronyism. It is well over a decade since Mr. Biya's propagandists have ceased extolling the virtues of this pseudo-technocracy.

There has, in recent years, been a remarkable shift in semantics from technocracy to technology and the latest moonshine he has embarked on selling the youths is a virtual universe called technopoly.

Addressing the nation on the occasion of the National Youth Day last week, Mr. Biya, who was visibly less buoyant and triumphant than usual (probably because of the Lion's inability to bring home the Cup of African Nations), sounded so unconvincing as he struggled to paint a bright future for the youths. The portrait of paradise was peopled, not by angels and cherubim, but by faun-like images he conjured with his frequent references to a world of uncertainties, a future of uncertainties and other uncertainties.

Mr. Biya has dubbed his proposed technopoly a University Free Zone that would train technologists and high-level technicians to supply specialised manpower to business enterprises. At face value, one would get the impression that he was promising a new project to resolve the country's chronic unemployment problem. Far from it. The technopoly project is in effect a variation of the information and communication technology, ITC, programme he has been singing ever since the Internet invaded our cultural space.

270

Having run out of fresh ideas and having failed to deliver on previous promises of economic salvation, Mr. Biya and his spin doctors are merely churning and recycling stale stew to serve very disappointed but highly expectant youths who rightly suspect somehow that the government is taking them for a ride.

In reality, the University Free Zone is just another name for the computerised distant learning centres, which the six State universities are supposed to have been putting in place for the past several years. Distant learning itself is not a new educational system. It used to be done by postal correspondence before the invention of its electronically mediated counterpart. Call it electronic distant learning, technological learning or academic free zone; it is all a matter of semantics. All we know for now is that the proposed virtual university or University Free Zone would be located in Yaounde as its technopolis.

So, we can joyfully look forward to a capital city which has steadily moved from a village to a township, to a metropolis and finally to a technopolis endowed with a luxurious cyberspace with bright superhighways, toll-gates and checkpoints manned by polite scientists dressed in white overalls and bow ties, not some rude bunch of hostile forces of law and order.

The prospects of digital advancement are very enticing, until we bother to examine what behavioural scientists and media researchers have observed about it. Social scientists have posited that digital technology promotes social stratification and widens the gap between the rich and the poor and the knowledge gap. By providing equal and affordable access to the technology, we would still perpetuate social inequalities.

Various schools of thought have observed that computer literacy training is really fulfilling a hidden curriculum that imposes the values of a dominant culture by teaching people, especially marginalised groups to obey commands and accept repetitive tasks. It teaches students to accept the authority of those who define computer applications and provide user assistance.

271

Thus, according to this argument, well-intentioned efforts to promote computer literacy for marginalised groups, the have-nots, really conditions them to accept their place in a system of economic exploitation (Roszack, 1994).

Likewise, wishful thinking about improving society through the Internet may be propaganda by a "virtual class" of business people and bureaucrats who control the Internet and seek to exploit it for their own mercenary ends. (Kroker and Weinstein, 1994)

We would always be on our guard every time we hear a high-tech company such as Apple or Microsoft has donated computers to a school, college or university. The recipients are happy to get the computers as they see them as a key to the future while the high-tech company gets tax rebates and favourable public relations, the taxpayers save money and everyone is apparently a winner.

French sociologist, Jacques Ellul, (1990) has argued that the pursuit of technological improvement led to the social dominance of an elite of scientists, engineers and managers - a technopoly - for whom technology became an end in itself, devoid of moral foundation. For Ellul, technology is a bluff and the efforts of technologists were ultimately ineffective. Technologists promise a great deal to assure their status in a society conditioned to welcome technological progress, but they deliver very little.

The question as to how the would-be graduates of the proposed Free Zone would be absorbed in the economic sector is still moot. Ever since we began marking time to the dictates of the IMF and World Bank by closing down dozens of State-owned enterprises such as the tanning and beef canning, paper pulp, bagging and agricultural tools factories, and now that we are left with a very weak industrial production sector, one wonders if we are not training people to swell the ranks of economic refugees in the Diaspora.

S-N F.

67

No Peace without Justice
Friday, 07 March 2008

Those who make peaceful change impossible, make violent change inevitable. The acts of violence perpetrated on the streets of some major towns throughout the country early last week by youths who were taking advantage of the sit-down strike by the road transporters' union to vent their anger and frustrations against Biya's callous regime, were a clear warning to the leadership to stop taking the much trumpeted peace and stability of Cameroon for granted.

It was indeed a very rare piece of dramatic irony when two ambassadors who were presenting their letters of accreditation slavishly stuck to their prepared speech by referring to Cameroon's legendary peace and stability, while streets of Douala and elsewhere were going up in flames.

A falsehood perpetuated by the regime that Cameroon is an island of peace just because there is absence of civil war has been debunked by the recent incidents of violence, which may not be contained soon enough even though we are told the Government and the transporters' union have struck a deal to call off the strike.

They may have called off the strike but putting a stop to the spontaneous street violence is quite another matter. For one thing, the perpetrators of last week's violence were not union members who merely grounded their vehicles and stayed at home. So to have suggested that the youths' agitation was beyond the control of the union is an overstatement because they were never in control of the situation in the first place.

The danger involved in the current spate of violence was the total lack of guidance by political and civil society organisations. In venting their long suppressed anger on the streets, the youths were only hoping that the Government would, for once, begin to seriously address their grievances.

If you randomly asked ten youths to say why they were bitter about the regime, you were likely to get ten different answers ranging from unemployment, corruption, spiralling inflation, very low purchasing power, police harassment and brutality, discrimination and favouritism in the educational system and inadequate training opportunities, etc.

The catalogue of grievances the populace has stomached for the past two decades is taller than Mount Cameroon, yet the regime keeps pretending that all is well or would have been well were it not for the wrong-headedness of a certain opposition party which has instigated the youths to violence.

It is very unfortunate that the Government is now refusing to assume its direct responsibility for the current malaise in the country by pointing a finger at the opposition. People are even wondering whether Cameroon of today can boast of an opposition party despite the registration of about 200 political organisations, the majority of which exist only on paper.

The current burst of anger sparked off by the unending rise in the price of petrol, food and essential commodities has nothing to do with the political agenda of the opposition party. The blame for socio-political and economic degeneration of the country lies squarely on the shoulders of the ruling CPDM regime, which has depended heavily on the brute force of the army and police to impose a reign of terror in order to govern without the slightest sense of accountability.

And now that the tail has begun to wag the dog, it has resorted to unleashing its dogs of war on innocent citizens instead of organising a genuine national dialogue to critically examine the issues plaguing the country. What has aggravated the unbearable social condition is the cavalier manner in which the regime has decided to perpetuate its grip on power by trifling with the Constitution.

Every right thinking citizen sees the current moves by the regime to indefinitely prolong Mr. Biya's presidency as an attempt to deprive the populace of hope. After a quarter of a century of hopelessness

274

under the Biya regime, people are too exhausted to carry the cross for yet another generation of helplessness.

The absence of dialogue among the political class and between the leadership and the people is primarily responsible for the inevitable process of collapse the country is witnessing at present. Ever since he came to power in 1982, President Biya has always acted as if it was beneath his dignity to concert with the active political forces.

Since, in reality, power was merely handed to him on a silver platter, he has never felt that he was accountable to the people he is supposed to be ruling. He owes his allegiance to the neo-colonial powers in France and to the vicious centres of international capital, not to the people who have slaved and made enormous sacrifices so he and his cronies can live in style.

The sheer arrogance of his leadership and the contempt he holds for his countrymen constitute the stumbling blocks of his downfall. Pride goes before a fall. If Biya had the slightest concern for the wellbeing of the people, he would have taken bold measures to cushion the severe economic hardship facing his countrymen.

His spin doctors have preferred to absolve him of bad governance by laying the blame for our economic woes on the IMF and the World Bank. Who asked him to go to the World Bank in the first place? The World Bank is not a charitable organisation. It is an institution designed to perpetrate the inequalities between the rich North and the poor South and to keep the Third World in the position of suppliers of raw materials and cheap manpower.

The World Bank was conceived and designed to perpetrate Western capitalism and Western economic hegemony and world view. Forget about the so-called Asian Tigers who yesterday were the hewers of wood and who today are said to have made remarkable economic progress.

Do we really know the real standard of living of the masses in those Asian countries? It does not suffice to erect skyscrapers in the capital city and refer to them as proof of economic advancement.

What Cameroonians are clamouring for is not the Hollywood version of life, nor the glamorous lifestyle of the likes of Mr. Biya and his cronies. The natural wealth of Cameroon can ensure a decent and healthy standard of living for its citizens, but these natural resources such as petrol or crude oil have been mortgaged by an unscrupulous and greedy leadership whose days are numbered.

What is happening on the streets today is the writing on the wall and whatever message Mr. Biya and his clique decide to make of it, is entirely their cup of tea.

P/S. This article was written before Mr. Biya's televised statement on Wednesday 27. We all know the incendiary effect of that bellicose pronouncement which was sans objet.

S-N F.

68

Too Little, Too Late
Saturday, 15 March 2008

Cameroonians are very fond of the phrase "better late than never." Going by this dictum, we ought to applaud President Biya for the belated measures he has taken to cushion the excruciating effects of the chronic economic crunch the nation has borne since the IMF imposed its structural adjustment programme in 1987.

The 15 percent increase in civil service salaries and the suspension of customs duties on certain essential commodities such as rice, wheat flour, sugar and cement, are laudable measures which have come a little too late and whose impact would largely depend on their effective implementation.

Critics have likened the government's reaction to the week-long violent street protests that rocked the major urban centres of the country last month to a negligent doctor who, instead of incising a tumour when it was still benign, preferred to dilly-dally until it became cancerous before he began prescribing palliatives for the patient.

How far these palliatives would go to reverse the chronic ailment that has plagued the country is anybody's guess. It would be recalled that earlier measures to check the galloping price of foodstuff had failed because of the unscrupulous manoeuvres by some importers and wholesalers who are in the practice of hoarding commodities or selling their goods to neighbouring countries for higher returns after benefiting from tax incentives.

Instead of setting the law in pursuit of such recalcitrant traders who have proven to be part of the cause of the general economic malaise, Cameroon and the international community are being treated to a melodramatic spate of kangaroo trials of more than 1,500 youths alleged to have perpetrated the street violence in which more than one hundred young persons are said to have lost their lives as a result of police brutality.

The Cameroon Bar has condemned the summary trials for lack of due process, but this does not seem to have impressed the authorities who have consistently demonstrated contempt for human rights. Reports of the seizure at the airport of the passport of opposition SDF MP, Jean Nintcheu, his arrest and handcuffing in public by uncouth security operatives are all acts of primitive governance, which go to demonise the nation's already soiled image.

I still find it difficult to believe government's insistence that the SDF and Honourable Nintcheu in particular were responsible for the bloody protests which, by all accounts, were spontaneous and lacked a sense of direction. If the government truly believes the SDF was behind the unrest, then I fear it is crediting the party with an extraordinary power to mobilise the masses; an influential force which the regime had previously refused to acknowledge if one were to rely on the fraudulent results of last July's general elections.

The SDF did call for a public demonstration in Douala to protest against plans by the regime to panel-beat the constitution so that Mr. Biya can become life president. Independent TV footage showed a rather scanty protest march that quickly aborted when it was confronted with tear gas and water cannons.

Two days later the urban transporters' strike came into effect and hordes of angry young men took advantage of the empty streets to express their bitterness over their meaningless condition of life. The forces of law and order even registered a scant presence on the streets in the early days of the strike given that their mobility was severely restricted by the strikes.

This would teach the government to start considering the building of barracks in order to facilitate the mobilization of the army in future. Given this state of affairs, it is hard to see the SDF's hand in the recent turmoil. Perhaps in a desperate search for a scapegoat, the government has conveniently forgotten that not long ago, it had stigmatised the SDF as a regional (Northwest) party.

If truly, the SDF were responsible for instigating and mobilising the strike which degenerated in some cases to deplorable acts of vandalism and that the SDF, as charged by Mr. Biya, was trying to gain power which it failed to obtain through the ballot box, then the regime is tacitly admitting that the SDF is a credible alternative political force to reckon with; a force that can create a veritable earthquake and not just a storm in a tea cup!

The whole idea of singling out the SDF, as if the rest of the opposition parties were unconcerned about the socio-political decay, is a cheap tactic of divide and rule. It is a futile attempt to demonise; to give a dog a bad name and hang it.

While the government is making frantic attempts to control damage, zealots of President Biya's tribal clique, taking cover under the banner of the ruling CPDM party, are busy provoking the tempers of other Cameroonians by publishing threats of ethnic cleansing. The hate literature published in the state-owned daily newspaper Cameroon Tribune early this month by an ad hoc group going under the name of "Elite (Forces Vives) of Mfoundi Division," is a dangerous move to Rwandanise a socio-political crisis which, from all indications, did not arise from ethnocentric considerations.

If, as they claim, the meeting which issued the declaration brought together "sons, daughters, elite etc., of all social status and all political shades of opinion", why then did they choose to meet at the CPDM party house? They talked of manipulators who deliberately sent children to their deaths. Who killed them?

They said they were strongly "opposed to those fomenting trouble and authors of all forms of vandalism on people and their property in our city." Whose city were they referring to? Is it the city which they aptly describe as the seat of national institutions? The so-called elite of Mfoundi warned "those forces of destruction to immediately leave our land because it is no longer secure for them."

They threatened to return act for act and swore to extract an eye for an eye and a tooth for tooth. Are they now advocating the replacement of the rule of law by Hamurabi's law? The excessive use of the phrase 'our land', 'our city' is an obvious

279

consequence of Mr. Biya's indigenisation of national politics. The ethnocentric overtones and the parochial possessiveness expressed by these elite smacks of childishness and immaturity.

They sounded very much like spoilt brats and over pampered tribesmen when they complained that "neither we, nor our children will be forced to trek, after sacrificing so much to acquire the means of movement in relative comfort." Were they referring to the luxury cars and SUVs acquired with ill-gotten state money? This reminds me of one woman who, after queuing for long to buy bread at a bakery in Douala, complained before TV cameras that no one was willing to serve her and her kids were so used to bread that they won't stop howling until she brought some home. She complained that even the soldiers who were around the bakery also refused to help her obtain bread, the ultimate symbol of gastronomic sophistication. In her ordeal of bewilderment, she did not realise that she was dressed in CPDM party uniform, crowned with a CPDM baseball cap, the arrogant symbol of political monopoly.

Even Biya has forever been very sceptical about appearing in public in the rags of his party emblem, a signal which his blind followers have failed to apprehend. The lesson to be drawn from the recent social upheaval is that if the opposition parties and civil society were to seriously contemplate a seizure of power, since the regime has distorted the democratic process and made nonsense of the ballot box, no amount of bullying and threat of ethnic cleansing can stop them.

S-N F.

69

When Dialogue Is Meaningless
Friday 28 March 2008

The decision by the Executive Council of the Social Democratic Front, SDF, to authorise party Chairman John Fru Ndi to seek audience with the Head of State, Paul Biya, sounds like a non-starter in many respects.

Critical observers are asking to know what in God's name is the Chairman hoping to achieve by a presidential audience, should Mr. Biya condescend to grant him one. Precious little or nothing, I dare say.

True enough, the lavish accusations leveled against the SDF Chairman by certain members of government of being the brain behind the recent violent street demonstrations that nearly brought the nation to a standstill were very vexatious especially as they were unsubstantiated.

While we do understand the righteousness of the Chairman's anger at the whimsical nature of these accusations, the public is yet to understand why he has decided to carry his case to the presidential palace in order to clear his name.

The Chairman, like everyone else, knows that his accusers were merely echoing their master's voice and that to seek audience with President Biya is like petitioning against Caesar to Caesar. The presidential palace is not a courtroom which has jurisdiction over matters of defamation.

Ostensibly, the Chairman wants to meet the President to discuss the situation in the country. Since when did Biya start discussing issues of national interest with outsiders when he seldom discusses them with his inner circle?

The man is a highly individualistic and secretive character and ever since he announced in an interview with radio Monte Carlo during a visit to Paris in early 1992, that he was looking forward to meeting with leaders of the opposition in Cameroon, that promise has remained a dead letter up till today.

In one of his campaign speeches for the October 1992 presidential election, Mr. Biya, in response to opposition clamour for a level political playground including an unbiased electoral code and an independent electoral commission, said he could not understand why the opposition was complaining about the democratic process.

He claimed that he had very generously brought democracy to Cameroon and could not understand what democracy the opposition was griping about, quipping that maybe they were more interested in coveting his presidential seat.

The one thing Mr. Biya has never made a secret of is his obsession with power. You are free to form all the political parties you want; create all the trade unions you want; shout at the top of your voice about bad governance; write all the rubbish you care to write about his regime; steal all the state monies you can steal as long as you don't get caught; but "for Heaven's sake, leave my seat alone!"

Given this situation and the prevailing atmosphere of calm that precedes a storm, what does the Chairman expect to achieve by meeting President Biya whose strong-headed determination to remain in power forever constitutes the main obstacle to democratic change? Does he intend to persuade the President to renounce his ambition and if so, how does he propose to formulate his plea? How do you plead to someone to relinquish the one and only thing he has come to see as his reason for living?

We are told the Chairman, as he has repeatedly said on previous occasions, would like to meet the Head of State in the presence of a third party. What a cheek! The last time the Chairman expressed a similar wish, he gave his Bamenda residence, Ntarikon Palace, as the preferred venue for the encounter.

So far, it has never been clear in my mind as to the nature of this third party the Chairman has been fond of referring to. I am equally ignorant about certain practices in state house protocol and presidential audiences, but I have a feeling that one does not seek a presidential favour by posing preconditions.

Fru Ndi's insistence on a third party as a precautionary move can be understood in the sense that government propaganda machinery cannot be trusted to render a truthful account of the proceedings of such a meeting. But then, why should one expect Mr. Biya to be interested in granting audience to Fru Ndi if he cannot twist it to serve his purpose?

Shortly after the recent unrest, Fru Ndi flexed his muscles and threatened to "expose the lies of the government." He was widely perceived as the aggrieved party in the verbal crossfire that ensued between the government and the SDF.

The Chairman was truly suffering from a persecution syndrome that won him a lot of public sympathy by proposing to meet Biya for a dialogue, the purpose and outcome of which cannot be clearly defined and discerned. The Chairman is showing signs of flinching. By failing to make political capital out of his political persecution, he seems to have lost the vantage point he had won by forfeiture.

Should Biya condescend to meet Fru Ndi, it would not be difficult to imagine the trend of their conversation. After the usual niceties of salutation, Biya would enquire "Yes, Mr. Chairman, what can I do for you?" And the Chairman would politely thank His Excellency for granting him audience.

"Oh, don't mention, Mr. Chairman. You know, my doors have always been open to all who believe in dialogue and especially to those who are willing to join hands with me in building this nation. I am quite aware of the silly things some of my ministers have been saying about you concerning the recent unfortunate incidents.

As you might have heard, I told them in no uncertain terms in my last cabinet meeting that the responsibility for the street protests was the result of their incompetence. You don't have to worry. One of these days I am going to nod my head and to be sure several heads will roll on the ground."

Then Fru Ndi would express appreciation that he was going to be avenged by no less a personality than the president of the republic himself. He would then timidly plead with the president to kindly reconsider the question of constitutional amendment.

"Please, Mr. President, if you sincerely love the people of this country and for the love of God, and speaking on behalf of the masses, it would be a great mark of statesmanship if you stepped down in 2011 and take a well deserved rest." At which Mr. Biya would, in a most thoughtful manner, remind Fru Ndi that his only reason for seeking to prolong his presidential mandate was the profound love he has for his countrymen.

"Mr. Chairman," he would say, "Can you imagine the chaos that would ensure if I decided to step down? Do you realise how many greedy people have been eyeing my seat since I came to power, including you, Mr. Chairman?"

"But Mr. President, there would be chaos if you decided to stay in power indefinitely."

"Who says I want to stay in power indefinitely. I have simply said I need a little more time to clear some unfinished business. After that, I quit. And by the way, if you are expecting me to hand over power to you, Mr. Chairman, then you must be dreaming.

One, there is no constitutional provision for that. Two, you don't command the majority in the Assembly. Three, you have your own palace in Ntarikon, why are you not satisfied with that? Why do you covet my palace, Mr. Chairman? Who even told you the Francophones are prepared to tolerate an Anglophone Head of State? Mr. Fru Ndi, you know we have always been friends and I have always provided assistance every time you ran into financial problems etc, etc."

This is the kind of meaningless dialogue that is likely to take place should Biya care to grant Fru Ndi audience. The Chairman should have held on to his position of moral high ground and waited for Biya to invite him for talks. By seeking an audience with Biya, the Chairman has lost the initiative and can hardly be in a position to squeeze any political concession from President Biya.

S-N F

70

China's Verbal Acrobatics on Sports and Politics
Friday 25 April 2008

Never before has there been such a heated and widespread controversy surrounding a sporting event as has been the case with the upcoming Beijing Olympics, which has been dogged by disruptions of the itinerary of the Olympic Torch and strident calls by human rights activists worldwide for a boycott of the games.

It would seem that the Olympic Games hardly come and go without some controversy or scandal to mark the event, but very few have mobilised world attention such as that of 1934 in Berlin during which the founder of Nazi Germany, arch anti-Semitist, Adolf Hitler, who had turned racism into a national religion, refused to shake hands with African-American sprint gold medallist, Jesse Owen.

Prior to the current Beijing controversy, the 1980 Moscow Olympics was mired by an unprecedented highly vocal campaign for boycott that was championed by the US and some of its allies. The Soviet Union, before Glasnost and Perestroika, was the evil empire which had instituted hundreds of subhuman concentration camps for political prisoners, the gulags, and was intolerant of divergent opinion.

Because of its despicable human rights record, the US even dispatched a rather reluctant messenger to Africa, the one and only Mohammed Ali, to campaign for a boycott of the Olympic Games. Coincidentally, and in the heat of the boycott campaign, the Supreme Council for Sports in Africa, SCSA, under the chairmanship of its President, Abraham Odia of Nigeria, was holding its summit meeting in Yaounde with the Moscow Olympic boycott featuring at the top of its agenda.

The international news media had virtually invaded Yaounde for the event, and as a young ambitious reporter for Radio Yaounde at the time, I was determined to be ahead of the pack of wolves to get the scoop and the exclusive interview; after all this was my territory and I knew the ropes. After tailing Old Man Odia, from one function to the other, we finally settled in his hotel suite at Mont Febe at midnight for the exclusive.

I went straight to the point. Should politics be mixed with sports? The old man asked me how I could imagine the organisation of sports and sporting events without government's involvement. Governments provide infrastructure, the enabling environment, finances and what have you, to promote sporting activities, how then can government be involved without politics coming into play?

Next question: Was Africa going to boycott the Moscow games or not? Of course not! cried the Old Man. Africa, he explained, was not going to get caught in super power politics. The SCSA was going to steer its own course and not be influenced by Western whims and caprices.

He cautioned me to beware of Western media propaganda which had disingenuously misled international public opinion to believe there was going to be a collective African boycott of the Moscow Games. Old Man Odia reminded me that we were dealing with the era of the Cold War; the super power rivalry between Washington and Moscow, adding that Africa must deal with the situation with circumspection.

At the end of the 90-minute interview, I had got my scoop and learned a lot about sports and politics; I had learned enough to know that any attempt to separate sports from politics is not only facetious but dishonest.

Ever since the end of the Mao Tse Tung era of isolationism, China has been gradually worming its way into the global arena of capitalism, not by mere political pronouncements, but by staging international spectaculars as an international public relations ploy to gain world visibility.

One of the landmarks of China's visibility exploits was the staging of the UN-sponsored International Women's Conference in Beijing in 1995 that produced resolutions and a code of conduct on matters related to the rights of women. We cannot forget the highly mediatised Sino-African Summit in Beijing last year, too.

China's lobby to host the 2008 Olympic Games has been motivated by political considerations, not the mere love of sports. Its ambition to host the Games is both politically and economically motivated and its outcome is intended to confer on China the status of a big world player in the field of international politics.

The whole purpose of the Games is to consolidate its position in the committee of civilised nations and it would be deceiving itself by seeking high visibility on the world arena and believing it can escape scrutiny. China ought to have been prepared to come under inevitable scrutiny over its international and bilateral relations and its adherence to the international norms, values and best practices.

Everyone would agree that sport, in general, is meant to promote human interaction, competition, tolerance, camaraderie and physical well-being. However, any sporting event that is staged against a background of unwholesome morality and disregard for universal values on the part of the host is bound to raise questions, criticism and controversy.

China has repeatedly declared to whoever cares to listen that its diplomatic and trade relations with the outside world are predicated on non-interference in the international affairs of other nations. China is overly sensitive and highly irritable whenever the issue of human rights is raised.

It becomes quarrelsome and intransigent whenever the issue of its subjugation of the autonomous province of Tibet and other provinces is raised. It is highly defensive whenever its relations with brutal, genocidal regimes in Africa are put to question. China's cosy relations with the Sudanese regime to which it supplies arms that are being used for the massacre of hundreds of thousands of its citizens in the Darfur region of Western Sudan considered to be second class citizens, is abominable.

287

Yet, China, knowing fully well the end purpose of those military supplies, has insisted in claiming that it is only respecting the terms of its bilateral relations and does not interfere in the internal affairs of Sudan.

Just the other day, Mozambique and South Africa refused a Chinese shipload of arms destined for Zimbabwe to anchor and offload the shipload at their sea ports. We hear the shipload later headed for Angola with which it has bilateral relations since the 1970s and in which it has significant investments.

I recently watched the Director of China's Institute of International Relations on TV expounding on his country's foreign policy. He castigated Western nations for dictating policy in Africa because of their historical relationship of colonialism and neo-colonialism. He gloated that while China is free from such colonial stigma, it was pursuing quite a different diplomatic course in Africa; a pragmatic course based on trade and devoid of interference.

China may not have been involved in the slave trade or the 19th century Scramble for Africa by European powers, but by definition, its relations with Africa are obviously not different from a colonial relationship wherein Africa is regarded as a source of raw materials, especially petroleum and a dumping ground for Chinese manufactured goods.

China's wobbling attempts to dissociate politics from sport, or trade for that matter, may appear to be pragmatic but pragmatism without morality, without ethics, without concern for the human being, boils down to unscrupulous pragmatism and must be condemned by the civilised comity of nations. By probing dictatorial regimes whose modus operandi is brutality and crimes against humanity on the capricious excuse of pragmatism and non-interference, China's diplomatic acrobatics is not only outdated; it is unacceptable.

China, in hosting the 2008 Olympic Games, has been given a sporting chance to gather its act together, shape up and amend its deplorable human rights record. China should be reminded that it is the oldest cradle of civilisation after Africa, irrespective of the latter's down-trodden position today.

China should do well to borrow a leaf from the African Union which, under the distinguished leadership of Alpha Konare, adapted the humanitarian philosophy of non-indifference, which goes far beyond the mercantile notion of non-interference.

Non-indifference signifies the primacy of humanity over mercantilist pursuits and upholds the truism that man lives by man; that you are your brother's keeper. Long live Ubuntu, the principle that good men shall not remain silent in the face of man'

S-N.F.

The Bolloré Mafia and French Imperialism
April 2008

The sacking over the weekend of the General Manager of the Autonomous Port of Douala, Mr. Etoundi Oyono, came as a sharp reminder of the French stranglehold on Cameroon's economy and, by extension, its political dispensation.

It can be said in all honesty that Etoundi Oyono is a victim of French imperialistic designs and mafia intrigues. Mr. Etoundi, who took over the management of the Douala Port from Mr. Alphonse Siewe about three years ago, was assigned the salutary mission to clear up the mess that had been piled up by his predecessor. He was in the process of reviewing the dubious 8-billion-a-year contract awarded to the French Bolloré Group to dredge the 50-km long waterway of the Wouri estuary. The contract carried the stench of corruption and Etoundi Oyono was about to sanitise the air when the axe fell without a warning.

His sack came as a shock especially at a time when President Biya has been showcasing his half-hearted fight against corruption as part of his credentials for demanding support for his ambition to remain President for life; at a time when everyone expects a more transparent and profitable management of State corporations.

Mr. Etoundi was knocked out by Biya's royal nod because someone had to be sacrificed on the altar of French imperial interests to appease the wrath of Mr. Bolloré, the notorious business magnate who is said to have bankrolled French President, Nicholas Sarkozy's, electoral campaign. Hours after he was declared winner of the May 2007 elections, Mr. Sarkozy lied to pressmen that he was retreating to a monastery for a day or two to meditate the task ahead. Smart investigative journalists who refused to swallow the bait, later spotted

Mr. Sarkozy and his girlfriend cruising on Mr. Bolloré's luxury yacht and having a real ball. Bolloré is Sarkozy's 'paddyman' and President Biya would think nothing of bending over backwards to kiss Bolloré's arse, just to be in the good books of Mr. Sarkozy, whom he has been desperately wooing for support, even though the French President has openly castigated African leaders who want to cling unto power forever, despite their deplorable stewardship.

Mr. Sarkozy, in his characteristic sarcastic manner, once remarked that he first heard of President Bongo of Gabon when he (Sarkozy) was still a college student and was truly amazed that he too, has become President, when, Mr. Bongo is still clinging unto power, refusing to relinquish it. President Biya has boastfully announced the impending official visit to Cameroon of Mr. Sarkozy and is ready to crush anyone who would attempt to compromise his diplomatic 'honeymoon' with the French leader. You can go to hell with political niceties like good governance, transparent management, anti-corruption, blah blah. You are free to intone the virtues of plural democracy, free and fair elections, separation of powers and decentralisation; as long as you don't rock the Biya-Sarkozy boat—no problem.

President Biya has set a very expensive public relations machinery to move forward his bid for life presidency. On the frontline of his strategy at present, are the Indomitable Lions, backed up by the musical artistry of Manu Dibango at the current continental soccer jamboree in Ghana; the upcoming extraordinary congress of the ruling CPDM party, Youth Day celebration on February 11, and Sarkozy's promised visit, which is likely to take place after the March session of parliament that is expected to rubber-stamp the constitutional amendment to pave the way for Mr. Biya to accede to his coveted throne.

When one takes a close look at the big picture, it is hardly surprising that the GM of Douala Port got the sack, despite the fact that Biya singled him out as an example of a good manager in the November interview he gave the French TV channel, France 24, said to be owned by Bolloré. Mr. Biya had precious little to boast about in that interview and cited the Douala Port and the Cameroon Shipyard and Industrial Engineering Corporation as the only redeeming sectors of the national economy. During his relatively short term of office at the Douala Port, Mr. Etoundi is reputed to have remarkably streamlined expenditure, increased worker's salary and stepped up maritime traffic. Contrary to accusations by his detractors that he did not fully appreciate the importance of dredging the estuary which accumulates huge quantities of silt that could hinder the navigation of ships, Mr. Etoundi merely wanted to review the terms of the Bolloré contract which knowledgeable insiders confirm was excessive at FCFA 8 billion.

Just for the record, Mr. Etoundi was not the first manager to realise the wastefulness of contracting foreign companies for the dredging exercise. When Mr. Dibong took over from Mr. Ngann Yonn as GM in 1985, he terminated the dredging contract with a Dutch firm Boscalis, which was scooping an untidy sum of FCFA 600 million per month while using equipment and machinery owned by the Douala Port. He investigated and discovered that there was, and still is, a Cameroonian shipping pilot who could operate a dredger and he did it. It is alleged that the Dutch contractors were so incensed that they poisoned the trays of shrimps and lobsters that had been supplied for their farewell dinner organised by Douala Port. Thanks to a vigilant steward who sent a warning signal to all the staff after noticing that the foil used in covering the trays had tiny perforations, disaster was averted.

It would be recalled that the Bollore Group has faced two major setbacks recently in the United States and in Senegal it was outbidded in a contract for the management of the Dakar Port by a more enterprising company from Dubai. While Bolloré has always contented itself with reaping windfall profits where it did not sow, the Dubai group is said to be coming to Dakar with a 50-billion dollar investment package to modernise the container terminal and an onshore technology transfer.

Transnational corporate financial interests and their agents are notorious for exterminating entire villages and communities in Third

World countries, just to safeguard and promote their insatiable penchant to accumulate wealth.

They would go to any lengths to maintain their grip on Third World countries which have yet to achieve real independence in order to have freedom of choice of economic partners.

72

Bakassi and the Principle of Derivation
Friday, 08 August 2008

There is a prevalent and somewhat misleading notion that the legal and diplomatic resolution of the Cameroon-Nigeria conflict over the oil-rich Bakassi Peninsula would guarantee a durable peace and stability in the area. Far from it.

The recent successful Cameroon military exploit that neutralised an armed insurgency in Bakassi by a Nigerian rebel group opposed to the August 14 official handing over of the Peninsula to Cameroon in accordance with the 2002 ruling of the International Court of Justice at The Hague and the Green Tree Accord of 2006, was highly commendable.

It was a good move, but not enough to ensure durable peace and development of the region. The very fact that the so-called Delta Defence and Security Council embarked on armed insurgency in the area only in November 2007 in which more than 20 Cameroon soldiers were killed and irrespective of reports, confirmed in parliament by the Minister of Defence, of illegal arms deals between some elements of the Cameroon army and Nigerian rebels, the details of which have yet to be made public, the Nigerian rebel belligerency is an indication that there is more to the Bakassi problem than meets the eye.

By undermining the Nigerian and Cameroonian governments, the insurgents have inadvertently sent a signal to Yaounde that inter-governmental solutions which royally snub the genuine aspirations and welfare of the people affected by such solutions are destined to fail.

The Bakassi problem is a mild symptom of the broader Southern Cameroon's question, which cannot be merely swept under the carpet by legal and diplomatic expediency but must be resolved by an honest, profound and comprehensive political settlement that should seriously take into account, the historical, cultural and socio-political parameters that have been deliberately ignored by the Cameroonian political class.

The imponderable factor in the Nigerian rebel action in Bakassi is the question as to why a dissident group that is opposed to a territorial settlement with a foreign (neighbouring) country should embark on a guerrilla warfare with that neighbouring country, instead of attacking its home government which entered the agreement in the first place.

If, truly, the contention of the Delta group is the handover of the Peninsula to La République du Cameroun, one would, therefore, expect the rebels to take their own government to task instead of provoking a situation pregnant with international repercussions that could compromise efforts to restore a durable peace.

It would be reasonable to assume that insurgents of the Delta Defence and Security Council are bona fide inhabitants of Bakassi who are vehemently opposed to the idea of being governed by La République du Cameroun. They are truly scared of what they perceive as the brutality of Cameroon gendarmes and their extortionist proclivity.

These fears have been compounded by the fact that the people of Ndian Division in which Bakassi is located have been left to their own devices since the unification of the British Southern Cameroons and the French-administered Cameroon in 1961.

And even after the area began producing oil in the mid-1970s, Bakassi remains the most backward enclave of the nation where the only reward, like the rest of the Southern Cameroons, the rightful owners of the Peninsula, has been the relegation to the status of second-class citizens.

During the early months of the Bakassi border conflict which erupted in late 1993, Nigeria's Nobel laureate for Literature Wole Soyinka suggested the holding of a plebiscite in the area as a means to determine the political aspirations of the inhabitants of Bakassi.

Soyinka stopped short of recommending the same solution for the entire Southern Cameroons which at the time was at the early stages of nationalist revival, encapsulated by the emergence of the All Anglophone Conference now known as the Southern Cameroons National Council, SCNC.

It is worthwhile recalling that during the February 11, 1961 plebiscite in which the Southern Cameroons voted to join La République du Cameroun in a federation of two states with equal status, what is now known as the Ndian Division (Kumba Southwest) cast a vote of 2,424 to remain as part of Nigeria as, against 2,227 in favour of joining French Cameroon.

Their deep-seated suspicion and distrust of the Francophone style of governance was, and remains unmitigated by irredentist colonial sentiments. The feelings of nationhood are not born out of mere cartographic configurations, national flags and anthems, legal and diplomatic mastery, but by a sense of belonging arising from the establishment of a level political landscape of equal opportunity, fairness, justice and above all the freedom of self-determination.

The lopsided pattern of unbalanced development, the unmitigated quest for wealth accumulation by political predators and greedy bureaucrats who do not in any way represent the interest of the citizenry, have all contributed to the alienation of the vital components of society.

And the Bakassi region stands out as naked evidence of gross socio-economic injustice. This sorry state of affairs inevitably leads to the radicalisation of the active forces of every society which ignores the principles of good governance. The Nigerian daily newspaper This Day of July 9 has a very instructive anecdote that illustrates this radicalisation process.

The story goes that the late Nigerian Head of State, General Sani Abacha, had invited some Ijaw youths of the Delta region of Nigeria to Abuja to participate in the three million-man march meant to drum support for his bid to transform himself from a military to a civilian ruler. There, the youths saw how Abuja had been transformed into what they saw as small London or America and suddenly realised how backward and desolate the Delta region, the source of Nigeria's formidable oil wealth, was. When they returned to their region, they rearranged themselves, held conferences and issued a declaration in which they advanced 100 reasons why the government and the oil companies could not continue to ignore their region.

They also issued an ultimatum to the oil companies to either do something or move out of the region. Instead of the government inviting them to the negotiating table, it drafted Federal troops to the area in November 1998, vandalised and looted the villages, shot and maimed thousands of people.

The government in the long run realised the futility of this policy of extermination and while it did not completely abandon its strong arm tactics, it all the same introduced a policy of derivation whereby 13 percent of oil proceeds were to be ploughed back for the development of the region.

That figure is said to have been revised upward to 50 percent except that the mechanisms established to ensure that the benefit trickles down to the grassroots, have woefully failed in their mission, hence the continued atmosphere of tension and conflict in the oil producing areas characterised by the kidnapping of oil company personnel and the disruption of pipelines.

It is up to the Cameroon government to learn from the Nigerian experience and to be conscious of the fact that any attempt to bring peace and stability in the Bakassi region must be backed by meaningful developmental projects within the framework of a derivation policy which so far has been restricted to timber producing areas.

Should government fail to do that, then it should not be surprised to witness the escalation of insurgency.

S-N F.

298

73

Had Barack Obama Been Born a Cameroonian
Friday, 29 August 2008

When one observes the meteoric rise to political stardom of Barack Obama, one must admit that the phenomenon could not have occurred elsewhere in the world than in the United States.

For this offspring of an African (not African American) father and a white woman who is barely rounding up his first term in the American Senate, and who, prior to becoming senator was little known out of his Chicago constituency; for him to have won the admiration of Americans and the international community and to have obtained the ticket of the Democratic party to run for next November presidential elections is a most extraordinary feat that could only be achieved in America, the land of opportunities, even if these opportunities are not always equal.

The manner in which Obama has succeeded in articulating his vision for change and rekindling faith in the American dream, the candidness of his speech, the sincerity of his winsome smile, his ability to connect and identify with the preoccupations of the ordinary man-in-the-street and his ability to deflect below-the-belt punches have combined to make him the wonder-boy of the 21st century.

As the 20th century rounded up with the world paying homage to an ageing political colossus, South African freedom fighter, Nelson Mandela, the 21st century seems to have been ushered by the emergence of a youthful visionary who has succeeded in electrifying the collective imagination of the world; a world that has begun to lose faith in man's humanity.

In trying to fathom the Obama phenomenon, I have on several occasions tried to imagine what could have become of him if he had been born a Cameroonian or just an African, living in Africa, especially when, we recall the fate of similar visionaries like Thomas Sankara of Burkina Faso and the Steve Bikos.

He would simply have been shot to death, maimed or vilified and imprisoned or, if possible bribed to shut up. The fate of Africa's heroes and fledging leaders is a tale of tragic proportion that has set the continent back to the Dark Ages when barbarism was the order of the day in Europe, while Africa held high the torch of enlightenment.

Had Obama been born a Cameroonian, let alone a second class citizen of Cameroon, such as the Anglophones have been honoured with, he would have been flogged, humiliated, thrown in prison for trying to assert his human right and dignity. The authorities would have banned his political rallies, brutalised his followers and sympathisers, and ordered to toe the line.

When John Fru Ndi of the Social Democratic Front, SDF, began spearheading the movement for change in Cameroon in 1990, the regime went on a collision course to break down the man in headlong confrontational attitudes and bloody clashes which made rubbish of genuine efforts to install a healthy democratic culture in the country.

Today, 18 years after his charismatic rise to the front line of social change, he is standing trial on cooked-up charges, after having been scathed by compromising allegations of accommodation with the very regime he initially set out to replace.

The regime has so very well excelled in the art of denigration, vilification, and personality destruction that even members of the civil society and intelligentsia have adopted its modus operandi as a means of survival. Members of the professional class have also been constrained to throw ethics to the dogs and are actively engaged in the game of dog eat dog, under the pretext of "survivalism."

This is in no way suggesting that even in America, the land of opportunity, Obama has been spared the cloak and dagger tactics of detractors and the hidden hand of the degenerate white racist sentiment of the Ku Klux Klan or what remains of it. This is not to suggest that Obama has not been badmouthed by self-seeking detractors, underachievers and the dregs of society.

Somehow, he has been able to rise above pettiness and mudslinging and has charmed the devil in its lion's den because, irrespective of deep seated racial, religious and social prejudices, the American mainstream are united under a common denominator that is: "give opportunity a chance."

It is not uncommon in Cameroon to hear remarks such as "who does he think he is?", "Look at that one; he thinks he knows too much. We have seen his betters come and go," "Look at him; he thinks he can change society," "Look at that one; he drinks like a fish, drunkard, and good-for-nothing." They forget the biblical injunction that, "It is not what goes into the mouth that counts; it is what comes out of it."

Vilification, badmouthing, mudslinging will lead us nowhere if we hope to have the likes of Barack Obama to dream dreams, articulate selfless visions for the advancement of society. If we hope to attain greater heights, we must refrain from being intimidated by those who are perceived to incarnate qualities of greatness, progressiveness and a genuine commitment to share and impart what the Almighty endowed each one of us to have as individual talents and capabilities.

If we must allow our Obamas to flourish and accomplish their humane visions of society, we should eschew pettiness.

S-N F.

74

Reinforcing Transparency and Accountability
Friday, 17 October 2008

Gone are the days when a certain Jean Assoumou of late, and at the time the General Manager of the National Hydrocarbons Corporation, SNH, could defiantly announce to Cameroonians over the State-owned television that matters related to petroleum production and marketing were a subject of taboo which only him and the President of the Republic were exclusively privy to.

He said it with such authoritative impunity that Cameroonians simply shut their big mouths and inquisitive eyes and accepted the pronouncement as an article of faith.

Between 1976 when it was officially acknowledged that Cameroon was an exporter of crude up till the mid 1990's when the Bretton Wood financial institutions, notably the International Monetary Fund and the World Bank imposed the obligation of disclosure in the oil sector as one of the conditionalities for access to the Structural Adjustment Programme, the subject of oil production was such a highly classified State secret that a mere query by any enterprising or curious journalist could earn him severe administrative sanction.

There was this famous anecdote concerning the late politician, Honourable Lobe Nwalipenja from the oil producing Ndian Division who at one time was summoned by the fearsome President Ahmadou Ahidjo who castigated him for questioning the inequitable distribution of wealth accruing from oil exploitation and the fact that Ndian Division was one of the least developed parts of the country.

After bullying the poor fellow and warning him for his own good to desist henceforth from mentioning the issue of oil and sternly reminding him that petroleum production was none of his business,

Ahidjo summarily dismissed him from his royal presence with a token envelop to appease his deflated ego.

The one-time ace broadcaster of Radio Cameroon, Asonglefac Nkemleke would always have a tale or two to tell concerning the lack of transparency which marked the oil sector in the 1980's. He was removed as station manager of Radio Buea for questioning the fact that Cameroon had adopted the unconventional policy of recording its oil production in millions of tons per annum instead of the common practice of other world producers who recorded production in number of barrels per day.

What was implied in Asonglefac's question was that government policy was intended to befuddle ordinary Cameroonians by making it difficult for them to assess their oil producing status in comparison with other world producers.

The coming of Transparency International and the rise of critical civil society organisations in Cameroon has had the salutary effect of instilling a culture of transparency and accountability in the conduct of public affairs and even though the government is yet to fully rise up to the challenge, there are some timid signs that the State is gradually realising that it would eventually have to shred its shroud of secrecy over issues concerning the commonwealth of the nation.

It is in the interest of government to not only exercise transparency in its method of governance, but also to make information of vital interest available to the public. Cameroonians and especially media practitioners were given a sign of hope with the recent international conference on the Freedom of Information held in Yaounde which aimed at promoting the culture of open government and the improvement of relations between citizens and the administration through the adoption of laws and institutional practices designed to guarantee unfettered access to information.

In the days of the Southern Cameroons and later, the federated State of West Cameroon, it was the normal practice for government to publish white papers on specific areas of policy as well as the findings of commissions of enquiry on matters of corporate mismanagement, graft, embezzlement and so forth. The coming of

304

the Unitary State in 1972 put paid to such practices of good governance.

The national gazette, for example, ought to be a regularly published document containing all legislation passed by parliament, executive ordinances, decrees and circulars governing the conduct of the administration. How regularly the official gazette is published and how available it is to the public is a question to moot.

The habit of conducting State matters as if they were confined to the realm of occultism is largely responsible for the total confusion that reigns supreme in Cameroon wherein the leaders are moving in one direction and the followers are moving in the opposite direction.

Concomitant to the right of information is the need for government to set up mechanisms in all its departments to monitor, assess and respond to public feedback. Feedback, short of clairvoyance, is the only reasonable mechanism for government to assess and adapt its performance and this is where the role of the ombudsman comes in.

The job of an ombudsman is to receive, examine and report complaints by ordinary citizens about the harmful and damaging acts of government or public authorities and to ensure that such complaints are given attention by the appropriate quarters.

In the light of the above, we can happily commend the Director General of Taxation, Laurent Nkodo, and the Minister of Finance, Essime Menye, for launching two communication services last week that would facilitate the reporting of cases of harassment, fraud and other abuses by tax agents to officials of the Taxation Department.

The decision to set up a toll-free telephone number 8200 and a website www.impots.com to provide access to fiscal information related to tax codes, the finance law and other relevant information is a praiseworthy innovation of the Inoni government as long as such complaints as may eventually be reported will not be swept under the carpet by officials, who, for solidarity considerations, would seek to protect their colleagues.

The choice of ombudsman in this case and his terms of reference are crucial to the success of this laudable initiative. We enjoin the

Prime Minister, Chief Ephraim Inoni, to institute the service of ombudsman in all government departments providing services to the public.

It would seem that attempts by the Ministry of Public Service and Administrative Reforms to provide access to career information by civil servants have failed to check the influx of government functionaries to Yaounde for the purpose of "chasing" their personal files. This should not, however, provide an excuse for not setting up mechanisms for checks and balance because it is the right thing to do.

If ombudsmen are charged with the duty of producing a monthly assessment of their activities and publishing government response to public feedback, we will have reasonable grounds to hope that the culture of good governance has come to stay in Cameroon.

S-N F.

75

Agenda for Pope and Paul
Friday, 31 October 2008

News of the impending visit to Cameroon of Pope Benedict XVI has come as a breath of fresh air and hope to a desolate populace whose struggle for survival and prospects for poverty alleviation are bleak.

The imminent papal visit is seen as a source of spiritual strength to a people, who have just been told by the International Monetary Fund to expect a dismal economic performance next year, a prediction which Cameroonians have been constrained to accommodate for more than two decades.

Even though we are told that the Pope's planned visit is at the invitation of President Paul Biya, presumably with the backing of the clergy, one can safely assume that it is the Vatican that would draw up the agenda of the visit after having condescended to grant us the rare favour of accepting the government's invitation.

Several critics have wondered aloud whether Cameroon truly deserves the favour, especially as next year's visit will make the third papal sojourn to the country; a country managed by a dubious, avaricious and vicious class of politicians and their appointees. Cameroonian faithful strongly believe, however, that it is thanks to this papal visit that the country has miraculously avoided plunging into an abyss of irreversible doom.

They strongly hold that it is thanks to this visit of the Holy Father that despite the proliferation of satanic cults and devilish practices including ritual murders, sodomy, incest, brazen armed robbery, bribery and corruption, callous exploitation of man by man, inordinate wealth accumulation and you name the rest, Cameroon has barely managed to avoid falling over the precipice.

Some observers of world affairs have concluded that the world is ruled by three super powers, namely; the United States, the United Nations and the Vatican. The Vatican, the repository of spiritual power which claims supremacy over temporal power, draws inspiration from God and it could be argued that like the good Jesus himself said, he had come to earth to save the sinners not the righteous.

Pope Benedict like the good shepherd has chosen to come to Cameroon, a country that is solely in need of spiritual, socioeconomic and political salvation. The Vatican, we are told, is a state endowed with the most efficient intelligence gathering apparatus in the world and we can confidently expect that the Holy Father will be thoroughly briefed on the most sensitive and intimate dossiers on the Cameroon situation.

It would not be a redundant exercise, however, to reiterate the expectations of Cameroonians with regard to the agenda of talks between the Pope and Paul Biya. The Pope is a superstar in his own rights but by virtue of the humility associated with his position, we cannot expect him to play to the gallery or to shout on the roof top how he is going to tell off Biya and warn him to toe the line of civilised governance.

Some have suggested that the Holy Father ought to threaten the wayward son of a catechist with excommunication, but such a line of action may cut no ice with a fellow like Biya whose sole purpose of inviting the Pope is to make political mileage out of a pastoral event.

I would strongly urge the Holy Father to provide spiritual counselling and exorcise Mr. Biya from the grip of demonic forces that have taken up residence in the country. He should persuade Biya to cast off his illusion of grandeur and to stop believing in the fiction that those who are clamouring for him to perpetuate his stay in office genuinely love him.

President Biya ought to know by now that his close associates and hangers-on are mere eye servants who are simply afraid to tell him that the king is naked. It is not a valid argument to justify his prolongation in office on a whimsical belief that it is the popular wish of the citizens.

We expect the Holy Father to persuade Biya to desist from taunting the Maker of Heaven and Earth who has tolerated Biya's illusion of a demi-god with mild amusement and to advise him to call for early presidential election which he shall gracefully desist from contesting.

The United Nations, through the voice of its former Secretary General, Koffi Annan, has made its position clear and unequivocal with regards to the externalization of power. We expect the Vatican to follow suit and hopefully Barack Obama would provide the last straw that will break the camel's back as soon as he accedes to the White House next January.

Another proposed point on the papal agenda is the issue of justice and social justice. The Presidency and the executive in general should curb their interference in the machinery of justice. Justice should be allowed to function normally, because there can be no peace without justice. Administrators of justice should apply the law with a human heart.

A certain English writer once suggested that judges of the law courts should make it a habit to place a roll of toilet paper on their high tables to remind them of their humanity every time they are about to pass a verdict. There is a mistaken belief in Cameroon today that magistrates and judges are above the law and that they cannot be prosecuted because they enjoy immunity. Far from it.

It would be recalled that in the days of the defunct Federated State of West Cameroon with its Anglo-Saxon legal system, Chief Justice Mensah, a Ghanaian by nationality, opted to escape from Cameroon because he faced imminent prosecution for driving a car without insurance.

The Anglophone Cameroon system of justice, was guided by certain norms and principles generally referred to as the accusatorial system which held that an accused person was presumed to be innocent until proven guilty beyond reasonable doubt by the prosecution.

The notion of habeas corpus ensured that suspects were not unduly held in detention for unspecified lengths of time. Freedom of movement was the rule, while detention was the exception. In short, it was a legal system that upheld and protected human rights and the rights of the individual.

It is the Anglo-Saxon legal philosophy, we are told, that influenced the new Cameroon Criminal Procedure Code which went into effect in January 2007. Somehow, it seems the Francophone administrators of justice have yet to attune themselves to this civilised legal approach.

It was shocking to hear that in the case of the State versus Fru Ndi and 22 others which came up for public hearing in Yaounde last week, the prosecution opposed preliminary objections raised by the defence with regard to certain procedural miscarriages at the onset of the Diboule murder, and subsequent arrests and detention.

The defence held that the manner in which evidence were adduced involved duress, torture and linguistic incomprehension - all of which violated the provisions of the new criminal procedure code. The prosecution is said to have raised a lame argument that at the time of the commission of the offence, the criminal code was not in force.

One wonders whether the prosecution is not confused between the substantive criminal law which is not retroactive and a new criminal procedure which in effect abrogates and repels previous provisions of the patch work of procedures which hitherto obtained in Francophone Cameroon.

One also wonders whether the prosecution was suggesting that torture as a method of investigation and adducing evidence was an acceptable practice in the Francophone legal system and if so, whether we should in the 21st century continue to countenance such a barbaric system.

The Holy Father would certainly not be able to afford the time to waste on minute details of justice, but we hope he will advise President Biya to temper justice with mercy and not use the judiciary as a means to settle scores with his political adversaries. Long Live "Papa for Rome".

S-N F.

76

The Audacity of Obama
Friday, 07 November 2008

Barack Obama is brighter by far than a star and the spectacular manner in which he has shot his way from the outhouse to the White House constitutes an unprecedented landmark in World History.

He has made history as the first Blackman to become President of the United States. What makes the guy tick is a combination of character, charisma and composure. The prevailing socio-economic conditions in America have also been quite conducive.

In the early days of the presidential campaign, he once said, in response to remarks about his stature, "I may be thin, but, I am tough. I come from Chicago!" At that moment I thought he really was going to need all the audacity of a Chicago gangster to knife his way through the rough terrain of political campaigning.

That the son of an African (not African-American) father and an American mother had dared to consider running for the highest office in the United States required a driving force that is by far deeper and stronger than a mere belief in the American dream. It is a driving force that is anchored in old time religion, profound compassion, and full-blooded empathy.

In his book published in 2006, "The Audacity of Hope" which can be considered as his political manifesto, Barack Obama explores the contours of his religious faith: "There are some things that I am absolutely sure about - the Golden Rule, the need to battle cruelty in all its forms, the value of love and charity, humility and grace."

He explains that "when I read the Bible, I do so with a belief that it is not a static text but the Living Word and that I must be continually open to new revelations..." While Obama keeps his mind open to new revelations, he says he is "not willing to accept a reading of the Bible that considers an obscure line in Romans to be more defining of Christianity than the Sermon on the Mount."

In short, he believes that the Biblical injunction that "Love thy neighbour as thyself" and the lesson drawn from the parable of the good Samaritan form the core of the guiding principles for all humanity and do not lend themselves to any ambiguous interpretations.

Obama's bid for the American presidency did not emerge on the spur of some whimsical urge to undertake an adventure for the sake of adventure. His bid was rooted in a well calculated design to shatter the centuries-old myth of racism and racial stereotypes.

Obama's audacity is rooted in the ancient iconoclastic tradition of Prometheus, the anti-slavery advocacy of Graville Sharp, Clarkson, and William Wilberforce - all white men who gave meaning to the religious assertion that all men are equal in the eyes of God.

They were encouraged in this by a little known black slave from Nigeria, Olaudah, Equiano aka Gustav Vassa, who bought his freedom and wrote an account in 1788 (the first novel by an African) of his experience of the Trans-Atlantic Slave Trade.

What Obama has done is to accomplish the centuries-old belief of the founding founders of the United States, the Thomas Jeffersons, Alexander Hamiltons, Benjamin Franklins, the architects of the American Constitution (the Federalist Papers) also unequivocally declared that "we hold this truth as self-evident that all men are created equal..."

What Obama has done is to accomplish the decades-old dream of the black civil rights leaders, the Martin Luther Kings, W.E.B. Du Bois; African leaders like Kwame Nkrumah, Nelson Mandela; Black Power activists like Nat Turner, Harriet Tubman, Malcom X who all swore by the principle of the equality of man.

Breaking away from the shackles of racism, man's most dangerous myth, has been the most difficult step Obama had to overcome to undertake his short, but daunting walk to the White House, the path to which had been partially cleared by an earlier pathfinder, the Reverend Jesse Jackson in 1984.

314

In his recollection of the funeral for Rosa Parks, the black seamstress who sparked off the civil rights movement by refusing to surrender her seat in a bus to a white boy in 1955, Obama had this to say: "The choir sang; the pastor said an opening prayer.

Former President Bill Clinton rose to speak and began to describe what it had been for him as a white southern boy to ride in segregated buses, how the civil rights movement that Rosa Parks helped spark had liberated him and his white neighbours from their own bigotry.

Clinton's ease with his black audience, their almost giddy affection for him, spoke of reconciliation, of forgiveness a partial mending of the past's grievous wounds." The significance of the above event and the impact it had on Barack Obama who witnessed the event from the privileged position of a Senator cannot be overemphasised.

Obama's choice to enter politics was not accidental. It was deliberate. He first ran for political office at the age of 35, four years after graduating from the University of Harvard Law School where he headed the Harvard Law Review, a prestigious and authoritative publication which was an enviable passport to any lucrative white collar job in America.

On the contrary, Obama decided to engage in low-income civil rights activities among the underprivileged neighbourhoods of Chicago. When he decided to run for the legislature of Illinois State, he was faced with cynicism and scepticism from the grassroots communities who had lost faith in the failed promises of politicians, who saw politics as a dirty game and could not understand why a well accomplished academic like him should bother to go into politics.

Obama's response was that; "I understand the scepticism but that there was - and always had been - another tradition to politics, a tradition that stretched from the days of the country's founding, to the glory of the civil rights movement, a tradition based on the simple idea that we have a stake in one another, and that what binds us together is greater than what drives us apart, and that if enough people believe in the truth of the proposition and act on it, then we might not solve every problem but we can get something meaningful done."

The theory of what might be termed the least common political denominator seems to inform Obama's political ambition and he went about it, neither by recruiting the Chicago mafia nor by resorting to the strategy of religious extremism. He has knifed his way to the White House not like Mac the knife, but by the sheer force of argument, crystal clear and articulated argument; the power of his tongue, his composure and infinite compassion.

Unlike in Cameroon where a self-seeking public servant was handed power on a silver platter 26 years ago by dint of a wishy-washy constitutional arrangement that absolved him of any allegiance to the citizenry he is supposed to be leading, Barack Obama has diligently worked every inch of the way to the White House by winning the admiration and genuine support of the electorate.

The overwhelming solidarity he enjoys from the whole of Africa and the rest of the world is based on the genuine feeling of pride and prestige his victory has instilled in the Blackman. It is not so much because Africa expects bigger hand-outs from the Obama administration. Far from it.

The most important impact expected of the Obama administration in Africa would be the isolation, disapproval and castigation of perpetual, autocratic rulers and the political gangsterism that has hampered the progress of the African continent whose dictators were unfortunately comforted by the indifference of outgoing president George W. Bush.

S-N F.

316

77

26 Years of Agony
Tuesday, 18 November 2008

President Paul Biya says he would like to be remembered as someone who brought democracy to Cameroon. Tough luck. One of his detractors sought to know from me if I could recall the type of bag in which the man had carried democracy and where he got the bag from. I was at a loss.

When the democratic wind of change swept across the world after the collapse of the Soviet communist system, Cameroonian banker and columnist for Le Messager newspaper, Celestin Monga, who now lives in exile in the US, published an open letter to President Biya in 1990. He described Mr. Biya as an incompetent leader, saying he should resign.

Monga and Pius Njawe the publisher were later tried on charges of contempt of authority and were sentenced to six months in jail. Another Cameroonian writer, the renowned novelist, Mongo Beti, who returned to Cameroon in 1991 after a long exile in France, did not, unlike most Cameroonians, warmly welcome Mr. Biya's accession to power in 1982. He described Biya and his predecessor Ahmadou Ahidjo as two sides of the same coin – "bonnet blanc, blanc bonnet".

Mongo Beti said Ahidjo had handed over power to Biya as if it were some bequest to enable the latter to perpetuate post-colonial autocratic rule. When the writer died in 2001, the government attempted to make political capital out of the event by sending a top official to confer a posthumous medal of honour on the fallen hero. The official was severely chastised by the writer's widow who warned the fellow to take his medal elsewhere and refrain from insulting the image of her late husband who was a virulent critic of the Biya regime.

Vincent Satz, an indefatigable correspondent of Reuters, who covered Cameroon in the heady days of the early 1990s, described Biya as a right royal president whose style of governance was not only autocratic, but also monarchical. Monarchs are usually disdainful of the common man. They are aloof, cynical and more concerned about preserving their throne than anything else. Paul Biya seems to fit the bill.

President Biya and his predecessor Ahidjo developed a dangerously conflictual relationship because of the latter's continuous presence on the political scene. Ahidjo had exploited his position as leader of the ruling CNU party to maintain a high profile, which had the effect of belittling and overshadowing his successor, his appointee.

Biya, as president and chief executive, did not have elbow space and had to consult Ahidjo on the least executive decision he took. Matters got to a head when, in blatant violation of the constitution, Ahidjo was about to introduce an amendment that would endorse the primacy of the party over the state.

In short, Ahidjo had handed the presidency over to Biya but was not prepared to relinquish the seductive charms of power. He wanted to continue ruling by remote control with Biya as a mere figurehead.

A new set of lexicons had suddenly been introduced into the Cameroonian political vocabulary and words like diarchy, bicephalism, and dualism kept cropping up in the press and in every group conversation and a variety of political caucuses that had emerged as a result of the friction between Ahidjo and Biya.

Cameroonians, who in their majority had welcomed the transition with much enthusiasm, were not prepared to entertain Ahidjo's political chicanery. Ahidjo had ruled for 24 years and Cameroonians thought he ought to take a well-deserved rest and stop meddling with politics.

Cameroonians were then creating newspapers every other day as the government adopted a policy of tolerance. Biya needed the press very badly to help him in the fight against Ahidjo's overbearing presence on the political scene.

318

Every progressive-minded Cameroonian, the academia, civil society and the press took a strong position in favour of legality, in favour of Biya who was looked upon by the populace as someone who might lead the country away from neo-colonial dictatorship and usher an era of democratic freedoms.

At the height of the Ahidjo-Biya conflict, Ahidjo backed down and went on voluntary exile in July 1983 as the argument for legality won the day. Ahidjo's partisans were not about to let up and in August, the government uncovered a coup plot and the following year in April, a pro-Ahidjo faction in the army attempted a coup d'état. The rest is history.

During his maiden nation-wide familiarisation tour, President Biya exhorted the crowd that had come out to welcome him in Garoua to take cognisance of the fact that "no tribe should take upon itself the right to dominate the others and that no tribe should presume to have a legitimate right to rule the others..."

Ever since Biya emerged victorious in the political struggle with Ahidjo, Cameroon has witnessed a steady monopolisation of the political and administrative arena by his Beti tribesmen. They dominate the government at cabinet and other levels. They control the lion's share of state corporations and the military hierarchy.

They have a disproportionate access to bank loans which they squander like nobody's business. Because of their easy access to state funds, they undoubtedly dominate the list of looters of state coffers. It is not surprising that Mr. Biya's tribesmen form the majority of scapegoats that have been caught as sacrificial lambs in the current anti-corruption campaign that has been imposed on the government by Western creditors and donors.

If Biya wants to take credit for bringing democracy to Cameroon, a phenomenon that was evidently beyond his control, so be it. He should, however, be honest enough to admit that he has contributed immensely in stifling the democratic process by attempting, like his predecessor, to use the constitutional instrument to perpetuate his grip on power.

This year's constitutional amendment, which allows him to seek another term of office when the current one expires in 2011 is the most grievous political sin he has committed so far. Even his most ardent supporters have lost enthusiasm for him and the lacklustre manner in which his 26th anniversary was celebrated last week is a clear indication that the man has outstayed his welcome.

Cameroonians have been going through a severe economic recession for more than two decades. Unemployment has been on a steady rise and instead of poverty eradication, we now talk of poverty reduction. Public utilities are grossly inadequate and unaffordable. The greed of public officials has taken a heavy toll on the nation's resources. Despite all these, Mr. Biya does not think it is time to quit.

All great leaders know exactly when to quit power before it quits them. A good actor leaves the stage before the audience turns its back on him.

S-N F.

78

Memories of Miriam
Sunday, 23 November 2008

No amount of eulogies and tributes in honour of Miriam Makeba can be considered enough to match the fame and fortitude of that Grand Old Lady who dropped dead a fortnight ago in Italy doing what she loved doing best - using her musical talent to fight a noble cause; the cause of freedom from oppression, freedom from racism.

She checked out of this sinful world in a spectacular manner at the age of 76 shortly after a stage performance in honour of six Africans who were assassinated in a racially motivated attack in the South of Italy and her dramatic exit was a tragic reminder of the popular saying that a Spartan dies but never surrenders.

My memories of Miriam stretch back to sometime in November 1974 when she visited Cameroon on the invitation of late President Ahmadou Ahidjo and during a subsequent trip several years later, I had an exclusive interview with her in the studios of Radio Cameroon in Yaounde.

At the time of her 1974 visit, she had already taken up permanent residence since 1969 in Guinea-Conakry from where she toured many African countries whose leaders were vying with one another to host the Queen of African music.

Miriam was fêted by the likes of Julius Nyerere of Tanzania, Jomo Kenyatta of Kenya, Kwame Nkrumah of Ghana, Abdel Nasser of Egypt, Jafaar Nimeiri of Sudan, William Tubman of Liberia, Kenneth Kaunda of Zambia, Muamar Khadaffi of Libya, Emperor Haile Selassie of Ethiopia - in short, she was the darling of all African Heads of State except her native South Africa that was under the evil spell of apartheid. In this competition by African leaders to bask in

321

the sunshine radiated by Miriam, our own Ahmadou Ahidjo was determined not to be left out.

The annual Red Cross ballroom dance was the only truly non-political, social and recreational outing Ahidjo permitted himself and, in 1974, Miriam was invited to thrill the occasion. I was in my second year at the International Higher School of Journalism Yaounde (ESIJY now ASMAC) that was established by a convention of six African countries including Cameroon, Chad, Gabon, the Central African Republic, Togo and Rwanda. The school's dynamic director at the time, Hervé Bourges, an accomplished public relations stuntman, had succeeded to woo Myriam to give a pep talk to the students and staff, the substance of which can be found in the December 1974 edition of ESIJY FORUM I discovered by chance in my personal archives.

Miriam Makeba's message to journalists was as follows: "President Ahmed Sekou Toure (of Guinea-Conakry) reminds us that culture is a fundamental weapon in our revolutionary struggle for total liberation. Consequently, those of us Africans who are scattered across the globe because of the nefarious action of European imperialism must make use of our culture as a weapon of liberation.

In this regard, the journalist must act as an intermediary, the mobiliser of the masses. Any African journalist who does not see his role in this context should be considered as passive and cannot make the least contribution to the emancipation of his people, in particular, and to history, in general.

"Common-sense teaches us the duty of a communicator is to be active; history has decided it, a sense of humanity has imposed it, our people demand it and expect much from us. The people look up to journalists to demonstrate that they recognise, understand and master the need to propagate the positive aspects of African culture across the world.

"It has been said of the Blackman that he is the music maker of the world. In effect, the reality is that without Africans, American culture, and especially American music, would never have attained the level it has reached in the world today. The capitalist system, as

322

vicious as it is, does not only exploit artists of all categories, including journalists, but seeks also to destroy the authentic inheritors of the African revolutionary culture. It is appropriate here to mention the case of Paul Robeson.

"I call on you, my brothers and sisters of the International Higher School of Journalism of Yaounde to join the ranks of those who make history. You ought to be conscious of the power you possess, and believe me, my brothers and sisters, you possess great power. This power ought to serve the interest of the suffering mass of our people.

"I extend to you my greetings and gratitude. I urge you to be intransigent in the struggle for the promotion of our African culture."

Needles to recall that her message was greeted by a standing ovation after which she settled down to field questions in an impromptu press conference that spanned issues related to her precarious upbringing in apartheid South Africa, her experience in racist America, her musical career and her return to Africa, though not her native South Africa to which she returned only after the release from jail of Nelson Mandela.

That day, she spoke of many things; fools and kings; her trials and tribulations, the kindness, warmth, and understanding she felt in Africa, her wish to one day see South Africa being ruled by Africans. That wish was eventually fulfilled in her life time. Speaking on problems facing the African continent, Miriam had this to say: "We have a lot to do with regard to the economic independence of Africa which is still under domination.

Whether you are a journalist or a musician, no one should tell himself that 'I don't want to be involved in politics, I just want to sing about love or I just want to write what would please everybody.'

"Drawing inspiration from the people, it is our duty, in a positive way, to restore meaning in the lives of our people. That is what I try to do for my brothers and sisters and for myself. If some of my songs militate in favour of the advancement of the African woman, I do sing primarily for the struggle of mankind (man and woman), the joy and the sadness of life in general."

323

Talking about the apartheid system, she confessed that she found it painful to speak about apartheid which she noted was a terminology used by the Dutch, European and American colonialists who seized our lands and practised a policy of racial segregation. These colonialists, she said, have attempted to relate the anti-apartheid struggle to the black civil rights movement in America, but beyond the issue of civil rights, the problem in South Africa has to do with the restitution of land to the rightful African owners.

She pointed out that the racist regime was interpreting the black struggle as a fight for the independence of the Bantustans (African village settlements created by white rulers) whereas the real struggle was aimed at recuperating lands that white settlers had expropriated.

On the question of African unity, Miriam Makeba lamented over the fact that the continent was the richest in the world but that, unfortunately, its inhabitants were the most deprived and the poorest in the world because it was not united and, unlike Europe and the Arab World, it lacked solidarity.

My memories of Miriam Makeba, like everyone else, are unforgettable. That day, in 1974, she wore a black ankle-length dress, a necklace of African beads and ear-rings to match, and her hair was plaited rasta, no threads, no superfluous make up like Michael Jackson. She spoke with a languorous strain which barely disguised the volcanic energy of her soul.

Her voice could tame a lion to sleep, but her vocal inflections, timbre and tone could move the mountain to the ocean. Like another great African musician, Manu Dibango of Cameroon who put African music on the world map, Miriam was a simple, unassuming talent of Olympian dimension. Plain red beans and rice that she was, she has left an artistic legacy that would remain unrivalled for a very long time to come.

S-N F.

79

Bali Boundary Disputes: Lessons From Bakassi**

December 2008

Ever since the final handing-over of the Bakassi Peninsula to Cameroon by Nigeria on August 14, President Biya has been strutting about like a peacock and basking in the glory of the diplomatic and legal victory scored by Cameroon at the end of the 15-year-long border dispute.

A few months ago, he mounted the rostrum at the UN General Assembly to blow his trumpet as a Messiah of Peace and to be lionised by his peers as a champion of the rule of law and a proponent of dialogue as a civilised means of resolving conflicts.

While Mr. Biya should be given credit for having initiated a peaceful resolution of the conflict, we should not overlook the fact that it also took the political will of the Nigerian leadership to arrive at a solution and that Cameroonians can, henceforth, look forward to seeing their Head of State applying the same principles that guided his approach to the Bakassi dispute in resolving other internal matters of national interest.

These principles that emerged from the peace process include the respect of territorial boundaries inherited from the colonial era, respect for the rule of law and the pursuit of dialogue in times of conflict.

In referring to the outcome of the Bakassi dispute, the official media have even usurped the slogan:" the force of argument" which, incidentally, is the motto of the Southern Cameroons National Council, SCNC, which is being persecuted for asserting the self-determination of the former UN Trust Territory of Southern Cameroons through the force of argument instead of the argument of force.

The resolution of the Bakassi dispute should not only be highlighted as an example for Africa and the rest of world to emulate, but, primarily, as a golden yardstick for the resolution of all other land disputes within the national territory. After all, what is good for the goose is good for the gander.

It has taken close to 15 years from the time Nigerian troops took up position in a section of the Bakassi Peninsula in 1993, through the verdict of the International Court of Justice in favour of Cameroon in 2002, the signing of the Green Tree Peace Accord in 2006 which laid down conditions for the complete withdrawal of the Nigerian Army and civilian

Administration from the disputed territory to arrive at a durable solution of the conflict in 2008.

By contrast, perennial internal land disputes which were resolved in the colonial and post-independence eras in Cameroon have had the uncanny habit of resurfacing their ugly heads in recent times, putting to question the integrity of local administrators as impartial arbitrators of disputes and keepers of law and order and the honesty of certain influential politicians who manipulate situations to achieve their ambitions.

There is general consensus that most local administrators, especially in the Northwest Province where land disputes are notoriously rife, have more often constituted part of the problem rather than part of the solution for very selfish reasons.

In a study of land disputes and boundary conflicts in the Northwest Province conducted by a civil society organisation LUKMEF-Cameroon in 2007, the organisation recommended that boundaries should be established "as generally long-lasting unchangeable facts, getting away from the idea that boundaries could be changed whenever some discontent with the existing boundary arises.

It states further that, "in line with attempts to create a legitimate, permanent boundary regime, transparent, reasonable and verifiable policies for the decision on land and boundary issues should be set up.

326

These policies should clarify the way on how changes are to be done and when a change of boundaries is justifiable or not, in order to prohibit a sense of 'all is possible if enough is paid.' These rules should include serious and verifiable details on how to prevent undue side-taking by administrative personnel (e.g. decision by Commissions instead of decisions by individuals)".

It is logical to deduce that the perpetual recurrence of land disputes that had long been settled in colonial times can be attributed to either the ignorance or greed of corruptible administrators who are susceptible to manipulation by professional trouble makers who thrive on such disputes to raise funds for personal gains or in some cases, by influential politicians who take advantage of their position to achieve a hidden agenda.

Such administrators are likely to throw caution to the wind, knowing that, at any given moment, they can be transferred to new postings, leaving behind a pile of confusion for their subsequent replacements to disentangle.

The Case of Bali Nyonga and Its Neighbours

A clear example of the recurrence of long-settled land disputes in the Northwest Province is the one involving Bali-Nyongha Fondom on the one hand and the surrounding Ngemba, Menemo and Moghamo clans of the Widekum tribe on the other hand.

In the aftermath of a violent land dispute in which the Bali Fondom was attacked by neighbouring clans in March 1952, the colonial administration ordered an official inquiry the following month which came up with a number of findings, namely, that the Balis acquired their land in the latter half of the 19th century by conquest and enjoyed a position of paramountcy long before the arrival of German colonialists and that the boundaries of Bali Nyongha had been demarcated as the result of a series of actions in Native Courts, of decisions given under the Inter-Tribal Boundaries Ordinance and by administrative action.

It concluded that the attacks on Bali property which led to the death of several Bali people were planned and concerted and were carried out by a large number of persons over a period of more than one week. Responsibility for the disturbances, it noted, lay with the Moghamo, Menemo and Ngemba clans of the Widekum tribe with the exception of Ba-Pinyin, Bambullue (Awing), Bagangu (Akum), Santa, Nkwen, Abakpa, Bamenda government station, Bafawkum, Banjong and Bafawmissang.

The details of this dispute which occurred under the British administration of the Trusteeship are contained in the Nigeria Gazette No. 45 Vol. 39 of August 26th, 1952. A more elaborate commission of inquiry instituted by the colonial administration in 1953 and headed by the Commissioner of the Southern Cameroons A.G.B Manson came out with a number of findings notably, that, "there are no grounds to support the allegations of the Widekum people that the boundaries between the Bali Nyonghas and their Widekum neighbours were unfairly or improperly determined and that there are no compassionate grounds - such as discriminatory treatment against, or unjust oppression of Widekums by Bali Nyonghas - which, in justice, require that any Widekum people (in the disputed area) should be allotted any special portion for their own exclusive beneficial enjoyment or which justify any readjustment of the Bali boundary."

Incidentally, the principle recommended today by LUKMEF-Cameroon as a parameter for durable settlement of boundary disputes had long been suggested by the 1953 Manson Report which, among several recommendations, urged the Governor-General in Lagos to make a formal declaration to the effect that "the Widekum people should be informed that their claims to a title whether statutory or customary, to occupational rights in the disputed area or any portion of the disputed area cannot be entertained."

The report further emphasised that "as security of tenure is indispensable to the future wellbeing, tranquillity and quiet, progressive development of the Bali people, and with a view to the avoidance of continual friction with their Widekum neighbours in the years ahead, it is essential that Your Excellency should make a formal positive declaration or acknowledgement to the effect that you deem it expedient that exclusive rights of occupancy over the land in dispute shall be vested in the Bali Nyongha people subject, at all times, to their native laws and customs and to the provisions of the Land and Native Rights Ordinance."

Curiously enough, and irrespective of the painstaking findings and recommendations made in the colonial and the post-colonial eras, the people of Ngyen-Mbu recently stormed the Northwest Governor's office to protest against purported encroachment on their land by the Bali Nyonghas.

Whereas there is a presidential decree of 1977 demarcating the boundaries between Bali Nyongha and its neighbours that is; Baforchu, Chomba, Mbatu and Nsongwa in Mezam Division and Ngyen-Muwa and Ngyen-Mbo in Momo Division and whereas the 1977 decree, which ceded certain portions of Bali land to its land grabbing neighbours stated in Article 8 that, "natural persons in zones affected by the modification of the territorial boundaries made in this decree may remain where they are on condition that they submit themselves to the authority of their new traditional ruler having jurisdiction over the area in which they reside and provided that a person who so wishes may go and settle on the land administered by their former ruler, in which case he shall receive compensation if he shows proof that he owns a dwelling house built of permanent materials or has perennial crops such as coffee at the place from where he has moved," local administrators, without exception, have failed to fully implement the provisions of that presidential decree.

It is interesting to note in passing, the striking similarity between Article 8 of the Presidential Decree and Article 3 of the 2006 U. N.-sponsored Green Tree Accord which confirmed Cameroon's authority over the Bakassi Peninsular.Art.3 (1) of the Accord states that" Cameroon, after transfer of authority to it by Nigeria, guarantees to Nigerian nationals living in the Bakassi Peninsular, the exercise of their fundamental rights and freedoms...Art 3(2a) In

329

particular, Cameroon shall not force Nigerian nationals…to leave the zone or change their identity. (b) Respect their culture, language and beliefs.(c) Respect their rights to continue their agricultural and fishing activities. (d) Protect their property and customary land rights etc. etc.

On the contrary, and in violation of the presidential decree, the Sub-prefect of Mbengwi issued an order in March 1983 banning farming activities on the parcel of land handed over from Bali to Ngyen-Mbu village, thus, giving the Ngyen-Mbu people the false impression that they had a right to expel Bali people who opted to remain on the land and pay allegiance to Ngyen-Mbu as stipulated by the decree.

In the normal hierarchy of laws, it is evident that the sub-prefectural order was in violation of and repugnant to a higher instrument of law, that is, a presidential decree and that such an order was automatically null and void.

Legal Consequence

Before examining the legal consequence of the Prefectural Order, it is worthwhile to take a closer look at the terms of the 1977 Presidential Decree. In the typical language and style of despotic regimes, the decree, without stating the cause or justification, bluntly stated in Article 2 that "the Baforchu village…shall comprise the former area making up Baforchu village *plus a parcel of land carved out from the Bali area.*" Article 3 says *"a parcel of land carved out from the Bali area…is hereby attached to the Chomba Mbatu and Nsongwa villages.."* and Article 4 refers to *a parcel of land carved out from the Bali area is hereby added to the Ngyen Muwa area in Batibo Sub division",* while Article 5 spoke of *two parcels of land carved out of the Mankon and Bali areas respectively shall be added to Ngyen Mbo in the Mbengwi Sub division."*

The above scenario can be viewed as some kind of a local version of the 1884 Berlin Conference during which some powerful potentates pulled out their hunting knives and proceeded to carve out Bali as a sacrificial lamb to appease the appetite of a demi-god who

330

was out for revenge. Otherwise, how else can we explain why all of a sudden, Bali territory became the subject of boundary modifications a quarter century after it had been established by previous legal and administrative instruments that its neighbours had no legal, customary, or compassionate grounds to lay any claims whatsoever to any portion of Bali territory which the Bali people were entitled to peacefully enjoy according to their native laws and custom. And since some influential neighbours, in connivance with some unscrupulous administrators thought that Bali was not entitled to the peaceful enjoyment of its territory, two Bali indigenes who were affected by the 1983 prefectural order decided to pursue the path of justice by taking the matter before the Mbengwi High Court presided over by the Honourable Chief Justice F.A K. Monekosso.

The applicants, in a motion ex-parte, applied for an order of certiorari in the matter of the aforementioned prefectural order. The applicants stated in a 6-paragraph affidavit that they were farmers and compound heads resident in Bali and owning land and houses that were the subject of the 1977 Presidential Decree. Counsel for applicants argued that the prefectural order cited above was made without jurisdiction in that it violated the terms of Article 8 of the Presidential Decree. He further argued that applicants had not refused to submit themselves to the natural ruler of the affected area. He stated that the prefectural order adversely affects the property rights of the applicants in that Ngyen-Mbo villagers have taken advantage of the order to occupy applicants' houses and farms. Delivering his judgment, Justice Monekosso remarked that "the question that has been posed to this court and for determination by this court is whether the decision of the Prefect was of a judicial character to attract the order of certiorari in the circumstances of its nature." The Judge observed that "the Prefect is a justice of the peace of the area." After an exhaustive citation of case laws, the learned Judge stated that the prefectural order though administrative in form, has a quasi-judicial nature. He agreed with counsel for applicants' prayer that the relief sought should be granted and an order to this effect reads: (1) that the order of certiorari as prayed for by the

331

applicants has been issued against the decision of the Prefect of Momo (2) The said decision is hereby removed into this High Court and quashed by reason of illegality.

** *This article was initially published in LELA magazine in December 2008*

S-N F.

80

Bawocks- The Unruly Friends of Bali-Nyonga
December 2008

Most Fondoms in the North-West have to cope with internal and external disturbances and Bali-Nyongha is no exception. Bawock is village in the heart of Bali-Nyongha inhabited by a Mendumba-speaking group who arrived in Bali sometime around 1905 from the Bagangte area in Nde Division. They had arrived as a destitute band of refugees seeking asylum after having been evicted by the Bangante for causing disturbances and damage to lives and property. According to a mimeographed study titled " A History of a People: The Secret Behind the Bali Nyonga and the Bawock Nfen Gai Nfai Affair", written by *two Bawock elites, Limen George and Njonji Richard, the authors state that the Bawock people were the most aggressive group in that they were prepared to fight anyone at any time. With their dexterity in war fare, they dug trenches around their land to keep permanent boundaries from their neighbours...Sometimes the Bawock people would fill some trenches and dig other ones to reclaim land from weaker neighbours.*"

They clearly state that *"the Bawock man is bad tempered* and fund (sic) of keeping secrets with little or no trust for strangers and is quite unlike his Bagangte brother." We learn from the study that the Bawocks originally came to Bangangte from Bafang and that "the reason why neighbours of the Bawock people developed some hatred for them came as a result of *their aggressive nature.* Bawock was very proud because she was able to fight and win wars and for that reason they occasionally raised provocation by trying to extend land boundaries."

The above explicit and unequivocal account does not require any interpretation to place the current misunderstanding between

Bawock and Bali whose origin can be traced to 1974. In 1969, the Bawocks dethroned their chief, a certain Athanasius Ntankeh II for living like a profligate, who, in order to indulge in his" love for luxury "sold off traditional artefacts and antiquities to tourists. Bawock elders then resorted to invite a successor from a hitherto unknown Bawock group in exile in Mbouda in the person of Nana Jacob Wanda who seemed to have come with a strange agenda to show Bali people wonders. According to the historical account cited above, the new chief did not deem it proper to present himself to the Fon of Bali , the Paramount ruler of the sub division, because the Bawock claimed it was not necessary. Chief Nana Wanda did not only ignore the paramountcy of the Fon of Bali but proceeded to disrupt the Bali annual festival of Lela in 1974, an incident which called for the deployment of the armed forces. The chief of Bawock had "informed the administration that if the Bali, in coming to carry out their traditional libation in his land, would interfere with the culture of his people, he would not allow them pass. They should stop coming to Bawock land since the stream (where the libation takes place) also passes through their land." So, clearly, the Bawocks were now prohibiting the Bali from performing a rite they had been observing for more than half a century before the arrival of the Bawocks in Bali as refugees. This was unfortunately a replay of story of the Arab and the camel who, in the bitter cold of the night in the desert had begged the Arab to allow it warm its ears in his tent. The Arab obliged. Soon after, it begged to warm its head. The Arab obliged. Thereafter it was the neck, and then the chest etc. etc. until in the end, the Arab found himself in the cold, outside his tent.

In January 1975 and under the auspices of the Mezam administration, the Fon of Bali and the chief of Bawock issued a joint communiqué pledging to promote peaceful coexistence. In October of the same year, the Senior Divisional Officer for Mezam, Mr. Alexander Motanga issued a prefectural decision stating among other points that(1) though there is no demarcation boundary between Bali and Bawock, there is an area known as Bawock in which the chief of Bawock has jurisdiction. (2) The Bali people shall continue to carry out their annual acts of libation at the usual place. (3) The Fon of Bali is the Paramount Chief of the Bali District (now sub-division) with the chief of Bawock as his second in command etc. etc. Thirty-one years after this prefectural order (Dec. 6, 2006), the Mezam administration, along with the traditional rulers of Bawock, Mbu (Baforchu) and Pinyin attempted, without informing and in the absence of the Fon of Bali, to demarcate a boundary between Bali and Bawock which is in the heart of Bali and cannot conceivably have a boundary with any other village, let alone Mbu and Pinyin. Barely three months after the aborted demarcation attempt, the Bawock people, in defiance of the 1975 prefectural decision, made bold to disrupt a procession of members of the Voma fertility cult of Bali Nyonga who were about to perform libation at the usual place. The Bawock committed the sacrilege of assaulting members of the cult and destroying their sacred paraphernalia. On March 6, 2007, three days after Voma was attacked, a sanctuary housing Bali traditional sacra, artefacts, antiquities and hunting trophies was set ablaze, presumably by some vandals from Bawock. It should be quickly pointed out that the majority of Bawock people do not subscribe to these atrocious acts and it would seem that for fear of reprisal or as a planned act intended to gain public sympathy, the Bawock ring leaders destroyed parts of their village and coerced their reluctant kith and kin to embark on a mass exodus to Bamenda town.

It also emerged from all these gimmicks that the Bawocks, under the influence of some politicians in neighbouring villages, were calculating to gain administrative and public support for their ambition to have not only a demarcated boundary with Bali-Nyonga but also to be attached to Mbu and Pinyin villages in order to form a separate administrative division and a separate electoral constituency. The latter was in view of the general election of June 2007. This view of the situation was concurred by a highly reputable Barrister, Ntumfor Nico Halle, the consecrated Spokesman of the North-West Fons' Union and the Regional Representative of the National Electoral Commission who fought hard to uplift the sagging image of traditional rulers by preventing some of them from meddling in the electoral process.

It would be recalled that in 1986, the chief of Bawock petitioned the sub divisional officer of Bali for the demarcation of his village " with survey pillars" The Bawock petition spoke of "new tactics being adopted by our neighbours with a view to assimilate our village and change its identity and culture which we very much want to preserve." Their decision to petition, they explained, "was arrived at, not in an attempt to make an extra inch of land for our village, but rather because the age old boundaries of trenches and hips(sic) of stones have outlived their usefulness in modern times, hence the many moral and physical encroachment into our village by our neighbours." It should be quickly pointed out that what the Bawock petition refers to as trenches and fences of loose rocks were not boundaries but safeguards to prevent the Fon of Bali's dwarf cattle in the olden days from straying into farmland. It is also intriguing to figure out just how the Bawocks intend protect themselves from moral encroachment with "survey pillars".

However, the only evidence of moral and physical encroachment the petition cited was that all government projects in Bali sub division carry the name Bali and none carries the name Bawock. In response to the petition signed by the chief of Bawock and the chairman of his traditional council, Peter Limen, the then Divisional Officer for Bali, Mr. Peter Oben Ashu, convened a joint meeting of the chief of Bawock and the Fon of Bali and their respective traditional councils at the Bali Town Hall. After listening to both parties, the D.O. explained that all government projects bear the names of the chief towns of the project area, hence the appellation: Bali Water Supply, Bali Hospital, Bali Government Secondary School etc. etc. Mr. Oben Ashu read the official text creating the 2nd class chiefdom of Bawock with a population of 1880 inhabitants and attached to the 1st class chieftaincy of Bali Nyonga having jurisdiction over the entire Bali sub division with a population of 26825. He reminded the chief of Bawock of the loyalty and respect that he owes to the Fon of Bali and advised him to accept his position as a subordinate to the Fon of

Bali. Twenty-two years after this advice, can it be said that the chief of Bawock has heeded to the call for loyalty and respect?

S-N F.

81

Stop These Agents of Confusion: The Farce about British Northern Cameroons**

April 28th, 2009

The diversionary activities of a certain Martin Ateh Chia (said to be the leader of an obscure movement called British Cameroons, (Britcam) which seem to have been allowed to go unchallenged in recent times, are now becoming a grave cause for concern and may in the long run prove to be inimical to the Southern Cameroons' nationalist struggle. We have been made to understand that the said Mr. Chia has been peddling a rather dangerous political doctrine that has begun to sow seeds of discord within the ranks of bona fide Southern Cameroonian nationalists. This dangerous doctrine consists in deceiving unsuspecting Southern Cameroonians who may not have taken the trouble to learn and understand the contours of their tortuous history, a history bedevilled by self-seeking revisionists, collaborators, fifth columnists and congenital traitors.

Mr. Chia's deceitful ploy consists in spreading the false theory that the restoration of Southern Cameroons' independence cannot be achieved without the involvement of what was once known as Northern British Cameroon which today forms parts of three different states in Northeastern Nigeria. It would seem that Mr. Chia arrived at this conclusion by satanic inspiration or simply by reading the United Nations instruments on decolonisation upside down. We have a bounding duty to challenge and put a halt to this tendency to distort or misinterpret history, which in this case is playing in favour of our common adversary who can only rejoice in the dissipation of our collective energy and resources resulting from these diversionary activities.

Nowhere was it ever suggested or implied in the UN Charter or resolutions that the administering authorities of Trust territories i.e.

Britain and France were to grant independence or autonomy to these territories simultaneously or en block. With regard to British Southern Cameroons and British Northern Cameroons, it must be pointed out that at no given period were the two administered as one territory. When the Allied Forces i.e. Britain and France sacked Germany out of its protectorate of Kamerun at the beginning of the First World War, France took the greater part of the booty to the east while Britain contented itself with two strips of territory to the west that were contiguous to the eastern border of the British so-called protectorate of Nigeria. The southern strip stretching from Rio del Rey in the Gulf of Guinea to Nkambe was simply named the Southern Cameroons while the northern strip stretching from the Adamawa area through the Benue right up to Bornu and the Lake Chad region was called Northern Cameroons. From the outset, Britain had found it expedient to administer Northern Cameroons as part and parcel of northern Nigeria and the Southern Cameroons as part of southern Nigeria at first and later as part of the Eastern region when Britain split its Nigerian possession into three main administrative units in 1946. The borders separating the British Northern and Southern Cameroons were formally established in that same year. There was no political or administrative interaction between the two entities and the only thing they shared in common was the name Cameroon because even during the German era ,the Reich had not had the opportunity to set up any meaningful administrative , economic or communications network in its relatively vast protectorate of Kamerun. In effect, the two territories had followed separate paths to self-determination. When Southern Cameroons representatives in the Eastern Nigerian House of Assembly in Enugu declared that enough was enough and walked out for good from the House in 1953, an act that was meant to assert their personality as representatives of a UN Trust territory who wanted to wash their hands off the politics of Nigeria (a British colony) and called for a separate House of Assembly in Buea (Southern Cameroons), they did not call on Northern Cameroons to join them.

Self-determination is a principle applied on a case by case basis, taking into consideration the peculiarities of each aspiring territory and the expressed wishes of its inhabitants. How Mr. Martin Ateh Chia came about the idea that the restoration of Southern Cameroons independence cannot be valid without involving the defunct Northern Cameroons can only be the work of the devil. The man has conveniently forgotten that UN-sponsored plebiscites to determine the wishes of the peoples of the two territories were organised separately and that the Northern Cameroons had even had a previous one in 1959 which was considered inconclusive and had to repeat the exercise on 11th Feb. 1961in which it decided to join Nigeria.

It does not require much imagination to see the path of disaster to which people like Mr. Chia are trying to mislead Southern Cameroonians. By preaching a doctrine that advocates a split in the Nigerian polity when there is no evidence of a groundswell of opinion to that effect originating from there is tantamount to steering the Southern Cameroons on a collision course. If Mr. Chia wants to fish in troubled waters, he should paddle his canoe alone and let well-meaning Southern Cameroonians go about their genuine struggle without the luxury of his confusionist agenda which can only produce the negative effect of alienating Nigeria, their most strategic ally.

** *This article was originally published in The Frontier Telegraph*

S-N F.

82

A Crisis of Ethics and Credibility in Cameroon's English- Speaking News Media: An urgent need for critical self-examination. *(Paper presented by Sam-Nuvala Fonkem at the Bamenda Colloquium to mark the World Press Freedom Day jointly organized by Cameroon Multi-Media Council CMMC and Global Information Network GLOBINET on May 8, 2009 at the Jua Hotel).* **

Throughout this week and in all the four corners of the globe, media practitioners and civil society have been organizing activities to mark the World Press Freedom Day; an occasion set aside by the UN for the public to reflect on the significance of press freedom and take stock of the ground so far covered to safeguard this freedom and to map out a course of action to promote its ideals. As we observe this day which we, as practitioners, should consider as a day of rededication to the lofty principles of human rights and dignity, it is our sacred duty to critically examine media practice within our local context and provide a clear-sighted perspective regarding the way forward.

December next year (2010) will mark the 20th year since the Cameroon National Assembly hurriedly passed a body of laws, pompously referred to by officialdom as Liberty Laws, spelling out the broad outlines of the freedom of association, freedom of movement, and the freedom of the press among others. The public began to witness the mushrooming of political parties, trade unions, and dozens of newspapers sprouting all over the place. This was subsequently followed by the liberalization of the audio-visual media in the year 2000 and we have since witnessed the emergence of dozens of private radio and television stations as well as non-profit community radio stations.

In terms of numbers, we can truly assert that the media landscape has undergone a revolution compared to the era of state monopoly

343

over the main channels of mass communication. Many more voices can now be heard in the open market of ideas even though a significant portion of the population can still be considered as voiceless for various reasons.

One would have imagined that with this pluralism in media ownership, the autocratic regime of President Paul Biya, who wants to be remembered as the one who brought democracy to Cameroon by his own volition, would at least demonstrate a greater responsiveness to the voice of the people and adjust government policies in accordance with the expressed wishes of the people with regard to the electoral process, the fight against poverty, the respect of human and peoples' rights and the right to a decent standard of living. Far from it. The exercise of executive powers, according to him, ends with the conjuring of freedoms with the stroke of the pen and any attempt to draw his attention to ensure the respect of those freedoms is an act of sheer ingratitude.

Even though Cameroonians speak more freely today than in the previous Ahidjo regime, today's ruling class has refused to fully respect its side of the bargain, i.e. the social contract regarding the freedom of the press.

It has even refused to make a reality of the Right of Information which should allow pressmen and the public access to vital information of public interest. A glaring example of this refusal is the failure to make public the result of a population census conducted in 2005.

Although censorship or more precisely prior restraint was only scrapped from the statute books six years after the enactment of the so-called Liberty Laws, the issue of libel and defamation still remains a criminal offense and unless libel is decriminalized, the task of exposing public authorities to public scrutiny remains an uphill task.

While it has been quite fashionable and easy to criticize the government for complicating the duties of the media, the media and media practitioners themselves are not entirely blameless and have conveniently avoided the difficult task of critical self-examination in order to identify the bad and ugly side of their practice.

The press is the watchdog of society and the question has always arisen as to who should watch over the watch-dog. By nature, the press or the news media do not lend themselves to any institution of oversight other than itself, while the public acts as the collective body that has power to grant or withdraw patronage. The duty to safeguard the freedom of the press lies squarely on the shoulders of the press and media practitioners ought to realize that the protection and respect of press freedom is a sacred trust that has been placed on them by the public.

In order to deserve this public trust, media practitioners have the duty to respect professional ethics, high professional standards and maintain credibility. A media without ethics is a media without a heart and a media without credibility is a media without a head.

The ethics of journalism enjoins practitioners to report news in a truthful, objective and fair manner. Truth, objectivity and fairness are the cardinal ethics of professional journalism. While it is very important to be truthful, the journalist must exercise care and strive to achieve balance and fairness. It was John Dumoga, the Ghanaian journalist, who coined the maxim that "it is good to be truthful but better to be fair."

A casual glance at our papers today gives one the impression that the media have shoved ethics to the back burner in hot pursuit of financial reward or what is generally referred to in Cameroon as 'gombo'. This 'gombo' journalism or "cheque book" journalism as it is called elsewhere has been shamelessly justified on grounds of pragmatism, survivalism and realism. Pragmatism may sound like a practical principle, but when pragmatism becomes unscrupulous, it is nothing short of brazen prostitution. A journalist has the right to earn a decent living from his works or stories especially if the publisher is the one paying for the stories. But when the newsmaker starts paying for the stories, we have a situation where the tail is wagging the dog and as the saying goes, "he who pays the piper calls the tune'. When the newsmaker or manipulator, spin doctor or agent of disinformation starts to call the tune, the journalist loses his independence and becomes a mindless tool in the hands of political jugglers, white collar robbers, cut throat artists and conmen.

On several occasions, I have read stuff in newspapers which gives me the creeps. Recently I read an article in The Post newspaper (a paper to which I have a special attachment) about the views of a certain faction of the North West Fons' Union concerning one of their peers, Fon Chafah of Bangolan. The views expressed gave the impression that His Royal Highness, Fon Chafah, was exploiting the Union for personal material gains aimed at acquiring sumptuous palaces and luxury automobiles. I was quite dumbfounded to read a corrigendum in a subsequent edition of the paper stating that the views expressed by the detractors of Fon Chafah were unfounded. The corrigendum even took the trouble to remind readers that Fon Chafah was a reputable magistrate- grade- 3; a rather clumsy suggestion that because he is a magistrate grade-3 , he did not deserve the rather uncharitable image that was painted by some of his compeers. The corrigendum was signed by the editor, a title which is nowhere to be found on the imprint of the newspaper in question. The Post has an executive editor, an editor-in-chief, desk editor, bureau chiefs and all what not, but no such position as editor. In which case, the signatory of that corrigendum can logically be considered anonymous.

We have every reason not only to question the identity of "editor" but also to question the use or abuse of a corrigendum. A newspaper corrigendum is simply a short notice carried by a newspaper to rectify an error that might have inadvertently cropped up in a story that was published in a previous edition. For example a statement might have been inaccurately reported or attributed to the wrong person or some mix up of facts which needs to be rectified and is usually concluded with the apology: " We regret the error". But when a corrigendum concludes with the observation that the statements made by so and so were completely unfounded, then it is no longer a corrigendum. It could be an indictment or a judgment, but not a corrigendum and supposing that Fon Chafah had directly or indirectly caused the publication of the said corrigendum, the

346

editors of the paper or any news media under the circumstances and irrespective of the attractiveness of any inducement, should have politely directed Fon Chafah to avail himself of the right of response by writing a rejoinder or a disclaimer. When a news organ starts playing the role of defence lawyer, then the tail has begun to wag the dog. The Post or any newspaper for that matter is not competent and is hardly expected to assume the role of counsel for the defence.

Media organs are run by people, human beings who may feel like taking a stand on serious issues of public interest. Of course, they have a right to do so provided they take the pains to express their stand in a distinct space provided for that, but certainly not in the news columns. The editorial and opinion pages are meant for that.

Another circumstance in which I thought the English-speaking press was beginning to lose its professional bearings was the media hype surrounding the arrest and incarceration of Mr. Zacheus Forjindam, former General Manager of the Shipyard and Engineering Corporation on allegation of embezzlement. In as much as I condemn the violation of due process that has attended his case, I cannot help being suspicious of some newspapers which have given the impression that the violation of the new criminal procedure code which is predicated on the Anglo-Saxon legal principle of habeas corpus is singularly restricted to the Forjindam case. The entire Cameroon populace is a victim of the violation of due process. It is even more disturbing when Mr. Forjindam is being portrayed by certain press organs as a victim of Anglophone marginalization or as an Anglophone martyr. It is simply ridiculous for the fact that Mr. Forjindam has never been known to espouse, let alone sympathize with the plight of the oppressed people of the Southern Cameroons to which he belongs. It is a widely known fact that he did not only court the favours of the oppressors of Southern Cameroonians but had demonstrated his ambition to carve a niche among the ruling class.

What is disturbing to the keen observer is that several months before his arrest, Forjindam was copiously vilified in the independent media for strenuously advocating for a constitutional amendment

347

that virtually consecrated President Paul Biya as Life President of Cameroun.

The same press that castigated him for promoting such a retrogressive political agenda turned out to be the very same press that by the same miraculous twist of fate began portraying him as a victim of the very same political system for which he had sold his conscience.

In the two cases I have cited, we cannot fail to take note of the fact that we are dealing here with individuals who have had or still have access to a considerable amount of money, at least enough money to spread for image laundering.

Apart from the violation of ethics, there are other factors that erode the credibility of the press such as laxity in the handling of facts, laxity in the respect of rules of grammar, deplorable spelling and poor choice of words. The credibility of a news organ depends largely on its standard of professionalism and authoritativeness. Achieving an acceptable professional standard depends largely on reporting truthfully, accurately and objectively.

Carelessness with facts is unacceptable and carelessness with language relegates the practitioner to the category of gutter journalism.

And there is indeed a disturbing proliferation of gutter journalism as one notices the increasing amount of sleaze and filth that is reported in most of the English language news media.

The language in these media is far below standard and it is indeed an irony that whenever there is a general public outcry about the falling standards of English, the media noisily join the chorus instead of seriously reflecting on the role they have played in bringing down these standards.

Most often when one listens to or reads by-lines by the new generation of media practitioners, you wonder whether they have ever bothered to read anything other than their own shoddy reports or whether they have ever bothered to listen to other reputable radio or TV stations. They are so full of themselves and believe that the mere fact of going on the air or scribbling some mumbo jumbo in a newspaper confers them the right to be called journalists.

Every journalist worth his salt should be conscious that at any given time that he writes or goes on the air, there are millions of people out there who are by far more knowledgeable than they are. Avoid talking over the heads of your betters and endeavour to exercise a certain amount of modesty and humility. When you quit the microphone and retire to your favourite watering hole, you're likely to receive undue accolades from fans who are eager to offer you a round of beer with such remarks, like "hey man, I heard you blasting, man that was wonderful!" and when you ask the fellow what he thinks about what you blasted, he blinks, scratches his head and mumbles something unintelligible. He just cannot remember anything you said. Beware of gratuitous flattery.

Avoid the tendency to think that because you go on the air or write stories in a paper, you have automatically become a star. Flattery is one of the deepest pitfalls a practitioner should guard against. It breeds complacency and mediocrity.

Avoid imitating the wrong things and picking up the wrong vocabulary such as the word "denizen" just because it sounds exotic. That word has been overused to the extent that one wonders whether the journalists using it even know its meaning. Another word that has been abused beyond recognition is "lady". A prostitute steps on stage, does an erotic routine, proceeds to shred her clothing and at the climax of her sleazy performance, the journalist writes "that the lady pulled off her underpants, and exposed her what have you!". You can't help asking whether the journalist knows the definition of the word "Lady". A lady is a highly respected woman in society who is held in high esteem not just any strumpet who undresses in public to entice the men folk as a means of making a living.

Language is the substance and primary means of communications among human beings and every communicator, especially the journalist, must take the pains to learn to use and master it.

Another common habit among newspapermen and women is the frequent use of the phrase "in a chat with so and so, he revealed that..." This habit of gathering information by means of a chat betrays a certain casualness and informality which portrays the news media as being unserious. In reality, a journalist might stumble on some vital piece of information during a chat but for heaven's sake, spare your poor readers the impression that news gathering is a pedestrian process. It does not convey any sense of professionalism. You could simply state that Mr. X told The Post that such and such a thing took place.

If all along you have noticed that most of my illustrations have been drawn from The Post newspaper, it is not because the other papers are any better. I have chosen The Post because I am attached to it and because I do not want it to be said that I am taking advantage of this forum to denigrate other rival newspapers. When I stated in the title of this presentation that there is a need for critical self-examination, I meant it.

The news media must subject itself to regular self-examination because as the Fourth Estate, entrusted with the difficult and thankless duty to act as the watchdog of society, the news media must establish a self-regulatory mechanism because only a watchdog can watch out for itself.

In this light, I am humbly suggesting that the various media associations ought to put the issue of ethics high on their agenda.

** *This paper was initially published in the Frontier Telegraph in May 2009 and later in The Post in early December 2012*

S-N F.

www.ingramcontent.com/pod-product-compliance
Lightning Source LLC
Chambersburg PA
CBHW022133020426
42334CB00015B/882